162-0

A PHILLIES PERFECT SEASON

PAUL KURTZ

TRIUMPH
BOOKS

Library of Congress Cataloging-in-Publication Data

Kurtz, Paul, 1954-
162-0 : a Phillies perfect season / Paul Kurtz.
p. cm.
ISBN 978-1-60078-534-4
1. Philadelphia Phillies (Baseball team)-History. I. Title. II.
Title: One hundred sixty two to zero.
GV875.P45K87 2011
796.357'640974811-dc22
2010043744

This book is available in quantity at special discounts for your group or organization. For further information, contact:

Triumph Books
542 South Dearborn Street
Suite 750
Chicago, Illinois 60605
(312) 939–3330
Fax (312) 663–3557
www.triumphbooks.com

Printed in U.S.A.

ISBN: 978-1-60078-534-4

Editorial and page production by Red Line Editorial

Photos courtesy of AP Images unless indicated otherwise

CONTENTS

FOREWORD

This book is a collection of 162 of the Phillies greatest, wackiest, record-setting victories spread out over a calendar season. They include no-brainer games we remember such as the epic blowout of the Mets when Von Hayes hit two first inning home runs, Mike Schmidt's 500th homer, the division-clinching win in '07 and Mitch Williams' game-winning hit in the 10th inning that ended the longest doubleheader in team history in '93. There are also a lot of games here that many fans probably don't remember, such as Del Wilbur hitting three straight homers and accounting for all the Phillies runs in a 3-0 win in 1952 . . . and Kewpie Barret, a journeyman pitcher who threw a 14-inning shutout against the Reds in 1943.

I would bet that if you got a bunch of Phillies fans together they would all be able to talk about their own memorable games. As the son of a major league player, a batboy watching the 1980 team from the dugout, a player, and general manager celebrating the 2008 World Series at Citizens Bank Park, I recommend this great collection in one book for the Phillies fans to enjoy. It's about baseball in the great city of Philadelphia.

—Ruben Amaro Jr.

INTRODUCTION

When I was approached to take on this project, my first thought was "This would be a lot easier to write if we called it 0–162."

Sure, we're now going through a Golden Era (actually a second Golden Era), but the long history of the Phillies contains far more downs than ups.

Let's not forget that this is a franchise that's lost more than 10,000 games and had one lonely winning season between 1917 and 1949! And need I mention 1964?

Anyway, I put my cynicism aside and soon found that even in the lean years the Phillies produced some amazing victories that gave otherwise frustrated fans something to cling to as they waited for better days.

Great wins can be defined in many ways—fantastic finishes, singular moments of brilliance and record-breaking accomplishments, to name a few. Not coincidentally, I found some of the same names popping up continually with these games as this mythical season developed.

The truly fascinating and delightful part of this project was digging up the incredible stories that went down the memory hole and the players who made those games special, some of whom you will read about for the first time—players like like Del Wilber, Dave Watkins, Glen Stewart, and Kewpie Barrett.

These are guys who rose to the occasion for one game, performed remarkable feats, then retreated back to obscurity.

Put them all together and you have the ultimate season: 162–0. These are the greatest wins.

I hope you have as much fun reading these stories as I did collecting them.

ABOUT THE AUTHOR

A 32-year broadcast veteran, Paul Kurtz has been a mainstay at KYW Newsradio in Philadelphia since 1985. A journalism major at Temple University, he began his career at WBCB in Levittown. At age 24, Kurtz moved to Washington to become a morning drive anchor and reporter for the award-winning news team at WASH-FM. He returned to Philadelphia in 1984 and moved to KYW the next year. In his time there, Kurtz won numerous awards, including the prestigious Edward R. Murrow National Award for reporting. He resides in Bucks County, Philadelphia, with his wife, Kim Glovas (who also reports for KYW): four boys, Luc, Chris, Pete, and Eli; and two cats, Lucy and Mr. Chibs. In his spare time he coaches youth baseball and basketball.

APRIL

Hall of Famer Mike Schmidt, a 12-time All-Star, won eight home run titles

The World Series March Begins with Victory

A crowd of more than 45,000 on opening night packed the Astrodome, but Terry Mulholland gave them little to cheer about. The veteran lefty pitched a masterpiece, holding the Astros to four hits and one unearned run as the Phils embarked on their magical, improbable journey to the 1993 World Series. It was their first opening day win since 1984.

Mulholland was unflappable despite a raucous enemy crowd that included Texas Gov. Ann Richards and former President George H. W. Bush.

"I had a good spring and I told myself that I'm not going to let anything distract me from my goal, and that's to get myself and my team to the World Series," said Mulholland.

Houston scored its lone run in the first inning on an error by shortstop Juan Bell. But the Phillies bounced back and took the lead for good in the fourth.

Catcher Darren Daulton's presence was undeniable in the early 1990s. "Dutch" was named an All-Star in 1992, 1993, and 1995 and hit 24 homers with 105 RBIs in 1993 to lead the Phillies to the National League pennant.

John Kruk walked with one out, Dave Hollins singled and Darren Daulton doubled, knocking in Kruk. Jim Eisenreich, a key off-season acquisition, singled to left, scoring Daulton.

The Phillies scored their final run in the ninth. Kruk led off with a double and scored on a single by pinch-hitter Pete Incaviglia, who played for the Astros the year before. On the day he was signed by the Phillies, Inky predicted that he would beat his former team on Opening Day.

Mulholland ran into his only jam in the eighth inning. With two outs, pinch-hitter Chris James slammed a double and Craig Biggio reached on Bell's second error of the night.

With the Astros' faithful now in full-throated roaring mode, the stoic lefty simply went back to work.

"It could be storming out there and I'm in Tahiti," said Mulholland, who retired Steve Finley on a grounder to second to end the threat.

"When he is focused like that out there," said Daulton, "he just doesn't let anything deter him. That was one of the best games I've ever seen him pitch."

At a Glance

WP: Mulholland (1–0)

Key stat: Mulholland 4 hitter; Kruk 1-for-2, 2 runs

Manager Jim Fregosi had closer Mitch Williams warming up in the eighth and ninth innings but stuck with his starter.

"He is a horse," said Fregosi. "He was just outstanding. He had control of all his pitches."

It was a great start to a season in which the Phillies would win 97 games and the National League pennant, a remarkable turnaround for a team that finished last in National League East the year before.

April 6, 1974
Phillies 5, Mets 4

Opening Day a New Beginning for Schmidt

Opening Day at Veterans Stadium featured a matchup between two future Hall of Fame pitchers along with a future Hall of Fame third baseman who kick-started his breakout season with a walk-off home run.

More than 40,000 fans showed up on a damp afternoon to watch Steve Carlton and Tom Seaver work their magic. They also were curious to get a look at a new lineup that featured youngsters such as Mike Schmidt and Greg Luzinski, and veterans like Dave Cash. The veteran second baseman came over from Pittsburgh in an off-season trade for pitcher Ken Brett.

Carlton, the 1972 Cy Young Award winner, was coming off a disappointing season in which he lost 20 games. And in this season opener he struggled with his control and location. Lefty lasted just five innings, giving up three runs on seven hits. Seaver, meanwhile, appeared to be in complete control as he held the Phils to three hits and one run through five innings.

But all that changed in the sixth inning. Larry Bowa led off with a base hit and scored after Del Unser singled and left fielder Cleon Jones bobbled the ball. Luzinski then knocked in Unser by ripping a double to right-center field.

The Mets came back and took the lead in the top of the seventh.

Tug McGraw, who was one year away from becoming a Phillie, replaced Seaver and breezed through the eighth inning, retiring Luzinksi and Willie Montanez on strikes.

In the ninth, pinch-hitter Tony Taylor led off with a single and moved to second on Boone's bunt. Schmidt, coming off a horrendous rookie season in which he hit .191, had no thoughts of small ball. After taking a first pitch screwball from McGraw for ball one, he looked for a fastball, got it and nailed it. The home crowd rose to its feet as Schmidt triumphantly circled the bases.

At a Glance

WP: Scarce (1–0)

HR: Schmidt (1)

Key stat: Schmidt walk-off HR, 2 RBIs; Unser 2-for-4, RBI

He knew the ball was gone as soon as he it.

"It made me feel awful good," said Schmidt, who went on to lead the National League with 36 home runs in 1974.

Hometown Hero Glanville Delivers

Doug Glanville became a hometown hero in this home opener by knocking in the winning run with a 10th-inning single. Glanville's heroics capped a thrilling comeback for the Phillies, who had trailed 8–4 after five innings.

Glanville, a North Jersey native and University of Pennsylvania graduate, was picked up from the Cubs in a trade for Mickey Morandini. He was considered an important part of the team's effort to rebuild following a 94-loss season.

Early on, the Phillies still had the look of last year's losers as they fell behind 2–0 when starting pitcher Garrett Stephenson gave up singles to the first four Marlins he faced.

The Phils answered with a run in the third and three in the fourth to take the lead. But Stephenson couldn't hold it. The right-hander gave up a pair of walks, two singles and a grand slam to Derrek Lee. The Phillies were suddenly looking at an 8–4 deficit and a very ugly home crowd.

Frustrated fans started showering the outfield with souvenir team schedule magnets. Players ducked and the game was halted to allow the grounds crew to get out to the field and clean up the mess.

Bobby Abreu started the Phillies' comeback in the sixth with a leadoff single and moved to second on a base hit by Alex Arias. After pinch-hitter Ruben Amaro, Jr. walked, Glanville hit into a force play, allowing Abreu to score.

At a Glance

WP: Botallico (1–1)

HR: Lewis (1), Rolen (1)

Key stat: Abreu 4-for-4; Lewis 2-for-4, 2 RBIs; Rolen 3-for-5, RBI

In the bottom of the seventh, the Phils crept to within two on a solo home run by Mark Lewis, then staged a game-tying rally in the eighth. Third baseman Scott Rolen got things rolling with a one-out homer. The Phils then loaded the bases for Arias, who drew a run-scoring walk from Marlins reliever Jay Powell. The crowd that had been so hostile 30 minutes earlier was now cheering wildly.

Glanville stepped to the plate in the 10th with two outs and the bases loaded and delivered a line drive into left field, setting off a jubilant celebration that gave the Phillies reason to believe early in the season.

Ricky Botallico, Darrin Winston and Jerry Spradlin didn't give up a hit after the fifth inning. Botallico got the victory, throwing two scoreless innings.

First Some Ring Bling, Then a Victory

The Phillies received their World Series rings in an emotional on-field ceremony that preceded a nerve-wracking comeback victory over the Atlanta Braves.

A sold-out crowd watched as the rings were transported into Citizens Bank Park by a van led by a police motorcycle escort.

"A World Series championship ring is a most prized possession," said team president David Montgomery. "We wanted to present our players and others in the Phillies organization with a meaningful tribute."

The rings were made of 14-karat white gold and contained 103 diamonds, symbolizing the 92 regular season and 11 postseason games the Phillies had won in 2008. The players "oohed" and "aahhed" as they gawked at their bling. "It exceeds any expectation I could have had," said pitcher Jamie Moyer.

Their minds seemed to be more on their rings than the game when they went out to face the Braves in the third and final contest of the season-opening series. Phils starter Joe Blanton was torched for nine hits and seven runs in the first four innings. The Braves scored a pair in the first on a two-run homer by catcher Brian McCann, then erupted for five runs in the top of the third, two more in the fifth and one in the seventh to take a commanding 10–3 lead.

The Phillies' offense finally awoke in the bottom of the seventh. With one out, Chase Utley blooped a single off reliever Eric O'Flaherty and went to second after Ryan Howard was hit by a pitch. Peter Moyland was brought in to replace O'Flaherty and walked Jason Werth to load the bases.

Newly acquired left fielder Raul Ibanez then laced an RBI single to left, setting off a scoring frenzy that ended with eight runs crossing the plate on four hits and five walks.

At a Glance

WP: Condrey (1–0)

HR: Ibanez (1)

Key stat: Ibanez 2-for-3, 3 RBIs, 3 runs; Utley 2-for-4, 2 RBIs

The Phils added a crucial insurance run in the bottom of the eighth when Ibanez walked, advanced to third on a Pedro Feliz double, and scored on a sacrifice fly to center off the bat of Eric Bruntlett.

It turned out to be the winning run because closer Brad Lidge gave up a one-out, ninth-inning homer to Matt Diaz. Lidge retired the next two batters to preserve the 12–11 win.

Beware—These Are Not the Phillies of Old

The Phillies served notice to the National League that this was not the same dreadful team that lost 107 games the year before.

Led by their young manager, Gene Mauch, they ambushed the defending National League champion Cinncinnati Reds, scoring seven times in the first three innings to cruise to a season-opening win at Crosley Field.

Clay Dalrymple got the Phillies on the board in the second inning with a solo home run. They batted around in the third inning, stringing together seven singles for six runs off Reds starter Joey Jay, a 21-game winner in '61.

In the fourth, right fielder Don Demeter hit a two-run homer over the center-field wall, and the Phils added three more runs after that.

It was a relentless offensive attack for the Phils, who bludgeoned five Reds pitchers, collecting 15 hits and drawing 10 walks.

Tony Gonzalez led the assault, going 3-for-5 with two singles and a double. Demeter, Dalrymple, Johnny Callison, Ruben Amaro and rookie Ted Savage each had two hits.

At a Glance

WP: Mahaffey (1–0)

HR: Dalrymple (1), Demeter (1)

Key stat: Gonzalez 3-for-5, 3 runs; Demeter 3 RBIs; Dalrymple 2-for-4, 2 RBIs

All that offense made life easy for starting pitcher Art Mahaffey, who went the distance despite running into trouble early in the game. Mahaffey gave up one run in the third inning and three more in the fourth. He settled down after that, surrendering just two hits over the final five innings.

The Phillies were on their way to becoming one of the most improved teams in baseball, going from a record of 47–107 in 1961 to 81–80 in '62.

© Temple University Libraries, Urban Archives

First Game at The Vet a Success Thanks to Bunning, Money

More than 55,000 people turned out on a raw, windy day to see the Phillies beat the Montreal Expos in the inaugural game at Veterans Stadium.

The Vet was a spectacular new venue, standing in stark contrast to the Phillies' previous home—the ancient, decrepit Connie Mack Stadium.

Built on a 72-acre site in South Philadelphia at a cost of about $52 million, the multi-purpose stadium was the largest in the National League. It featured an Astroturf playing surface, multi-colored plastic seats and a high-tech, computerized scoreboard in addition to amenities such as luxury boxes and a picnic area.

The ceremonial first pitch was dropped out of a helicopter to catcher Mike Ryan, who bobbled the ball but managed to hang on.

Future Hall of Famer Jim Bunning gives way to reliever Joe Hoerner in the first game at The Vet on April 10, 1971.

Jim Bunning, 39 years old and in the final season of a Hall of Fame career, was given the honor of pitching the opener. And the aging right-hander was able to reach back for some of his old magic.

Bunning held the Expos to six hits, walked three and struck out four. He surrendered the first run at the new stadium in the sixth inning after giving up back-to-back doubles to Ron Hunt and Rusty Staub.

The Phils struck back against Expos starter Bill Stoneman in the bottom of the sixth, when third baseman Don Money led off with the first home run hit at the Vet.

"It was a fast ball, up around the letters," said Money, who drilled a 2–2 pitch over the left-field fence.

The Phils scored two more runs in the sixth and added another run in the seventh.

Manager Frank Lucchesi went to his bullpen in the eighth inning after the Expos put runners on first and second with one out. Joe Hoerner replaced Bunning and walked Ron Fairly to load the bases. But the side-winding lefty struck out Mack Jones and John Bateman to end the inning. Hoerner returned to retire the side in the ninth and earn his first save.

At a Glance

WP: Bunning (1–0)

S: Hoerner (1)

HR: Money (1)

Key stat: Bowa 2-for-4, run; Freed 2-for-3, RBI

Lucchesi singled out a number of players in addition to Bunning and Money, including Larry Bowa. The scrappy young shortstop recorded the first hit in stadium history in the bottom of the first and followed that with the first stolen base. He later belted a triple and made two slick plays in the field.

Rookie rightfielder Roger Freed had two singles and drove in the game-winning run in the sixth. Left fielder John Briggs came up with the game's best defensive play when he caught a ball against the wall to put down a possible Montreal rally in the seventh.

"If he doesn't make that catch," said Lucchesi, "it could have changed the complexion of the game."

Phils Shut Down Astrodome's Opening Night Celebration

Houston's new domed stadium opened to rave reviews, but the Phillies, led by Dick Allen and Chris Short, made sure that more than 43,000 Astros fans sat on their hands most of the night.

The Astrodome was unlike any other stadium. Dubbed "The Eighth Wonder of the World," it was enclosed by a ceiling that had transparent plastic panes to let the sun shine in, and was the first air-conditioned stadium to offer baseball, football, basketball, concerts and just about any other sporting or entertainment event.

It featured cushioned seats and 52 swanky suites. Team owner Roy Hofheinz lived in a luxurious apartment inside the dome. The centerpiece of the stadium was an enormous computerized scoreboard that entertained fans throughout the game with cartoons, messages, and wild, digitally displayed explosions after an Astro hit a home run.

But the only homer in this game came off the bat of Allen, the 1964 National League Rookie of the Year.

At a Glance

WP: Short (1–0)

HR: Allen (1)

Key stat: Allen 2-for-4, 2 RBIs; Gonzalez 2-for-4

Manager Gene Mauch decided to start Ruben Amaro at shortstop in place of Cookie Rojas, a move that paid dividends in the third inning when Amaro led off with a single. That brought Allen to the plate.

With a 1–1 count, the muscular third baseman had to duck out of the way of a chin-high fastball from Astros right-hander Bob Bruce. Allen dusted himself off and slammed the next pitch more than 400 feet over the center-field fence. It was the first regular season home run hit in the Dome. (Mickey Mantle had hit one a few days earlier when the doors were officially opened for an exhibition game between the Astros and New York Yankees).

"I don't know if he was throwing at me or not," said Allen, referring to the pitch that preceded his blast. "But I was mad. I was going to hang in there if he threw the next pitch through me."

Bruce denied throwing at Allen.

"I was pitching him in. He hit a breaking ball and he hit it good."

Allen's two-run homer proved to be more than enough support for the hard-throwing Short, who went all nine innings, surrendering just four hits while striking out 11 and walking three. After the game, Short said he enjoyed pitching in the spacious new ballpark.

"The dimensions are nice. Those batters don't get any cheap home runs," he said.

Short's shutout was the first by a Phillies pitcher in a season opener since Ken Heintzelman blanked the Boston Braves in 1948. He went on to post a record of 18–11 in 1965 with a 2.82 earned-run average and 237 strikeouts. Allen would hit 20 home runs, knock in 85 and hit .302.

Larry Bowa

One of the finest fielding shortstops in major league history, Larry Bowa transformed himself into an All-Star-caliber player through hard work and dogged determination.

Bowa broke in with a bad Phillies team in 1970 and became a mainstay as it evolved into a perennial pennant contender through the middle and latter part of the decade.

The winner of two Gold Gloves, Bowa led the National League in fielding percentage six times and was selected to the All-Star team five times.

Though fielding was his primary talent, Bowa could also ignite an offense with his fiery demeanor and ability to steal bases. He stole 20 or more bases nine times.

Bowa's finest season at the plate was in 1975 when he batted .305. He retired with a .260 average for his career.

Bowa turned to coaching and managing after his playing days ended. He managed the Phillies from 2001-2004, compiling a 337–308 record.

Young Christenson Goes the Distance in Debut

Nineteen-year-old Larry Christenson made his major league debut a memorable one with a complete game victory over the New York Mets.

The Marysville, Wash., native was the youngest player in the major leagues, but he pitched like a seasoned veteran in front of a sparse Veterans Stadium crowd of 7,127 fans.

LC surrendered just five hits and came within one out of a shutout.

Mets	AB	R	H	RBI
Harrelson ss	4	0	2	0
Millan 2b	3	0	0	0
Milner 1b	3	0	0	0
Staub rf	3	0	1	0
Jones lf	4	1	1	0
Fregosi 3b	3	0	1	0
Chiles cf	4	0	0	0
Dyer c	3	0	0	0
Matlack p	0	0	0	0
Stone p	0	0	0	0
Boswell ph	1	0	0	0
Sadecki p	0	0	0	0
Kranepool ph	0	0	0	0
McGraw p	0	0	0	0
Totals	**28**	**1**	**5**	**0**

Phillies	AB	R	H	RBI
Bowa ss	5	0	2	1
Tovar 3b	4	2	2	0
Montanez rf	4	1	2	1
Johnson 1b	4	1	1	3
Luzinski lf	4	1	0	0
Anderson cf	0	0	0	0
Robinson cf-lf	4	1	1	0
Boone c	3	0	0	0
Harmon 2b	4	1	3	1
Christenson p	3	0	0	0
Totals	**35**	**7**	**11**	**6**

NYM	0	0	0	0	0	0	0	0	1	-	1	5	2
PHI	1	0	0	2	3	0	0	1	X	-	7	11	0

Mets	IP	H	R	ER	BB	SO
Matlack L (1-1)	4	7	6	6	4	3
Stone	1	0	0	0	0	0
Sadecki	2	1	0	0	0	5
McGraw	1	3	1	1	0	1
Totals	**8**	**11**	**7**	**7**	**4**	**9**

Phillies	IP	H	R	ER	BB	SO
Christenson W (1-0)	9	5	1	1	6	3
Totals	**9**	**5**	**1**	**1**	**6**	**3**

E—New York Fregosi, Milner. DP—Philadelphia 3. 2B—New York Jones; Philadelphia Robinson, Harmon. 3B—Philadelphia Tovar. HR—Philadelphia Johnson (1). LOB—New York 6; Philadelphia 8. Attendance: 7,127.

"I was never nervous during the game," said Christenson. "How could anybody be nervous with seven runs?"

He had a point. The Phillies pounded Mets starter Jon Matlack. In the first inning, Cevar Tovar hit a fly ball to deep left-center field that took a high hop off the Astroturf. Tovar wound up at third with a triple and scored when Willie Montanez bounced a single up the middle.

In the fourth inning, Greg Luzinski hit into a force play and went to third on a double by Bill Robinson. Matlack then threw a wild pitch, allowing Luzinski to score and Robinson to move up to third. After an intentional walk, Terry Harmon hit a slow roller for a run-scoring infield single.

Deron Johnson made it a 6–0 game with a three-run homer in the fifth, and Larry Bowa drove in the Phillies' final run in the eighth.

Meanwhile, Christenson carved up a Mets lineup that would eventually come within a whisker of winning the '73 World Series.

He remembers relying primarily on a thunderous fastball.

"I could throw 100 miles per hour. I didn't really have any other pitch other than a little bit of a breaking ball," Christenson said.

His shutout was broken up with two outs in the ninth inning after Cleon Jones doubled and scored all the way from second on a wild pitch.

"Bob Boone couldn't find the ball, that was very odd," said Christenson, who represented a new generation of talented players performing under the tutelage of first-year manager Danny Ozark.

But Christenson's remarkable debut would turn out to be the highlight of his season. In his next eight starts he went 0–4 and was sent down to the minors in early June.

"I lost my confidence," he recalled. "I went down and had to kind of start all over. I had injury problems and had to work my way back."

Christenson spent the '74 season going back and forth between the minors and big leagues before sticking with the Phillies for good in 1975.

Did You Know?

The youngest player ever to wear Phillies pinstripes was Ralph "Putsy" Caballero. He was just 16 years old when he batted against the New York Giants on Sept. 14, 1944.

Putsy had the good fortune of coming along at a time when major league teams were strapped for talent with so many players off fighting in World War II.

He wasn't the only youngster out there. Three months earlier, in Cincinnati, 15-year-old pitcher Joe Nuxhall became the youngest player ever to appear in a game in the modern era when he made his debut for the Reds.

It's Déjà vu with Two More Homers by Utley

Chase Utley placed his season on an All-Star track by hitting two home runs for the second straight game to lead the Phillies to a win over the Rockies in Colorado.

"This is a great place to hit," said Utley. "There's a great background, and the ball definitely travels. There are a lot of hits out there."

Utley was slow out of the gate in '06, hitting just .200 with no home runs in his first eight games. But on April 13, he broke out of his funk against Atlanta with a pair of homers and four RBIs in four trips to the plate.

On this night, he was even better. The Phils had taken an early 4–3 lead on home runs by Aaron Rowand and Pat Burrell. Utley followed Burrell's third-inning blast with a solo shot to make it 5–3.

In the fourth inning, the Phils loaded the bases on walks to Rowand and Burrell and a single by Bobby Abreu. Utley then unloaded a 430-foot grand slam to give them a 9–3 lead. But big leads early in the game don't count for much in the mile-high air of Coors Field, as the Phillies soon found out.

Ryan Madson went seven workmanlike innings in which he gave up four runs (three earned) and 11 hits while striking out two. He also helped himself at the plate with three hits. Reliever Julio Santana threw a scoreless eighth but broke down in the ninth.

He plunked leadoff hitter Clint Barmes then walked Todd Helton. Garrett Atkins followed with an infield single and Matt Holliday cleared the bases by ripping a double down the left-field line. With the score now 10–7, manager Charlie Manuel went to his bullpen again, calling on southpaw Arthur Rhodes, who struck out Brad Hawpe.

Manuel came back out and lifted Rhodes for his closer, Tom Gordon, who retired Luis Gonzalez for the second out.

At a Glance

WP: Madson (1–0)

HR: Utley 2 (3,4), Rowand (2), Burrell (4)

Key stat: Utley 3-for-5, 2 HR, 5 RBIs; Rowand 3-for-4, HR

After walking Jason Smith, Gordon gave up a single to pinch-hitter Miguel Ojeda. Holliday scored but Smith foolishly tried to move from first to third. Left fielder Shane Victorino gunned him down for the final out.

The win went to Madson, his first of the season. Utley wrapped up an incredible two games in which he went 5-for-9 with four home runs and nine RBIs.

He went on to hit .309 with 32 home runs and 102 RBIs in 2006.

Carlton's Debut the Start of Something Big

Opening Day in Chicago saw the Phillies trot out their new ace. Steve Carlton made his highly anticipated debut, and the lanky lefty lived up to the hype as he held the Cubs to four hits over eight innings.

Carlton was traded by the Cardinals to the Phillies for Rick Wise in February 1972. At the time it was considered an even swap of two pitchers who'd been holding out for more money. But it eventually became the most lopsided trade in Phillies history.

Carlton immediately showed Phillies fans the form that would define his otherworldly season. Despite two weeks of inactivity due to a players' strike, he was able to pitch into the late innings.

"Hell, I could have finished the game, but the skipper said he didn't want to take any chances," said Carlton, who was able to last as long as he did because he was so efficient. His pitch count through six innings was 68.

The Cubs took an early lead, scoring one in the third but blowing an opportunity for more. With Rick Monday on first and one out, pitcher Fergie Jenkins hit a fly ball down the right-field line that fell in for an apparent double. But Jenkins neglected to touch first base. The Phillies appealed, and umpire Paul Pryor called Jenkins out and Carlton got out of the inning.

At a Glance

WP: Carlton (1–0)

HR: Luzinski (1)

Key stat: Luzinski 1-for-3, HR; McCarver 2-for-5, RBI; Carlton 5 Ks in 8 IP

In the fourth, 21-year-old Chicago native Greg Luzinski blasted a home run through the wind and over the bleachers in left to tie the game.

The Phils and Cubs each scored again to make it a 2–2 game entering the ninth. That's when Carlton's batterymate, Tim McCarver, took over.

The left-handed swinging McCarver delivered a drive to deep right field that bounced off the glove of Jose Cardenal and scored two runs.

Veteran reliever Joe Hoerner closed the game with a 1–2–3 ninth.

For Carlton, the win was his first in a Phillies uniform. In eight innings he allowed only four hits and struck out five. Lefty would go on to post 27 wins, nearly half the team's total (59), and pick up the first of his four Cy Young Awards.

April 17, 1976

Phillies 18, Cubs 16 (10 innings)

Schmidt's 4 Homers, 8 RBIs Too Much for Cubs

Spurred on by an epic performance from Mike Schmidt, the Phillies erased a double-digit deficit to beat the Cubs at Wrigley Field.

Schmidt became the 10th player in big-league history to slug four home runs in one game. He also matched a franchise record by driving in eight to help the Phillies win one of the wildest games in team history.

Ironically, when Schmidt looked at the lineup card that day he discovered that he been demoted from third to sixth in the order. In the previous four games, he had hit just .167 with nine strikeouts.

But the move didn't seem to bother him.

"I was feeling good and was nice and relaxed when I went up there," Schmidt said.

The Cubs seized control early in the game, hammering Steve Carlton for seven runs on seven hits in the second inning. Lefty was lifted for right-hander Ron Schueler, who was chased in the third after giving up three more runs.

The Phils trailed 12–1 after three innings and 13–2 after four. But strange things can happen at Wrigley when the wind is blowing out.

In the top of the fifth, Schmidt ignited an unforgettable comeback by slamming a two-run homer. In the top of the seventh he did it again, hitting a solo blast to trim Chicago's lead to 13–7.

The Fightins continued their resurgence in the eighth with a two-run single by Dick Allen and a three-run homer by Schmidt. It was now a one-run game.

In the ninth, the Phillies continued to pound as catcher Bob Boone

Tug McGraw

One of the top relievers in team history, Tug McGraw had a major impact on the Phillies' fortunes after the New York Mets traded him to Philadelphia in December 1974.

Over the next 10 years McGraw saved 94 games with an ERA of 3.10, reaching the apex of his career in 1980 when he saved 20 games with a microscopic 1.46 ERA in 92 innings.

In the postseason he was even better. McGraw saved two games in the 1980 League Championship Series and appeared in four World Series games against Kansas City. His strikeout of Willie Wilson for the final out in Game 6 remains one of the two most memorable moments in franchise history.

led off the inning with a game-tying home run. Bobby Tolan followed with a single and Larry Bowa tripled to give the Phils the lead. When Jay Johnstone knocked in Bowa with a bunt, it looked like they were ready to wrap up a miraculous victory.

But the Cubs refused to fold, scoring two runs in the bottom of the ninth to send the game into extra innings.

Allen led off the 10th with a walk, setting the stage for Schmidt. Facing Paul Reuschel, the powerful third baseman stepped into the history books as he drove a high, inside fastball into the left-field bleachers for his fourth home run of the day.

The Phils scored once more and held on to win 18–16.

The two teams combined for 34 runs and 43 hits. Schmidt's numbers alone were outrageous as he went 5-for-6 with eight RBIs and four runs scored.

His four home runs were the most by a Phillie since July 10, 1936, when Chuck Klein hit four against the Pirates at Forbes Field. Like Schmidt, Klein's fourth was a game-winner in a ten-inning contest.

The last major leaguer to hit four home runs in a game before Schmidt was Willie Mays (1961), and the last National Leaguer to hit four in a row was Bobby Lowe in 1894.

Schmidt confessed that he didn't believe the Phils had much of a chance after they fell behind by 11 runs.

"Maybe the lack of pressure helped," he said. "You just go up there and work on your swing. I needed a game like this to take off some of the pressure."

The win went to Tug McGraw, who pitched the eighth and ninth before being lifted for a pinch-hitter in the 10th.

Phillies	AB	R	H	RBI
Cash 2b	6	1	2	2
Bowa ss	6	3	3	1
Johnstone rf	5	2	4	2
Luzinski lf	5	0	1	1
Brown lf	0	0	0	0
Allen 1b	5	2	1	2
Schmidt 3b	6	4	5	8
Maddox cf	5	2	2	1
McGraw p	0	0	0	0
Underwood p	1	1	1	0
Lonborg p	0	0	0	0
Boone c	6	1	3	1
Carlton p	1	0	0	0
Schueler p	0	0	0	0
Garber p	0	0	0	0
Hutton ph	0	0	0	0
Reed p	0	0	0	0
Martin ph	1	0	0	0
Twitchell p	0	0	0	0
Tolan ph-cf	3	2	2	0
Totals	**50**	**18**	**24**	**18**

Cubs	AB	R	H	RBI
Monday cf	6	3	4	4
Cardenal lf	5	1	1	0
Summers lf	0	0	0	0
Mitterwald ph	1	0	0	0
Wallis lf	1	0	0	0
Madlock 3b	7	2	3	3
Morales rf	5	2	1	0
Thornton 1b	4	3	1	1
Trillo 2b	5	0	2	3
Swisher c	6	1	3	4
Rosello ss	4	1	2	1
Kelleher ss	2	0	1	0
R Reuschel p	1	2	0	0
Garman p	0	0	0	0
Knowles p	0	0	0	0
P Reuschel p	0	0	0	0
Schultz p	0	0	0	0
Adams ph	1	1	1	0
Totals	**48**	**16**	**19**	**16**

PHI	0	1	0	1	2	0	3	5	3	3	-	18	24	0
CHI	0	7	5	1	0	0	0	0	2	1	-	16	19	0

Phillies	IP	H	R	ER	BB	SO
Carlton	1.2	7	7	7	2	1
Schueler	0.2	3	3	3	0	0
Garber	0.2	2	2	2	1	1
Reed	2	1	1	1	1	1
Twitchell	2	0	0	0	1	1
McGraw W (1-1)	2	4	2	2	1	2
Underwood	0.2	2	1	1	0	1
Lonborg S (1)	0.1	0	0	0	0	0
Totals	**10**	**19**	**16**	**16**	**6**	**7**

Cubs	IP	H	R	ER	BB	SO
R Reuschel	7	14	7	7	1	4
Garman	0.2	4	5	5	1	1
Knowles L (1-1)	1.1	3	4	4	1	0
P Reuschel	0	3	2	2	0	0
Schultz	1	0	0	0	0	0
Totals	**10**	**24**	**18**	**18**	**3**	**5**

DP—Philadelphia; Chicago. 2B—Philadelphia Boone; Chicago Cardenal, Thornton. 3B—Philadelphia Johnstone, Bowa. HR—Philadelphia Boone (1), Schmidt 4 (2,3,4,5), Maddox (1); Chicago Monday 2 (2,3), Swisher (1). SH—Philadelphia Johnstone; Chicago R Reuschel. SF—Philadelphia Luzinski. HBP—Chicago Thornton, R. Reuschel, Monday. LOB—Philadelphia 8; Chicago 12. Attendance: 28,287.

April 18, 1987
Phillies 8, Pirates 6

Schmidt Joins the 500 Club with Game-Winner

Mike Schmidt joined the 500 Home Run Club in dramatic fashion with a game-winning, three-run blast in the ninth inning.

"Whoever wrote the script for this should be given the Pulitzer Prize," said Schmidt. "Because when I think of this at-bat, the most important thing to keep in mind is the game situation."

The ninth-inning fireworks began with two outs and the Phils trailing, 6–5. After grounding into a fielders choice, Juan Samuel stole second and went to third on a wild pitch. Charlie Hayes then walked, setting the stage for Schmidt, who stepped in to face Pirates closer Don Robinson. His approach was simple: hit the ball hard somewhere.

"If I did that and made an out, then I at least felt I had done what I had tried to do. I would have been disappointed if I had flied out."

Schmidt worked the count to 3–0, forcing Robinson to either walk him or throw the ball over the plate. Robinson chose the latter and Schmidt made him pay with a shot that landed far back in the left-field stands.

Second-guessers later criticized Pirates manager Jim Leyland for not issuing the walk, but Schmidt disagreed.

"They don't want to put the winning run at second base. And there's no reason to fear me, based on my at-bats today. The game situation dictates that they go right after me."

At a Glance

WP: Tekulve (1–0)

HR: Schmidt (5), Parrish (1)

Key stat: Schmidt 1-for-4, 3 RBIs; Hayes 1-for-2, 2 runs

Schmidt's homer averted what looked to be an ugly loss. The Phillies scored a run in the first inning, then added four more in the third. The big blow was a three-run homer by Lance Parrish.

With the Phils holding a comfortable 5–2 lead in the eighth inning, manager John Felske handed the ball to his closer, Steve Bedrosian. But Bedrosian gave up four runs, including a three-run homer by Johnny Ray.

Bedrosian was off to a terrible start to the season, having given up four home runs in 7 1/3 innings. But better days were ahead. Bedrosian would register 40 saves en route to winning the 1987 National League Cy Young Award.

Rookie Sensation Allen Lives Up to the Hype

The 1964 season was barely a week old and baseball was already buzzing with talk about a sensational rookie in Philadelphia named Dick Allen.

Playing in front of a national television audience, the 22-year-old third baseman raised his batting average to .429 after thumping a pair of home runs and an RBI single to help the Phils demolish the Cubs at Wrigley Field.

Allen hit his first homer in the fifth inning, a tape-measure shot that reached the back row of seats in left-center. The second one landed in the right-center field bleachers in the seventh.

After the game, players and coaches were comparing him to some of the greats of the game.

"I thought (Hank) Aaron had power to the opposite field, but that one Allen put out was a bomb," said Chicago coach Lou Klein.

Ernie Banks said Allen reminded him of Frank Robinson.

"He's too much," said Banks. "He attacks the ball."

Third baseman Ron Santo called him a can't-miss prospect.

Allen wasn't the only rookie involved in the blowout. Left fielder Danny Cater went 3-for-3 with two doubles, and center fielder John Herrnstein added a home run to left-center and a single in the second that led to a four-run rally.

At a Glance

WP: Bennett (1–0)

HR: Allen 2 (2,3); Herrnstein (1)

Key stat: Allen 3-for-5 3 RBIs; Cater 3-for-3

Pitcher Dennis Bennett was the beneficiary of all those runs. The southpaw gave up 12 hits but kept the Cubs at bay.

The victory left the Phillies with a record of 4–1 atop the standings in the National League. It was a position they'd become familiar with—at least for most of the season.

Cravath's Blast Provides Sweet Win over McGraw's Giants

Sometimes anger can be a great motivator. Phillies player-manager Gavvy Cravath channeled his rage into one mighty swing that gave the Phillies a jaw-dropping victory over John McGraw's New York Giants at the Polo Grounds.

Cravath's heroics broke a scoreless game dominated by pitchers Eppa Rixey and Rube Benton. Rixey, a left-hander who later found fame with the Cincinnati Reds, held the Giants to one hit over seven innings.

The Phils finally got a rally going in the eighth inning on singles by Dots Miller and Ralph Miller. With runners on first and third and one out, Mack Wheat hit a ground ball to third. Frankie Frisch's throw to the plate was high and Miller appeared to easily slide in safely under the tag.

But umpire Barry McCormick called Miller out. The Phillies' dugout erupted, as angry players and their manager stormed the field. They surrounded McCormick at home plate, screaming at him in protest. But the ump refused to budge.

An incensed Cravath then herded his players back to the bench, grabbed a bat and stepped to the plate as a pinch-hitter for Rixey. He might as well have called his shot because on the first pitch from Benton, Cravath swung and hit a line smash into the right-field grandstand for a three-run homer.

Intense rage now turned into joyous bedlam in the Phillies' dugout as players raced back onto the field to mob their leader.

George Smith held the Giants in check the rest of the way with two scoreless innings and the Phils went back to their hotel to celebrate one of the team's most unforgettable victories.

At a Glance

WP: Rixey (1–1)

HR: Cravath (1)

Key Stat: Cravath 3 RBIs

Cravath was the premier slugger of his day, the dead ball era. By the time he retired after the 1920 season, he had collected six home run titles and was tops on the all-time list with 119.

Team Meeting, 15 Ks from Hamels the Perfect Tonic for Phillies

Saddled with a 4–11 record, the Phillies skipped batting practice and held a team meeting before going out and smothering the Reds behind Cole Hamels, who struck out a career-high 15 batters in front of a sold-out crowd at Great American Ball Park.

"We'll have another meeting the next time Cole pitches," joked manager Charlie Manuel. "He pitched a hell of a game."

Manuel called the meeting to give the players a chance to clear the air and talk about the issues that were adversely affecting their performance. It clearly had a positive impact on Hamels, who was sensational as he overpowered the Reds with a crackling fastball and knee-buckling change-up.

"Just going out there with the motivation we had makes you relax a little more, because you know everybody is going to be behind you and we're going to play as one unit," Hamels said. "That's what puts that confidence in you."

At a Glance

WP: Hamels (2–0)

HR: Utley (3), Rowand (2)

Key stat: Utley 2-for-4, 3 RBIs; Victorino 2-for-4, run; Hamels 9 IP, 15 Ks

The Phils spotted Hamels a 2–0 lead in the first inning. Leadoff batter Shane Victorino opened the game with a single and Jimmy Rollins reached first on a throwing error. The runners then pulled off a double steal and came around to score when Chase Utley ripped a double to left-center.

The Phillies' two other runs came on solo homers from Utley in the sixth and Aaron Rowand in the eighth.

Hamels gave up his only run in the second inning when Jeff Conine homered to cut the lead to 2–1. He got into a jam in the fifth inning when the Reds' first two batters reached base, but was bailed out by his infielders, who pulled off the Phillies' first triple play in eight years.

David Ross hit a hard ground ball right at third baseman Abraham Nunez, who stepped on the bag for the force and threw to second baseman Chase Utley for the second out. Utley's relay to first was in plenty of time to nail Ross.

Nunez claimed that he saw the play in his mind before it happened. "Honest to God, I did. It's one thing to have it in the back of your mind. But I thought if this is going to happen, this is the time to do it."

The web gem seemed to re-energize Hamels. "Having that play just come out of nowhere was very helpful and so exciting," he said. "It saved probably 10 to 15 pitches, and I wouldn't have been able to go out in the ninth."

The 23-year-old southpaw compiled 115 pitches in throwing his first major league complete game.

Catcher Rod Barajas said it was one of the best games he'd ever caught: "You could tell with the change-up and the fastball that he was going to have an awesome night. For him to do what he did, you don't see it very often."

Did You Know?

Richie Ashburn built a Hall of Fame reputation as a slick center fielder, expert base runner and NL batting champion. But he was also known for his ability to foul off multiple pitches until he got something good to hit.

On Aug. 17, 1957, Whitey hit a pair of foul balls at Connie Mack Stadium that became legendary.

The first one hit Alice Roth in the face, breaking her nose. Roth, wife of *Evening Bulletin* sports editor Earl Roth, was watching the game with her two grandsons at the time.

As emergency workers carried her out on a stretcher, Ashburn fouled the very next pitch into the stands again, hitting Mrs. Roth in the knee.

Phillies 1, Cubs 0 (Game 1); Phillies 6, Cubs 0 (Game 2)

© Temple University Libraries, Urban Archives

Mahaffey Ties NL Benchmark with 17 Strikeouts

Flame-throwing Art Mahaffey put on one of the greatest displays of power pitching in baseball history as he established a new franchise record and tied a National League record by striking out 17 batters. Mahaffey's gem came in the second game of a doubleheader after Frank Sullivan blanked the Cubs in Game 1.

The 22-year-old right hander was simply untouchable as he struck out at least one batter in each inning and struck out the side twice. His total of 17 blew

Art Mahaffey strikes out Ron Santo of the Cubs, one of 17 strikeouts in Mahaffey's dominating performance.

away the team record of 13, set by Ray Benge, and matched Dizzy Dean's NL mark for a day game. He also came within one of tying the all-time strikeout record (at the time) of 18, held by Bob Feller and Sandy Koufax.

Mahaffey relied mainly on a fastball that was among the best in the major leagues.

"It was working so well I just kept throwing it," he said. "I didn't throw more than a couple of curves. All I did was to keep pumping."

The job of hanging on to all that heat went to catcher Clay Dalrymple.

"Art's high, inside fastball was jumping all over," he said. "It was handcuffing the Cubs. Then, for a change, I was giving him a low and away target. It was amazing the way he hit the corners. Later I started calling for the curve."

By the fourth inning, Mahaffey had already recorded nine strikeouts. He got number 10 in the fifth, then struck out five of the next six batters in the sixth and seventh.

The Phillies' offense gave Mahaffey an early cushion, scoring twice in the first two innings thanks to a pair of errors by third baseman Ron Santo.

They broke the game open in the fifth. Ruben Amaro started the rally by smacking a triple off the right-field wall. After a two-out walk to Tony Taylor, Johnny Callison hit a mammoth three-run homer into the upper deck in left-center field.

The Phils added one more run in the eighth on an RBI single by Tony Gonzalez.

By the top of the ninth, the 16,027 fans at Connie Mack Stadium were on their feet, screaming with every pitch. Mahaffey made leadoff hitter Don Zimmer his 17th strikeout victim, putting the all-time record squarely in his sights. He got two strikes on Santo but couldn't put him away as the third baseman hit an easy fly ball to left for the second out.

The next batter was Ernie Banks, a three-time strikeout victim. But not this time. Banks popped up to second to end the game.

At a Glance

Game 1

WP: Sullivan (1–1)

HR: Smith (1)

Key stat: Smith walk-off HR

Game 2

WP: Mahaffey (1–1)

HR: Callison (2)

Key stat: Mahaffey 17 Ks; Callison 1-for-2, 4 RBIs;
Taylor 1-for-2, 2 runs; Amaro 2-for-3, run

Manager Gene Mauch called it "the most powerfully pitched game I ever saw. And I've been in baseball for 20 years."

Utley Gets Career Started with Grand Slam

Chase Utley's first major league hit was a grand slam that propelled the Phillies to a 9–1 mauling of the Colorado Rockies.

"It's unbelievable. It's a great feeling," said the 24-year-old second baseman, who was so excited he nearly sprinted around the bases.

Manager Larry Bowa said he'd never seen anyone circle the bases so fast after a home run.

"That's got to be a thrill of a lifetime," he said. "I'm sure he'll remember that a long, long time."

Jim Thome was on third when Utley hit his blast.

"I was so jacked for him," said Thome. "I remember the same kind of feeling. My first one was a little quicker than they are now, but it was great."

Utley's third-inning slam gave Randy Wolf a comfortable 6–0 lead, allowing the left-hander a chance to relax and aggressively attack the strike zone. Wolf went 7 $^{2}/_{3}$ innings, allowed just one run on four hits to go along with eight strikeouts.

Utley added a leadoff double in the eighth inning to ignite a two-run rally and finish his memorable day by going 2-for-4 with four RBIs and two runs scored.

A first round draft pick out of UCLA in 2000, Utley was called up from Triple A Scranton/Wilkes-Barre after the injured Placido Polanco was placed on the 15-day disabled list.

He became the first Phillie to make his first major league hit a home run since Marlon Anderson on Sept. 8, 1998. Jim Command's grand slam was also his first major league hit, but it came on his seventh at-bat on July 11, 1954.

Bowa could see he had a special player in Utley.

"I've watched him for a few years. He's pretty intense. He makes an out, he gets mad. If something happens to Polanco I wouldn't hesitate to play him there every day."

That time had not yet arrived. Utley was sent back down to the minors after Polanco returned from the DL, but he was recalled in August after third baseman David Bell got hurt.

Herbert Scatters 15 Hits, Comes Away a Winner

It's not easy for a pitcher to give up 15 hits and still win a ballgame, let alone still be in the game in the ninth inning. But that's exactly what Ray Herbert did on a Sunday afternoon at sunny Chavez Ravine.

Herbert, a 35-year-old right-hander picked up in an off-season trade for Danny Cater and Lee Elia, was coming off a sparkling debut for the Phillies in which he went eight scoreless innings against the Astros.

But he struggled mightily against the Dodgers, giving up at least one hit in every inning and working out of jams all afternoon.

The Phils fell behind 1–0 in the first but bounced back against Don Drysdale to take command of the game with two runs in the fourth and four more in the fifth.

Herbert started the big rally with a line-drive double down the left-field line. He went to third on a single to center by Tony Taylor, then scored on an infield hit off the bat of Dick Allen.

After the Phils loaded the bases, Tony Gonzalez grounded into a force play at second, allowing Taylor to score. Dick Stuart ripped a two-run double into right-center field to open up a 6–2 lead.

Herbert returned to the hill and continued to flirt with disaster. In the eighth inning he gave up a double to Wes Parker and an RBI single to pinch-hitter Wally Moon before getting out of the inning.

He returned for the ninth inning and came within one out of a complete game after giving up a double to Dick Tracewski. Herbert was pulled after surrendering a run-scoring single to John Roseboro and a base hit to Maury Wills.

At a Glance

WP: Herbert (1–0)

HR: Stuart (2)

Key stat: Stuart 2-for-4, 4 RBIs; Gonzalez 1-for-4, RBI, 2 runs

Reliever Jack Baldschun preserved the 6–4 victory by retiring Parker on a pop-up.

Herbert was exhausted but satisfied after throwing more than 140 pitches.

"I don't think I've ever given up 15 hits and stayed in a ballgame that long," he said.

Ryan Maintains Hot Streak at the Plate

Another perfect day at the plate for second baseman Connie Ryan sparked the Phillies to a win over the Pirates and extended the team's winning streak to seven games.

Just 10 days after becoming the 31st player in major league history to go 6-for-6, the Phillies' leadoff hitter went 5-for-5 against the Pirates in the first game of a doubleheader at Shibe Park. Ryan also scored three runs and drove in a pair to help Robin Roberts earn his third win of the season.

His first hit was his longest of the day, a home run into the left-field grandstand off Pirates starter Bob Friend. It was also Ryan's first homer of the season.

Ryan had a hand in a second-inning rally that began when Granny Hamner walked and advanced to second on a fielder's choice. Smoky Burgess singled to score Hamner, then came around to score on Ryan's base hit to left.

By the seventh inning, Ryan was 4-for-4 as the Phils had built a 6–1 lead for a grateful Roberts, who ran into trouble in the final two frames.

Ralph Kiner cracked a two-run homer in the eighth to cut the lead in half. But the Phils bounced back with an insurance run in the bottom of the inning. Once again, Ryan was the catalyst as he bunted for a hit with two outs.

At a Glance

WP: Roberts (3–1)

HR: Ryan (1)

Key stat: Ryan 5-for5, 3 runs, 2 RBIs; Wyrostek 3-for-5, 2 RBIs

After Ashburn walked to put runners on first and second, Johnny Wyrostek knocked in Ryan with a single to left.

Roberts gave up a two-run homer to Ed Pellegrini in the ninth but gutted it out and picked up the victory. He finished the game with four strikeouts and one walk to improve his early season record to 3–1.

The first-place Phillies also took the second game of the twinbill to push the winning streak to eight, their longest in more than five years.

At the end of the day they were the hottest team in baseball, and had opened a two-and-a-half game lead over the Chicago Cubs. Phillies fans were having early season flashbacks to 1950.

But the magic wouldn't last. The Brooklyn Dodgers proved to be too much for the Phils or any other team in the National League in 1953 as they won 105 games and ran away with the pennant. The Phillies finished in third place, 22 games out with a record of 83–71.

April 27, 2003
Phillies 1, Giants 0

Ledee Lends a Hand, Bat to Millwood's No-Hitter

Ricky Ledee's first-inning home run provided all the run support Kevin Millwood would need as the Phillies' newly acquired ace became the ninth pitcher in franchise history to throw a no-hitter.

The 28-year-old Millwood, who came over from the Braves in a trade for catcher Johnny Estrada the previous December, relied on an overpowering fastball and pinpoint control to stifle a good hitting Giants lineup. He struck out 10 and threw 72 strikes out of 108 pitches.

The Phillies collected only four hits—two by Ledee, who also made a dazzling defensive play to preserve Millwood's no-hitter. It came in the top of the seventh, after Marquis Grissom hit a rocket to center field.

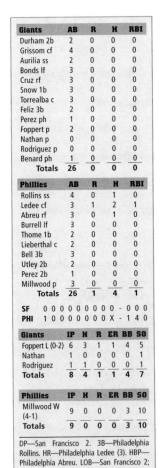

Giants	AB	R	H	RBI
Durham 2b	2	0	0	0
Grissom cf	4	0	0	0
Aurilia ss	2	0	0	0
Bonds lf	3	0	0	0
Cruz rf	3	0	0	0
Snow 1b	3	0	0	0
Torrealba c	3	0	0	0
Feliz 3b	2	0	0	0
Perez ph	1	0	0	0
Foppert p	2	0	0	0
Nathan p	0	0	0	0
Rodriguez p	0	0	0	0
Benard ph	1	0	0	0
Totals	26	0	0	0

Phillies	AB	R	H	RBI
Rollins ss	4	0	1	0
Ledee cf	3	1	2	1
Abreu rf	3	0	1	0
Burrell lf	3	0	0	0
Thome 1b	2	0	0	0
Lieberthal c	2	0	0	0
Bell 3b	3	0	0	0
Utley 2b	2	0	0	0
Perez 2b	1	0	0	0
Millwood p	3	0	0	0
Totals	26	1	4	1

SF	0	0	0	0	0	0	0	0	0	-	0	0	0
PHI	1	0	0	0	0	0	0	0	X	-	1	4	0

Giants	IP	H	R	ER	BB	SO
Foppert L (0-2)	6	3	1	1	4	5
Nathan	1	0	0	0	0	1
Rodriguez	1	1	0	0	0	1
Totals	8	4	1	1	4	7

Phillies	IP	H	R	ER	BB	SO
Millwood W (4-1)	9	0	0	0	3	10
Totals	9	0	0	0	3	10

DP—San Francisco 2. 3B—Philadelphia Rollins. HR—Philadelphia Ledee (3). HBP—Philadelphia Abreu. LOB—San Francisco 2; Philadelphia 6. Attendance: 40,016.

"I just started running," said Ledee, who turned and raced toward the fence, jumped up and came down with the ball.

"I thought it was a home run," said Millwood, who got right back to work by striking out Rich Aurilia and Barry Bonds to end the inning.

"Once I struck out Bonds I knew I had a shot," Millwood said. "It's probably as nervous as I've ever been. The fans were great. Once I got two strikes, I couldn't even hear myself think."

In the top of the ninth inning, more than 40,000 fans at Veterans Stadium rose to their feet, hoping to be witnesses to history.

Milwood faced two pinch-hitters, Neifi Perez and Marvin Bernard, and got both of them to ground out.

After walking Ray Durham, a visibly anxious Millwood gathered himself, and threw a fastball that Grissom lifted to center field. Ledee settled under it and made the catch. Millwood was mobbed by his teammates.

"Every starting pitcher, it's the goal to do it once," said Millwood. "This was like the playoffs, the World Series."

Ashburn Packs Power with 2-Homer Game

Richie Ashburn put on a rare display of power as he hammered two home runs into the upper deck and knocked in four in this victory over the New York Giants.

Ashburn carved out a Hall of Fame career as a speedy contact hitter. He compiled just 29 home runs over 15 seasons, which made his performance at the Polo Grounds all the more amazing.

Whitey's first blast in the top of the sixth inning cut a 2–0 Giants lead in half. The Phils tied the game in the seventh, thanks to some heads-up base running by Stan Lopata.

The big first baseman boomed a drive off the right-center field wall, some 450 feet from home plate. When Lopata tried to stretch a double into a triple, he appeared to be a dead duck after a marvelous relay by Willie Mays and Alvin Dark. But Lopata managed to kick the ball out of third baseman Foster Castleman's glove, then scrambled to his feet and scored.

In the top of the ninth, Lopata came up again with one out and broke the tie. He beat out an infield grounder and went to second after Hank Thompson, who had replaced Castleman, threw the ball past first base. Lopata advanced to third when Jim Greengrass grounded out.

The Giants decided to walk the No. 8 hitter, Andy Seminick, to go after pitcher Robin Roberts. But the strategy backfired.

At a Glance

WP: Roberts (3–0)

HR: Ashburn 2 (2)

Key stat: Ashburn 3-for-4, 2 HR, 4 RBIs; Lopata 3-for-4, 2 runs

Roberts hit a grounder to third that rolled up the glove arm of Thompson and landed behind him as Lopata raced home with the go-ahead run.

Ashburn then sent Giants fans to the exits by smashing a 3–2 pitch from Johnny Antonelli off a right-field upper deck girder for a three-run homer.

Antonelli, the great southpaw, was masterful handling most of the Philies lineup. But he had no answers for Ashburn and Lopata, who had three hits apiece.

On the other hand, Roberts had no trouble quieting the Giants' bats. His only mistake came in the second inning, when catcher Ray Katt hit a two-run homer.

Robby scattered 10 hits, struck out three and did not issue a single walk in improving his record to 3–0.

April 29, 1993
Phillies 5, Padres 3

Thompson Jumps the Fence for Game-Saving Catch in Eighth Inning

A spectacular catch by left fielder Milt Thompson saved the day as the Phillies hung on to beat the Padres and improve their record to a major league best 16–5.

Thompson's breathtaking play remains one of the most memorable of the '93 season and was a sure sign that this team seemed destined for greatness.

"It's unbelievable," said second baseman Mariano Duncan. "Every day, every game it's something different."

The Phils had built a 5–1 lead, thanks in large part to Thompson, who went 3-for-4 with three singles. One of those hits came in the middle of a four-run rally in the third.

With two outs and runners on first and second, Wes Chamberlain hit a slow roller to shortstop Craig Shipley for what should have been the third out. But Shipley bobbled the ball.

With the bases now loaded, Thompson stepped up and ripped a single up the middle to score two runs. Juan Bell followed with a two-run double.

At a Glance

WP: Jackson (2–0)

HR: Dykstra (3)

Key stat: Thompson 3-for-4, 2 RBIs; Hollins 2-for-5

The score remained 5–1 until the eighth, when starter Danny Jackson began showing signs of fatigue. With the bases loaded and one out, manager Jim Fregosi replaced the left-hander with Larry Andersen.

Guillermo Velasquez greeted L.A. with a two-run single to right, reducing the lead to 5–3. Fregosi dipped into the 'pen again. This time it was left-hander David West, who walked Ricky Gutierrez, then got Phil Clark to fly out.

The next batter, Bob Geren, smoked a 2–2 fastball to left. Everyone in the ballpark thought it was a grand slam as the ball soared toward the left-field wall. But Milt Thompson still believed he had a chance.

"I can't explain how I caught it," he said. "I just did."

Thompson arrived at the base of the left-field wall, leaped up and snagged the ball as it was going over the eight-foot high fence.

"I knew I had to get up in the air to get it because, you know, it was over the fence. I just happened to make the catch."

Thompson came down with the ball in his glove, pumped his fist and jumped for joy. Center fielder Lenny Dykstra dashed over and hugged him while the rest of the team ran out of the dugout to congratulate him.

Mitch Williams called it, "the greatest catch I've ever seen in person. I jumped up and down 10 feet in that bullpen."

The catch was a backbreaker for the Padres, who went down in order in the ninth.

For the Phillies, it was yet another magical moment in their young season.

"It's incredible, the things that are happening to us," said Andersen. "But when you're winning and you believe you're going to win, things go your way. It's a great feeling."

Did You Know?

The Phillies are co-owners of the major league record for the fastest nine-inning game ever played.

On Sept. 28, 1919, the Phils and New York Giants played the first game of a season-ending doubleheader at the Polo Grounds in just 51 minutes. The Phils lost, 6-1.

April 30, 1991
Phillies 11, Giants 9

Never-Say-Die Phils Put on Major Comeback

The Phillies broke out the heavy lumber to mount a ferocious comeback and stun the Giants in front of a home crowd of more than 15,000.

After falling behind 4–2 in the fourth, manager Jim Fregosi took a gamble and sent up a pinch-hitter for starter Pat Combs. There were two runners on and two outs at the time.

"I just felt we were in a game where we'd have to score some runs," said Fregosi. "It turned out to be one of those games."

The skipper looked like a genius after Jim Lindeman came through with a run-scoring single.

But the Giants clobbered relievers Darrel Akerfelds and Joe Boever in the fifth, scoring five times to increase their lead to 9–3.

The Phils used the long ball to launch their comeback. Dale Murphy and Ricky Jordan slammed back-to-back homers in the fifth to cut the lead to 9–5.

With two outs and two on in the bottom of the sixth, John Kruk crushed a ball high and deep down the right-field line toward the foul pole.

"At first I thought, 'Please stay fair,'" said Kruk. "Then when I saw how high it was and the fielder was there I thought, 'Please go foul.' Then when I saw it was staying fair I thought, 'Please be far enough.'"

It was. The ball landed in the bullpen, just inside the foul pole. With the Phils suddenly trailing by a run, the fans stood, cheering for more. And they got it.

At a Glance

WP: Boever (1–1)

HR: Murphy (4); Kruk (4); Jordan (1)

Key stat: Kruk 1-for-4, 4 RBIs; Murphy 3-for-5, 3 runs, RBI; Jordan 2-for-4, 2 RBIs

Dale Murphy singled to right, Jordan hit a scorching line drive to the center-field fence for a game-tying triple, and Charlie Hayes smoked a fastball into the left-center field stands to give the Phillies an 11–9 lead.

The bullpen took over from there. Roger McDowell pitched a scoreless seventh and eighth and closer Mitch Williams got the save in typical "Wild Thing" fashion.

Just like he did in the 1993 World Series, John Kruk had a knack for coming up with clutch hits during his six-year career with the Phillies. Kruk was selected to play in the All-Star Game in 1991,1992, and 1993.

29

After walking Kevin Mitchell, Williams gave up a two-out double to Kevin Bass to put runners on second and third. But he struck out Steve Decker to end the game.

The Phillies were full of optimism after the comeback win.

Kruk said, "if this was two weeks ago we would have lost today. We would've called off the dogs. But we feel like right now we're gonna go out and hit and it doesn't matter who's pitching."

MAY

May 1, 2008

Phillies 3, Padres 2

Howard's Slump-Breaking Game Puts Phils in First

Ryan Howard broke out of a brutal early season slump with two hits, including the game-winning homer, to lift the eventual World Series champs into first place for the first time.

"It's always good to be in first place," said manager Charlie Manuel. "Let's see if we can stay there until October."

Ryan Howard put his early-season slump to rest by hitting the game-winning home run in the eighth inning of a 3–2 victory over the Padres on May 1, 2008, in Philadelphia.

Howard came into this game at Citizens Bank Park hitting an anemic .172, but was feeling better about his swing after taking some extra sessions of batting practice.

That extra work came into play with two outs in the third inning and the Phillies trailing 2–0. Howard lined a double to center to score Shane Victorino from second with the Phillies' first run of the game. Pat Burrell followed with the third double of the inning to bring Howard home with the tying run.

The scored stayed that way until the bottom of the eighth when Howard led off with his sixth homer of the year.

"It felt good," said the big first baseman. "I'm seeing the ball better. But to come through in a situation like that, it only makes it that much better.

"When you're not seeing the ball, everything is tough. Now, I'm starting to kind of see it. Hopefully, the results will start to change a little bit."

Howard hit his game-winning blast off left-handed reliever Joe Thatcher. It was an encouraging sign for a slugger who was a notoriously slow starter.

"Toward the end of April I was starting to get better swings," he said. "It's a fresh start. It's a new month."

Tom Gordon picked up the win for the Phils in relief of Adam Eaton, who allowed two runs in six innings. Brad Lidge got his seventh save in seven opportunities.

At a Glance

WP: Gordon (3–2)

HR: Howard (6)

Key stat: Howard 2-for-4, 2RBIs, 2 runs; Burrell 2-for-4, RBI

The win was a sign of things to come. The defending NL Eastern Division champions didn't reach first place until Game 160 the year before. They were not yet in first place for good. Not yet. But the '08 Phillies were clearly headed in that direction.

Schilling Puts Strike, Injuries in Rearview

Phillies ace Curt Schilling signalled his return from injuries and a players' strike with this dominating performance against the Reds.

"It's starting to get fun again," said the right-hander, who battled elbow and knee problems before the '94 strike began. "And it's only going to get funner if we stay healthy, because we're going to win a lot of games."

The season was only about a week old when Schilling took the mound at Riverfront Stadium. The strike that began the previous August didn't end until April 25. Schilling opened the season the next day with five decent but unspectacular innings against St. Louis.

At a Glance

WP: Schilling (1–0)

Key stat: Eisenreich 3-for-4; Stocker 2-for-4, 2 RBIs; Hayes 1-for-3, triple, 2 RBIs

Showing his return to dominance after being slowed by injuries, Curt Schilling allowed three hits and no runs in seven innings against the Reds on May 2, 1995.

Facing the Reds, Schilling was superb as he gave up just three hits in seven shutout innings, struck out four and walked none. He retired the last 10 batters in succession.

Manager Jim Fregosi didn't want to take any chances so he pulled his starter after the seventh.

"He threw the ball extremely well but I thought he tired after the fifth inning," said Fregosi. "He's going to need another start or two before he's going full bore."

Fregosi was also impressed with the Phils' offense, which scored six runs, including four in the second.

Dave Hollins opened the inning with a walk and scored the game's first run on a double by Darren Daulton. After Jim Eisenreich singled, Charlie Hayes drove in two more runs with a triple to center field. Kevin Stocker brought Hayes home with a single.

The Phils padded their lead in the fifth when Gregg Jefferies doubled and raced home on a single by Hollins, who scored the Phillies' sixth run on Stocker's second RBI single.

Greg Harris relieved Schilling in the eighth and preserved the shutout with two scoreless innings.

Curt Schilling

When the Phillies acquired Curt Schilling in a 1992 trade with Houston, they envisioned a hard-throwing pitcher who could anchor the back end of the bullpen.

But by the middle of May, it became clear that the big right-hander was much more suited to anchor the rotation.

Schilling went 14–11 that season, then won 16 games in 1993 before bursting onto the postseason stage as an up-and-coming star.

The 26-year-old was named MVP of the League Championship Series after allowing just three earned runs in 16 innings. In the World Series, Schilling was brilliant as he threw a five-hit shutout in Game 5 against Toronto.

In 1997, Schilling exploded into a dominating power pitcher. He set a team record with 319 strikeouts while compiling a 17–11 record.

The next year he became only the fifth pitcher in major league history to strike out 300 batters in back-to-back seasons.

Schilling was a three-time All-Star with the Phillies.

Santiago's Unlikely Grand Slam against Maddux Lifts Phils

Benitigo Santiago's ninth-inning grand slam gave the Phillies a miraculous win over the Atlanta Braves and four-time Cy Young Award winner Greg Maddux.

It was an improbable blow off the best pitcher in baseball at the time. Maddux had never given up a grand slam in his career before facing Santiago with one out in the ninth.

His electrifying blast gave Terry Mulholland a much-deserved victory. The left-hander scattered nine hits over eight innings. His only mistake was serving up an eighth-inning homer to David Justice to give the Braves a 2–1 lead.

Santiago, an off-season free agent pickup, hit a game-tying home run in the fifth inning off Maddux.

"Both of those home runs were on good pitches," said Santiago, who went 2-for-4 and tied his career record for RBIs in a game with five.

Only two other players had ever homered twice off Maddux in one game—Luis Gonzalez in 1991 and Kal Daniels in 1990.

Overall, though, Maddux was in typical form as he carried a three-hitter into the ninth inning.

That's when the Phillies' offense awoke. The first three batters—Lenny Dykstra, Mickey Morandini and Mark Whiten—all singled. Dykstra scored on Whiten's hit.

At a Glance

WP: Mulholland (3–2)

HR: Santiago 2 (8,9)

Key stat: Santiago 2-for-4, 5 RBIs; Whiten 2-for-4, RBI

After Todd Zeile popped out, Whiten stole second. With runners on second and third, Braves manager Bobby Cox decided to intentionally walk Jim Eisenriech to set up a force.

The Phillies' catcher didn't take kindly to the strategy.

"I hate that," said Santiago. "I hate that when they walk somebody to try to get to me. Don't get me wrong. They have gotten me on double plays many times."

But not this time. Santiago jumped on Maddux's first pitch and sent it on a line over the center-field wall.

The Braves did not go down quietly in the bottom of the ninth. Dave Lieper came in for the save and was greeted with a leadoff home run by Ryan Klesko. After giving up a one-out double to pinch-hitter Jerome Walton, manager Jim Fregosi had seen enough and brought in his closer, Ricky Botallico, who got the final two outs to earn his 11th save of the season.

The Phils were on their way to a 95-loss season. But the bad days had not yet materialized. After beating Maddux, they were in second place with a record of 16–11, just one game out of first. For the moment, anything was possible.

Did You Know?

Vince DiMaggio holds the Phillies record for most grand slams in one season with four.

DiMaggio went on his binge in 1945, beginning on May 20 in a game against the St. Louis Cardinals.

He hit No. 4 on Sept. 1 during a seven-run rally against the Boston Braves.

Chuck Klein and Gene Freese share the No. 2 spot with three grand slams.

May 4, 1973
Phillies 5, Braves 4 (20 innings)

After 20 Innings and 5 Hours, Phils Leave a Winner against Braves

It took 20 innings over a period of five hours and 16 minutes for the Phillies to beat the Atlanta Braves in the team's longest game since April 30, 1919.

There were only 10,000 fans watching when the game began at Veterans Stadium on a Friday night and far fewer than that when Denny Doyle scampered across home plate with the winning run the next morning.

The Braves opened the scoring in the third inning with two unearned runs off starter Dick Ruthven.

With one out, Atlanta pitcher Ron Reed hit a slow roller toward third. Mike Schmidt bare-handed it, but his hurried throw pulled first baseman Willie Montanez off the bag.

Later that inning, Darrell Evans hit a bases-loaded double to give the Braves the lead.

Reed pitched shutout ball through seven innings before running into trouble in the eighth. Right fielder Mike Anderson led off with a double to right-center and scored on Doyle's single to right.

Braves manager Eddie Mathews called on reliever Danny Frisella to face rookie Mike Rogodzinksi, who was batting for Ruthven. "Rogo" bunted Doyle over to second.

Larry Bowa followed with a looping fly ball that center fielder Dusty Baker dropped, a two-base error that allowed the Phils to tie the game.

Atlanta appeared to put the game on ice in the 13th inning, when Oscar Brown hit a two-out single and third baseman Darrell Evans hit a 3–2 fastball off Billy Wilson over the right-field fence.

But the Phillies came right back in the bottom of the inning. Anderson led off with a line smash off the knee of pitcher Tom House, who hobbled off the field. His replacement, Ron Schueler, gave up back-to-back singles to pinch-hitter Tommy Hutton and Bowa.

With the bases now loaded, an unnerved Schueler threw a wild pitch to let one run in, then walked Cesar Tovar. Del Unser hit a sacrifice fly to once again tie the game.

Both lineups then went dormant. The Phils could not even mount a threat, while the Braves continually left runners on base. In the 18th inning they set a major league record by stranding their 24th and 25th runners.

The Phillies' rally in the 20th inning began when Doyle led off with a triple. Greg Luzinski and Bowa were then given intentional walks to set up a force at home. But Jose Pagan hit a fly ball deep enough to left field to send Doyle dashing home with the winning run.

Braves	AB	R	H	RBI
Garr rf	11	0	1	0
Jackson ss	3	1	1	0
Perez ph-ss	4	0	0	0
Aaron lf	3	0	1	0
Brown lf	4	1	2	0
Evans 3b	9	1	3	4
Lum 1b	8	0	3	0
Baker cf	8	0	1	0
Johnson 2b	8	0	2	0
Oates c	8	0	1	0
Reed p	4	1	0	0
Frisella p	0	0	0	0
Gilbreath ph	1	0	0	0
Niekro p	0	0	0	0
Dietz ph	0	0	0	0
Pierce ph	1	0	0	0
House p	0	0	0	0
Schueler p	2	0	1	0
Blanks ph	1	0	1	0
Kelley p	1	0	0	0
Totals	**76**	**4**	**17**	**4**

Phillies	AB	R	H	RBI
Bowa ss	8	0	1	0
Tovar lf	6	0	1	0
Lersch p	0	0	0	0
Robinson ph	1	0	0	0
Lonborg p	0	0	0	0
Pagan ph	0	0	0	1
Unser cf	7	0	0	1
Montanez 1b	6	0	0	0
Boone c	8	0	2	0
Schmidt 3b	7	0	0	0
Anderson rf	8	2	2	0
Doyle 2b	7	2	2	1
Ruthven p	2	0	0	0
Rogodzinski ph	0	0	0	0
Scarce p	1	0	0	0
Wilson p	0	0	0	0
Hutton ph	1	0	1	0
Harmon pr	0	1	0	0
Twitchell p	0	0	0	0
Luzinski ph-lf	2	0	0	0
Totals	**64**	**5**	**9**	**3**

ATL 0 0 2 0 0 0 0 0 0 0 0 0 2 0 0 0 0 0 0 0 - 4 17 1
PHI 0 0 0 0 0 0 0 2 0 0 0 0 2 0 0 0 0 0 0 1 - 5 9 4

Braves	IP	H	R	ER	BB	SO
Reed	7	3	2	1	2	2
Frisella	3	0	0	0	0	3
Niekro	1	0	0	0	0	0
House	1	1	1	1	0	1
Schueler	5	3	1	1	3	4
Kelley L (0-1)	2.1	2	1	1	2	2
Totals	**19.1**	**9**	**5**	**4**	**7**	**12**

Phillies	IP	H	R	ER	BB	SO
Ruthven	8	6	2	0	3	6
Scarce	3.2	2	0	0	3	4
Wilson	1.1	3	2	2	0	2
Twitchell	2	1	0	0	2	3
Lersch	3	4	0	0	1	0
Lonborg W (2-4)	2	1	0	0	1	0
Totals	**20**	**17**	**4**	**2**	**10**	**15**

E—Atlanta Baker; Philadelphia Doyle 2, Schmidt, Lonborg. DP—Atlanta. 2B—Atlanta Evans, Lum, Johnson; Philadelphia Boone, Anderson, Tovar. 3B—Philadelphia Doyle. HR—Atlanta Evans (7). SH—Atlanta Lum, Brown; Philadelphia Rogodzinski. SF—Philadelphia Pagan, Unser. HBP—Atlanta Johnson, Lum, Jackson. LOB—Atlanta 27; Philadelphia 11. Attendance: 10,158.

Phils Pull Victory from the Jaws of Defeat

Facing what appeared to be certain defeat, the Phillies rallied to score five times in the ninth inning and pull out a wild win in front of 12,000 crazed fans at Connie Mack Stadium.

The Cardinals scored a run in the eighth to break a 3–3 tie, then knocked Robin Roberts around for three more runs in the ninth to take a commanding 7–3 lead. The big blow was Ken Boyer's triple off the wall in left-center.

But the Phils wouldn't quit. Wally Post singled and scored after Harry Anderson doubled off the scoreboard.

Jim Brosnan was brought in to replace Cardinals starter "Vinegar Bend" Mizell, but he didn't fare any better. Willie Jones slammed a double to make it 7–5. Gene Freese, pinch-hitting for Sparky Anderson, hit a bouncer back to the mound for the first out, but pinch-hitter Dave Philley slapped a run-scoring single to cut the lead to one and send Brosnan to the showers.

Bob Bowman came in to hit for reliever Dick Farrell and singled to left field off Brosnan's replacement, Larry Jackson, sending pinch-runner Chico Fernandez to second.

Richie Asburn walked to load the bases and Granny Hamner drew another walk to force home the tying run. Ed Bouchee then hit a line drive over the head of center fielder Curt Flood to score Bowman with the winning run.

The late-inning fireworks delighted a home crowd that had been watching a fine pitchers' duel for seven innings.

The Cards took a 1–0 lead in the first when Alex Grammas singled and Boyer doubled into the left-field corner.

The Phillies grabbed the lead in the second on Jones' two-run homer into the lower left-field deck. But two innings later, the Cardinals went out in front again after scoring a pair of runs off Roberts.

At a Glance

WP: Farrell (1–2)

HR: Jones (5)

Key stat: Bouchee 3-for-5, 2 RBIs; Jones 2-for-4, 3 RBIs; H. Anderson 2-for-4, RBI, 2 runs

The Phils tied the game in the sixth on Bouchee's double to the bullpen.

The see-saw battle continued right up until the final rally in the ninth. Farrell got the win after throwing just one pitch, inducing Flood to ground into an inning-ending force out.

Brandt's Game-Saving Slide Caps Comeback

An offensive explosion by both teams in the 11th inning produced a combined nine runs, but the Phillies came up with the one that mattered most when Jackie Brandt slid into home with the winning run.

The game looked like a lost cause to nearly 19,000 fans at Connie Mack Stadium when the Pirates erupted for four runs in the top of the 11th.

Willie Stargell opened the inning with a double to right off reliever Roger Craig. Jim Pagliaroni singled to left to score pinch-runner Manny Mota.

After shortstop Dick Groat booted Donn Clendenon's grounder, Bill Mazeroski homered, sending thousands of fans to the exits. And why not? The Phils hadn't produced a base runner since the fifth, when Johnny Callison hit a one-out double. Callison scored on a single to center by Tony Gonzalez to give the Phils a 3–0 lead.

Those runs seemed to be enough until 37-year-old right-hander Bob Buhl ran out of gas in the seventh inning. Buhl, acquired by the Phillies in the infamous trade with the Cubs for future Hall of Fame pitcher Ferguson Jenkins, had pitched just an inning in relief before getting his first start as a Phillie.

Jim Pagliaroni led off the inning with a single. Buhl retired the next two batters but gave up consecutive singles to Bob Bailey and pinch-hitter Jerry Lynch. Matty Alou then cleared the bases with a triple to the tie the game.

Rookie left-hander Woodie Fryman came in and put the Phillies to sleep for the next four innings, retiring 12 batters in a row before the fateful 11th.

Trailing 7–3, Callison led off with a single to right. Harvey Kuenn then beat out a high chop-

Pirates	AB	R	H	RBI
Alou cf	5	0	2	3
Pagan ss	6	0	1	0
Clemente rf	5	0	1	0
Stargell lf	4	0	1	0
Mota pr-lf	0	1	0	0
Pagliaroni c	5	1	3	1
Alley pr	0	1	0	0
May c	0	0	0	0
Clendenon 1b	5	1	0	0
Mazeroski 2b	5	1	2	3
Bailey 3b	5	1	1	0
Schwall p	2	0	0	0
Lynch ph	1	0	1	0
McBean pr	0	1	0	0
Fryman p	2	0	0	0
Face p	0	0	0	0
Totals	45	7	12	7

Phillies	AB	R	H	RBI
Briggs cf	4	0	1	0
Brandt ph-cf	2	1	1	1
Groat ss	6	1	2	2
White 1b	5	0	0	0
Callison rf	5	2	3	1
Gonzalez lf	2	0	2	1
Kuenn ph-lf	2	1	1	0
Taylor 3b	5	0	1	1
Rojas 2b	5	1	1	1
Dalrymple c	2	1	0	0
Uecker ph-c	2	1	0	0
Buhl p	2	0	0	0
Craig p	1	0	0	0
Knowles p	0	0	0	0
Clemens ph	1	0	0	0
Totals	44	8	12	7

PIT	0	0	0	0	0	0	3	0	0	0	4	-	7	12	3
PHI	1	1	0	0	1	0	0	0	0	0	5	-	8	12	1

Pirates	IP	H	R	ER	BB	SO
Schwall	6	6	3	2	3	4
Fryman	4	2	2	2	0	2
Face L (3-1)	0.2	4	3	2	0	1
Totals	10.2	12	8	6	3	7

Phillies	IP	H	R	ER	BB	SO
Buhl	7	7	3	3	2	2
Craig	3.2	5	4	3	0	3
Knowles W (3-0)	0.1	0	0	0	0	0
Totals	11	12	7	6	2	5

E—Pittsburgh Clendenon, Pagan, Mazeroski; Philadelphia Groat. DP—Pittsburgh; Philadelphia. 2B—Pittsburgh Stargell; Philadelphia Callison. 3B—Pittsburgh Alou. HR—Pittsburgh Mazeroski (2). LOB—Pittsburgh 7; Philadelphia 7. Attendance: 18,982.

per to shortstop, prompting Pirates manager Harry Walker to make a pitching change.

Walker turned to his top reliever, Elroy Face, who was greeted with a run-scoring single by Tony Taylor. Cookie Rojas then broke an 0-for-17 streak with a base hit to left to plate Kuenn, making the score 7–5.

With the crowd (or what was left of it) now stirring, catcher Bob Uecker attempted to move the runners into scoring position. But his bunt went right back to Face, who turned and fired to third for the force. When Doug Clemens struck out, it looked like the Phillies were done.

But Jackie Brandt, who entered the game earlier as a pinch-hitter, hit a blooper into right field to knock in Rojas and scooted to second when Roberto Clemente's throw back to the infield caromed off the leg of Clendenon at first.

Up stepped Groat, who seared a ball to left field. Uecker crossed the plate with Brandt chugging hard right behind him. He slid in as the ball bounced off the hands of catcher Jerry May.

Brandt bounced up and was greeted by a throng of teammates who had streamed out of the dugout.

Afterward, Groat, the 1960 National League MVP, said, "I can't think of a hit that's pleased me more."

"It's like they say," said Cookie Rojas. "A ballgame is never over until the final out."

Ageless Moyer Throws Two-Hitter at Age 47

Jamie Moyer, the 47-year-old Ageless Wonder, turned in a masterful performance to become the oldest major league player to throw a shutout.

Moyer threw a two-hitter to move ahead of Phil Niekro, who previously held the record at age 46. Troy Glaus had both of Atlanta's hits—both singles.

Since age was no obstacle to Moyer, he took the historic moment in stride.

"Just doing my job," he said. "I changed speeds pretty well, kept the ball down and got ahead in the counts."

"Jamie carved us up tonight," said the Braves' Chipper Jones. "The guy is 87 years old, and he's still pitching for a reason. He stays off the barrel of the bat, keeps you guessing."

Moyer bamboozled the Braves all night with a fastball that barely broke 80 mph and an array of off-speed pitches thrown with pinpoint control. At one point he retired 17 straight batters.

Jamie struck out five and walked no one.

"I had fun," he said. "I probably had forgotten what that's like. It hasn't happened a whole lot in my career."

It was only the 10th shutout of his lengthy career, making Moyer the only pitcher to throw a shutout in each of four decades. He threw his first one against the Montreal Expos on Aug. 16, 1986.

The veteran lefty had lots of run support. Placido Polanco, Raul Ibanez, Chase Utley, Jayson Werth and Ryan Howard all had two hits apiece. One of Werth's hits was a three-run homer in the third inning. Raul Ibanez and Wilson Valdez each knocked in a pair of runs with singles in the fifth.

At a Glance

WP: Moyer (4–2)

HR: Werth (6)

Key stat: Moyer becomes oldest pitcher to throw a shutout; Werth 2-for-4, 3 RBIs

The Phils made it a short night for Braves starter Derek Lowe, lighting him up for 11 hits and seven runs. Lowe was lifted after five innings.

In the ninth, Moyer had a sellout home crowd of more than 45,000 behind him, chanting, "Jamie! Jamie!"

His final victim was Omar Infante, who grounded out. Catcher Carlos Ruiz pumped his fist and first baseman Ryan Howard trotted over and tossed Moyer the ball as the crowd went wild.

May 9, 1948

Phillies 14, Reds 2 (Game 1)

Pride of Egypt, Pa., Simmons Gets Early Birthday Present

Ten days short of his 19th birthday, Egypt, Pa., native Curt Simmons got his sterling career on track with this eight-hit gem against the Reds.

Pitching in the first game of a doubleheader at Crosley Field in Cincinnati, the young left-hander struck out six and was never in serious trouble. He gave up an unearned run in the fourth inning when first baseman Dick Sisler dropped the relay throw on what would have been an inning-ending double play, allowing Hank Sauer to cross the plate.

Simmons had a four-run lead when he walked out to the mound for the first inning, thanks mainly to a three-run homer by Del Ennis. It was the opening salvo of a 15-hit assault on four Reds pitchers, including starter Howie Fox.

Dick Sisler and Johnny Blatnick each had four hits. Richie Ashburn had three, while Ennis drove in five runs.

The Reds scored their other run in the seventh when Ray Lamanno doubled and came home on Virgil Stallcup's single. But by then the run hardly mattered.

At a Glance

WP: Simmons (1–2)

HR: Ennis (3)

Key stat: Blatnik 4-for-5, 4 runs, 3 RBIs; Sisler 4-for-4, 2 runs, 3 RBIs

The victory was the first of 1948 for Simmons and his second career complete game. He would go on to finish his first full season in the majors with a record of 7–13 and a 4.87 ERA.

Curt Simmons made his major league debut at age 18. He scattered eight hits in a 14–2 win over the Reds on May 9, 1948.

Padilla Lifts Phils to Seventh Win in a Row

The Phillies won their seventh game in a row behind the superb power pitching of Vicente Padilla, who came within four outs of throwing a no-hitter against the defending World Champions.

Padilla, who was obtained from Arizona in a blockbuster trade for Curt Schilling in 2000, wound up with a two-hit shutout.

"He took his game to another level," said manager Larry Bowa. "That's a good team over there, with a lot of good left-handed bats."

The right-hander struck out seven and walked three. His no-hitter was broken up with two outs in the eighth when Chris Donnels, pinch-hitting for Arizona starter Rick Helling, banged a first-pitch fastball into the left-field corner for a ground-rule double.

Donnels said he wasn't trying to think about the no-hitter.

"I had watched a lot of the game on TV in the clubhouse and I just tried to stay aggressive."

As more than 20,000 fans rose to give Padilla a long standing ovation, Bowa came out to remind his teammate it was a close game and he still had work to do. Padilla responded by getting Tony Womack to hit a ground ball to second and end the inning.

At a Glance

WP: Padilla (5–2)

HR: Abreu (3), Glanville (1)

Key stat: Padilla 2-hitter; Abreu 2 RBIs; Glanville 2 RBIs; Burrell 3-for-4

At that point, Padilla was nursing a 2–0 lead. But the Phils added two more in the bottom of the eighth to put the game away.

After catcher Mike Lieberthal hit a leadoff double to right, Arizona relievers Jose Parra and Eddie Oropesa lost sight of the strike zone as they combined to walk three batters and hit another, giving the Phillies a 4–0 lead.

The Phils scored their first run in the fifth inning on Bobby Abreu's opposite-field home run.

In the seventh, Glanville hit a ball that bounced past right fielder Danny Bautista and rolled into the corner. Glanville easily circled the bases for an inside-the-park home run.

Padilla's gem was the highlight of a 14–11 season and the capstone of the longest winning streak in seven years for the Phils, who finished third in the National League East with a record of 80–81.

Record 10 Homers Part of the Fun at Baker Bowl

The Phillies and St. Louis Cardinals went on a long ball rampage as they blasted a major league record-setting 10 home runs at Baker Bowl.

Center fielder Cy Williams led the barrage with three homers on his way to hitting a league-leading 41. He hit his first homer in the third inning, a two-run shot that followed Johnny Mokan's three-run homer. The five-run outburst erased an early 3–0 lead by the Cardinals.

From there the Phils kept pounding away. The Cardinals certainly got in their rips but couldn't keep up with this runaway train that piled on three more runs in the fourth, four in the fifth, two in the sixth and three each in the seventh and eighth innings.

Mokan hit two homers and matched Williams with seven RBIs.

There may even have been an 11th home run. Fans vehemently argued that a fly ball hit by the Cardinals' Milt Stock reached the left-field stands. But the umpires disagreed.

Needless to say, all that slugging made life miserable for pitchers on both sides that day as earned averages soared. Cardinals reliever Bill Sherdel took the worst beating. He was tagged for seven runs in just two innings and was charged with the loss.

Phils starter Petie Behan got the win despite giving up eight runs in five innings.

Cy Williams

Cy Williams was the Phillies' first true left-handed slugger, a dead pull hitter with a stroke that was perfect for Baker's Bowl short fence in right field.

The 6-foot-2, 180-pound center fielder broke in with the Chicago Cubs in 1912. Four years later, he led the NL with 12 homers. Williams was traded to the Phillies in 1918 and saw his home run production increase as the major leagues emerged from the dead-ball era.

With the Phillies, he hit double digits in home runs nine years in a row and led the league three times, hitting 15 in 1920, 41 in 1923 and 30 in 1927.

Williams hit 251 homers and knocked in 1,005 runs in a career that spanned 19 years.

At a Glance

WP: Behan (1–1)

HR: Williams 3 (10, 11, 12), Paxkinson (2), Mokan 2 (3, 4).

Key stat: Williams 3 HRs, 7 RBIs

Ring's Bat as Vital as His Arm

Pitcher Jimmy Ring continued his convincing impersonation of a slugger in this game by igniting a seven-run rally with a grand slam. It was the veteran righty's second home run in 10 days and went a long way toward Ring winning his first game of the season.

In the locker room after the game, Ring couldn't stop chattering about his newfound ability to hit the long ball.

"I guess I get more kick out of a home run or any timely hit than out of anything else. Two homers for me in the last week, too. Looks like I'm getting dangerous."

His boasting brought good-natured groans from teammates.

"It looks like a tough year," said catcher Jimmie Wilson. "We won't hear the last of that home run for a long time."

Wilson started the sixth inning uprising with a leadoff single. Heinie Sand and Clarence Huber also singled, setting the table for Ring, who hit a high fly ball over Baker Bowl's right-field fence onto Broad Street.

The grand slam broke a 1–1 tie and clearly rattled Pirates starter Vic Aldridge, who allowed two more batters to get on base before giving up a three-run homer to Phils cleanup hitter George Harper. Wilson came around again to double in the same inning but was left stranded at second base.

At a Glance

WP: Ring (1–2)

HR: Ring (2), Harper (3)

Key stat: Ring 4 RBIs; Harper 2-for-4, 3 RBIs, 1 run; Wilson 3-for-4

The Pirates made things interesting by scoring three times in the eighth inning and once more in the ninth. But Ring hung on get the win. He gave up five runs, 11 hits and struck out four to improve his record to 1–2.

Homer the Lone Blemish for Roberts in 1-Hitter

After surrendering a leadoff home run in the first inning, Robin Roberts settled in and sat down the next 27 batters en route to an 8–1 victory at Shibe Park.

The great right-hander said he was disappointed over giving up the homer to Bobby Adams, but not over losing the no-hitter.

"I threw it where I wanted it to go but Adams caught it," said Roberts. "I knew it was really tagged when it left his bat. Many of my pitches were curves but Adams hit a fast one."

His near-perfect performance amazed everyone in the ballpark that night, including Reds manager Birdie Tebbetts.

"You don't compare Roberts with good pitchers," Tebbets said. "You compare him with great pitchers."

"I never knew a pitcher could make a fastball move the way Roberts did tonight," said home plate umpire Bill Jackowski, who was also behind the plate on April 29 when Roberts one-hit the Milwaukee Braves.

The Phils took a 2–1 lead in the second. With runners on second and third, Bobby Morgan hit a one-out single to left to score Johnny Wyrostek. Roberts followed with a ground ball fielder's choice that allowed Smoky Burgess to cross the plate.

They broke the game open in the fifth, scoring five runs on three hits, including a triple by Earl Torgeson.

Meanwhile, Roberts was pounding the strike zone and sitting down one batter after the next. He needed only five pitches to get through the fourth inning, retiring leadoff hitter Roy McMillan on a first-pitch lineout, Gus Bell on a first-pitch fly ball to right, and Ted Kluszewski on three straight strikes.

At a Glance

WP: Roberts (4–3)

Key stat: Roberts throws perfect game after leadoff home run

"All during the game I felt better than I had felt at any time last year," said Robby. "My rhythm was just the way I wanted it to be."

A number of his victims remarked after the game that Roberts threw the most amazing slider they'd ever seen. The Phillies' ace claimed he didn't even know how to throw one but conceded that, "every once in a while my pitches take a sudden slide. I don't know what causes it."

May 14, 1950

Phillies 9, Giants 7

Konstanty Shows MVP Form in Lengthy Battle

Flashing the form that would make him the National League's Most Valuable Player, Jim Konstanty pitched three innings of solid relief in a weird game that the Whiz Kids didn't actually win until July 5.

After losing the first game of a doubleheader, the Phils and Giants battled for nearly three hours in the nightcap until umpire Bill Stewart invoked the Sunday curfew law and suspended play.

Things didn't begin well as starter Russ Meyer was rocked for four first-inning runs. Meyer failed to register an out and was replaced by Bob Miller, who then gave up a solo home run to Hank Thompson.

At a Glance

WP: Konstanty: (2–0)

HR: Ennis (5)

Key stat: Ennis 2-for-3, 3 RBIs; Ashburn 3-for-5, 2 runs

Jim Konstanty picked up the win on May 14, 1950. He appeared in 74 games, all in relief, and compiled a 16–7 record on his way to being named National League MVP.

Trailing 6–1, the Phillies' bats came alive in the fifth inning. Richie Ashburn got more than 25,000 fans at Shibe Park wound up by bashing a triple to deep center field. He then scored on a bunt single by Granny Hamner.

With one out, Del Ennis walked and came home along with Hamner on a single by Willie Jones and an error by Giants left fielder Whitey Lockman. Dick Sisler knocked in Jones with a double to right.

Konstanty replaced Bubba Church in the top of the sixth and retired the side in order after issuing a leadoff walk to Hank Thompson.

The Phils grabbed the lead in the bottom of the inning. After a walk to Ashburn and a single by Eddie Waitkus, Ennis slammed a home run off the facing of the upper deck bleachers.

A walk, a single and two Giants errors led to another run, making the score 9–6. The Giants scored one in the seventh when Bobby Thomson doubled and came around to score on a triple by Lockman.

With daylight fading, the umpire crew stopped the game at the end of the eighth inning. Had it been a weekday, they simply would have ordered that the lights be turned on. But state curfew laws at the time stated that no inning could begin after 6:44 on Sunday evening.

So the two teams headed back to their respective clubhouses, showered up and went home. The scored stayed 9–7 for more than seven weeks. They resumed play on July 5, with Robin Roberts making a rare appearance in relief. Robbie made short work of the Giants, retiring the side in order to end the game.

Jim Konstanty

Casimir James Konstanty will forever be remembered for one magical season when he rose from obscurity to win the National League Most Valuable Player Award in leading the Whiz Kids to the NL pennant.

Konstanty put together one of the all-time great seasons out of the bullpen in 1950. Armed with a palmball, the off-speed specialist became a workhorse for manager Eddie Sawyer, pitching 152 innings in 74 appearances.

Konstanty directly accounted for 38 of the Phillies' wins with a record of 16–7 and 22 saves. His earned run average was 2.66.

When the World Series rolled around Sawyer surprised everyone by naming Konstanty his Game 1 starter against the Yankees. Though the Phillies lost, the right-hander was superb, surrendering only one run on four hits in eight innings.

May 15, 1989

Phillies 3, Giants 2 (12 innings)

Dernier Provides New Look to Walk-Off Homer

Bob Dernier added a new dimension to the walk-off home run when he electrified a Veterans Stadium crowd with his three-run, inside-the-park run off homer in the bottom of the 12th.

Dernier's mad dash around the bases was one of the most unforgettable endings to a ballgame in the history of Veterans Stadium, and it happened just minutes after the Giants had taken a 2–0 lead in the top of the inning.

Before that, it was all about the pitching. Phillies southpaw Don Carman and the Giants' Scott Garrelts were outstanding. Both threw nine scoreless innings, with Garrelts allowing just three hits and Carman four.

The Giants finally broke through in the 12th when Will Clark and Kevin Mitchell hit back-to-back homers off Phils reliever Steve Bedrosian.

In the bottom of the 12th, pinch-hitter Dickie Thon and Steve Lake hit back-to-back one-out singles. After Steve Jeltz popped up for the second out, Dernier came to the plate and pulled a line drive down the left-field line for what looked like an easy double.

But the ball took a crazy hop off the wall and bounced away from Mitchell.

Third base coach Larry Bowa began waving his arms frantically to the base runners. Thon and Lake scored standing up, and when Mitchell had trouble picking up the ball, Bowa signaled to Dernier to keep on coming.

At a Glance

WP: Bedrosian (2–2)

HR: Dernier (1)

Key stat: Dernier walk-off inside-the-park HR, 3 RBIs

"I had thought triple as I left the plate, because I figured if I make them have a play on me at third, Laker might score," said Dernier. "But as I hit second, I saw Mitchell still chasing the ball and I picked up Bo waving me on. So I just hauled it and turned left at third."

With more than 15,000 fans cheering him on like a racehorse, Dernier headed down the stretch and slid head first into home ahead of the relay throw. The Phillies' dugout emptied as players and coaches mobbed the man of the hour.

Dernier's heroics ended a 20-inning scoreless streak and averted a record-setting fourth consecutive shutout at the Vet. All three games of their previous series against the Dodgers had ended in shutouts, with the Phils winning the first two.

Dernier also took the Phillies' closer off the hot seat.

"I'm just not throwing my slider the way I want," Bedrosian said. "Things haven't been too pretty lately for me, but I have to just keep battling."

Bedrosian worked his way out of a big jam in the top of the 10th, thanks to a terrific defensive play by Dernier. With one out, Clark boomed a double off the top of the top of the right-center field fence.

After a walk to Mitchell, Candy Maldonado singled to right. Dernier charged the ball, made a clean pickup and uncorked a strike to beat Clark at home plate.

Manager Nick Leyva called it a great win for his team and a much needed boost for Bedrosian.

"Here, he gave up two more homers and he would have had to try and sleep with that," said Leyva. "But winning like this has to make things easier for him."

Werth Posts Big Game: 3 Homers, 8 RBIs

Jayson Werth had the game of his life as he blasted three consecutive home runs and drove in eight of the Phillies' 10 runs in a rout of the Toronto Blue Jays. Werth's RBI total tied a franchise record.

His first homer was a three-run shot to right in the second inning. The second homer was a 425-foot grand slam to right in the third, and No. 3 was a solo belt to left-center in the fifth to give the Phils a 9–2 lead.

"Anything can happen on any given day I guess," said Werth. "It's not like I was trying to do anything like that. It just happened. I don't know what else to say. It's just crazy."

Werth had a chance to break the RBI record and reach the exclusive Four Home Runs in a Row Club in the seventh, but fouled out. He later admitted that he was a little too mindful of the moment.

"I swung at some pitches I probably shouldn't have," Werth said.

Still, he placed himself in some great company, joining Mike Schmidt (1976), Willie "Puddin' Head" Jones (1958), Gavvy Cravath (1915) and Kitty Bransfeld (1910) as the only players in Phillies history to knock in eight runs in one game.

Werth also became the 18th Phillie to hit three homers in a game. Ryan Howard was the last one to do it in September 2006.

"Jayson had a great night at the plate," Howard said. "It's a lot of fun to watch somebody who's that locked in. He deserves it because he's been working hard at it."

At a Glance

WP: Moyer (3–3)

HR: Werth 3 (7, 8, 9)

Key stat: Werth 3 HRs, 8 RBIs

All those early runs made life easy for starter Jamie Moyer. The 45-year-old southpaw went 6 2/3 innings, holding the Blue Jays to three runs on seven hits. He struck out five and walked two.

"I felt like I threw the ball a lot better than I have recently," said Moyer. "We won and that's the most important part."

They won because of a player who turned out to be a free-agent steal for the Phillies. Werth, a former Dodger, was plagued by injuries in Los Angeles. By '08 he was the Phillies' starting right fielder and a key element to the team's run to the World Series title.

Only Line Needed: 45 runs, 50 hits, 11 homers!

The Wrigley Field wind blew strong and steady all day long, helping the Phillies and Cubs combine for one of the most epic slugfests in major league history: 45 runs, 50 hits, 11 home runs!

Mike Schmidt hit the first homer of the day and the last. But the Cubs' Dave "Kong" Kingman won top honors by stroking three.

Schmidt's home run in the first inning appeared to be nothing more than a pop-up behind shortstop. But the ball got caught up in the howling wind and carried into the left-field bleachers for a three-run homer.

Three batters later, Bob Boone hit another three-run blast, and that was all for Cubs starter Dennis Lamp. Phils pitcher Randy Lerch then homered off reliever Donnie Moore to give the Phils an early 7–0 lead.

Lerch left the game shell-shocked in the bottom of the first after giving up four runs, including a three-run bomb to Kingman. The Cubs scored two more off Doug Bird to cut the lead to 7–6.

In the top of the third, the Phils erupted for eight runs on seven hits, including a three-run homer by Garry Maddox. They continued to pour it on, scoring twice in the fourth and four times in the fifth, increasing their lead to 21–9.

But Chicago counterpunched with a seven-run inning off Tug McGraw, four coming on a Bill Buckner grand slam. The Phils' legendary reliever could only laugh at the absurdity of it all.

"I saw everybody getting knocked around. I knew nobody could get anybody out," Tug said. "But I said this thing has to be stopped. And I was the man to stop it. And I did. They only got seven runs."

The Cubs tacked on three in the sixth, and after the Phillies scored a run in the seventh, completed their incredible comeback by scoring three more in the eighth to tie the game at 22.

Catcher Barry Foote, who hit the game-tying single off Ron Reed, said he was so tired, "I couldn't even put my fingers down anymore."

Reed, who gave up six runs in 3 1/3 innings, noticed how the wind emboldened anyone holding a bat that day.

"The wind turns .220 hitters into .320 hitters. It's a snowball effect, and pretty soon, there's nothing you can do."

No one scored in the ninth inning. But in the top of the 10th, Schmidt cracked what proved to be the game-winning homer off Chicago closer Bruce

May 17, 1979

Phillies 23, Cubs 22 (10 innings)

Phillies	AB	R	H	RBI
McBride rf	8	2	3	1
Bowa ss	8	4	5	1
Rose 1b	7	4	3	4
Schmidt 3b	4	3	2	4
Unser lf	7	1	1	2
Maddox cf	4	3	4	4
Gross pr-cf	2	1	1	1
Boone c	4	2	3	5
Meoli 2b	5	0	1	0
Lerch p	1	1	1	1
Bird p	1	1	0	0
Luzinski ph	0	0	0	0
Espinosa pr	1	1	0	0
McGraw p	0	0	0	0
Reed p	0	0	0	0
McCarver ph	1	0	0	0
Eastwick p	0	0	0	0
Totals	**53**	**23**	**24**	**23**

Cubs	AB	R	H	RBI
DeJesus ss	6	4	3	1
Vail rf	5	2	3	1
Burris p	0	0	0	0
Thompson ph-rf	2	1	1	0
Buckner 1b	7	2	4	7
Kingman lf	6	4	3	6
Ontiveros 3b	7	2	1	1
Martin cf	6	2	3	3
Sutter p	0	0	0	0
Foote c	6	1	3	1
Sizemore 2b	4	2	2	1
Caudill p	0	0	0	0
Murcer rf-cf	2	0	1	0
Lamp p	0	0	0	0
Moore p	1	0	1	1
Hernandez p	1	0	0	0
Dillard ph-2b	1	2	1	0
Biittner ph	1	0	0	0
Kelleher 2b	1	0	0	0
Totals	**56**	**22**	**26**	**22**

PHI 7 0 8 2 4 0 1 0 0 1 - 23 24 2
CHI 6 0 0 3 7 3 0 3 0 0 - 22 26 2

Phillies	IP	H	R	ER	BB	SO
Lerch	0.1	5	5	5	0	0
Bird	3.2	8	4	4	0	2
McGraw	0.2	4	7	4	3	1
Reed	3.1	9	6	6	0	0
Eastwick W (1-0)	2	0	0	0	0	1
Totals	**10**	**26**	**22**	**19**	**3**	**4**

Cubs	IP	H	R	ER	BB	SO
Lamp	0.1	6	6	6	0	0
Moore	2	6	7	7	2	1
Hernandez	2.2	7	8	6	7	1
Caudill	1.1	3	1	1	2	3
Burris	1.2	1	0	0	0	1
Sutter L (1-1)	2	1	1	1	1	1
Totals	**10**	**24**	**23**	**21**	**12**	**7**

E—Philadelphia Schmidt 2; Chicago Kingman, DeJesus. DP— Philadelphia 2. 2B—Philadelphia Boone, Rose 2, Maddox 2, Bowa 2; Chicago Martin, Foote, DeJesus. 3B—Philadelphia Gross; Chicago Moore. HR—Philadelphia Boone (2), Schmidt 2 (13,14), Maddox (6), Lerch (1); Chicago Buckner (4), Martin (3), Ontiveros (1), Kingman 3 (10,11,12). SF—Philadelphia Gross, Unser. HBP—Philadelphia Boone. LOB—Philadelphia 15; Chicago 7. SB—Philadelphia Meoli, Bowa. Attendance: 14,952.

Sutter. "He threw me that pitch of his (a splitter) on the inner half of the plate, and I just reacted," said Schmidt.

Rawly Eastwick closed the game with a 1–2–3 10th and made it look easy, unlike all the other pitchers that day.

"I've always pitched well here," he said. "I knew what was going on, but I don't care about conditions, circumstances. I just want to pitch."

Rare Win over Derringer Ends 0–11 Hex

After more than two years of torment, the Phillies finally figured out a way to beat Paul Derringer.

Cincinnati's hard-throwing right-hander had beaten the light-hitting Phillies 11 straight times, winning six in a row in 1939 and five straight in '38.

But on this warm spring day at Shibe Park, the Phillies hit Derringer early and often as they shocked the defending National League champions.

Cincinnati took a 3–0 lead in the first inning, but the Phils came back with two in the second and two in the third to take a 4–3 lead.

In the sixth, they exploded for four more runs and sent Derringer to the showers.

Years of frustration came to a head as every batter got a hit off Derringer, with the exception of Heinie Mueller, who was twice robbed in the field.

Phillies starter Hugh Mulcahy pitched his best game of the young season in running his record to 4–1 as he struck out four while holding the Reds to three runs on seven hits.

At a Glance

WP: Mulcahy (4–1)

Key stat: Atwood 2-for-3, 3 RBIs; Arnovich 2-for-4, 2 runs

Overall, it was the best performance by the cellar-dwelling Phillies in two years, and perhaps the highlight of the season for a team destined to lose 100 games for the third year in a row. Mulcahy wound up with a record of 13–22.

For the Reds, the loss stung, but it was really nothing more than a minor bump in the road. They would go on repeat as NL champs and defeat the Detroit Tigers in the 1940 World Series, led by their ace—Paul Derringer.

May 20, 1964
Phillies 7, Giants 2

Wine's Clutch Defensive Play Staves Off Giants

Timely hitting and a sensational defensive play proved to be a winning combination for Gene Mauch's star-crossed Phillies, who moved back into a tie for first after this early season showdown with their West Coast rivals at Candlestick Park.

San Francisco grabbed the lead in the bottom of the first when Jesus Alou led off with a single, moved to third on a bunt and a fly ball, and scored on Willie McCovey's base hit.

Giants starter Juan Marichal held the Phillies in check through the first four innings. But with two outs in the fifth, Dick Allen hit a solo home run, Johnny Callison singled and Wes Covington slammed a two-run homer to give the Phils a 3–1 lead.

The Giants were on the verge of tying the game in the bottom of the fifth. A leadoff single by Alou, a walk to Chuck Hiller and another RBI single by McCovey made it 3–2.

Mauch replaced his starter, Art Mahaffey, with Jack Baldschun, who hit the first batter he faced, Orlando Cepeda.

With the bases now loaded, Baldschun served up a 2–0 fastball to Jim Ray Hart, and the rookie third baseman smoked it up the middle.

"My heart just sank," Baldschun said. "I told myself, 'That's a base hit and it means two runs.' Then I saw Wine going after the ball."

The reliever was referring to shortstop Bobby Wine, who hustled behind second base, dove and gloved Hart's smash on the hop. He quickly flipped the ball to second baseman Tony Taylor for the force out.

At a Glance

WP: Baldschun (2–0)

HR: Allen (8), Callison (3), Covington (4)

Key stat: Callison 5-for-5, 3 RBIs, 2 runs; Allen 2-for-4, 2 RBIs

"The thought of a double play never entered my mind—until I saw Tony wheel and throw to first base to get Hart," said Baldschun. "It's the happiest thing for me that ever happened in a ballgame."

Catcher Clay Dalrymple had perhaps the best viewpoint.

"I still don't know how Wine got to that ball. It was hit like a shot. And it was only a foot or two from second base."

The inning-ending double play was a game-changer. In the top of the sixth, the Phils added three more runs to chase Marichal, who came into this game with a 12-game winning streak. His last loss was on Aug. 30, 1963.

In the eighth, Johnny Callison wrapped up a perfect 5-for-5 day at the plate with a solo home run to close out the scoring.

The team's overall performance made a big impression on Giants manager Alvin Dark.

"When I heard the Phillies got Jim Bunning, I knew they were going to be tough. And that's before I knew about Richie Allen," said Dark. "They're a good defensive team, too. They make the plays that have to be made and they have the neat knack of making the great play at the right time."

Dick Allen

One of the most talented and controversial players to ever wear a Phillies uniform, Dick Allen electrified fans with his powerful bat and polarized a city with his feuds with management.

No one was prepared for the impact Allen had when he arrived in Philadelphia in 1964 and nearly led the Phillies to the National League pennant. The Wampum, Pa., native batted .318 with 29 homers, 91 RBIs and 125 runs scored to win NL Rookie of the Year honors in 1964. Allen made his major league debut late in the 1963 season.

But things began to turn sour in 1965 after Allen got into a vicious pregame fight with teammate Frank Thomas after Thomas yelled racial slurs at him.

While his off-field escapades, suspensions and outspoken opinions infuriated many fans, no one could ignore Allen's breathtaking home runs and all-around game. His best season with the Phils was in 1966, when he batted .317, banged 40 homers and drove in 110 runs.

He was traded to St. Louis after the '69 season, after compiling 177 career home runs, 544 RBIs and a .300 batting average.

May 21, 1967
Phillies 2, Reds 1 (18 innings)

© Temple University Libraries, Urban Archives

Two Pitchers Plenty in 18-Inning Win

In a game that went 18 innings, the Phillies used only two pitchers to outlast the National League-leading Cincinnati Reds at Connie Mack Stadium.

Chris Short was outstanding for 12 of those innings, and reliever Dick Hall threw six scoreless frames to get the win. It was the Phils' longest extra-inning victory in 16 years.

"My goodness," manager Gene Mauch said of his pitchers. "What performances they put on."

The Reds went the more traditional route, relying on starter Milt Pappas and five relievers.

"Their pitching wasn't bad either," said Mauch.

Short took a 1–0 lead into the ninth and came to within a whisker of throwing a shutout.

Chris Short threw 12 innings in the Phillies' 2–1 win over the Reds on May 21, 1967, but didn't get the decision.

After giving up a leadoff walk to Tommy Harper, the big lefty struck out Vada Pinson and got Pete Rose on a grounder to shortstop.

But Tony Perez hit a slow grounder that scooted past third baseman Dick Allen and shortstop Bobby Wine, allowing Harper to score the tying run from second.

"Eight out of ten times it's an out," said a frustrated Short. "It was a slider—a good pitch—and he didn't hit it hard at all."

The Phils had several chances to win the game in extra innings. They had runners on first and third with two outs in the 11th, but Clay Dalyrmple fouled out to end the inning.

In the 12th, Cookie Rojas led off with a double and advanced to third when shortstop Leo Cardenas botched the relay throw from the outfield. The Phillies attempted a suicide squeeze, but Reds manager Dave Bristol had sniffed out the strategy and called for a pitchout. Rojas got caught in a rundown and was tagged out.

Taylor then flied out to end the inning.

The Phils loaded the bases in the 16th. With one out, Clay Dalrymple grounded into a home-to-first double play.

Finally, in the bottom of the 18th, the Phillies played small-ball to end the marathon. Allen drew a one-out walk and moved to second on Callison's slow roller to second. Don Lock then hit a line-drive single to center. Pinson came up throwing but had no chance to cut down Allen, who was running on contact.

"I was just trying to hit the ball hard," Lock said. "All I wanted to do was get a hit, any kind of hit."

Reds	AB	R	H	RBI
Harper rf	6	1	1	0
Pinson cf	7	0	0	0
Rose lf-2b	7	0	2	0
Perez 3b	7	0	3	1
May 1b	7	0	2	0
Pavletich c	6	0	2	0
Maloney pr	0	0	0	0
Nottebart pr	0	0	0	0
Robinson ph	1	0	0	0
Osteen p	0	0	0	0
Ruiz 2b	2	0	1	0
Johnson ph	1	0	0	0
Simpson lf	0	0	0	0
Shamsky ph-lf	3	0	0	0
Cardenas ss	7	0	0	0
Pappas p	2	0	0	0
Coker ph	1	0	0	0
Abernathy p	0	0	0	0
Helms ph	1	0	0	0
Queen p	0	0	0	0
McCool p	1	0	0	0
Edwards c	2	0	0	0
Totals	**61**	**1**	**11**	**1**

Phillies	AB	R	H	RBI
Gonzalez lf	5	1	2	0
Taylor ph	1	0	0	0
Hall p	2	0	0	0
Allen 3b	7	1	2	0
Callison rf	6	0	0	0
Briggs cf	4	0	2	1
Lock ph-cf	3	0	1	1
Francona 1b	5	0	1	0
Dalrymple c	5	0	1	0
Rojas 2b	7	0	2	0
Wine ss	2	0	0	0
White ph	1	0	0	0
Sutherland ss	2	0	0	0
Short p	4	0	0	0
Clemens ph	0	0	0	0
Brandt ph-lf	3	0	0	0
Totals	**57**	**2**	**11**	**2**

CIN 000000001000000000 - 1 11 1
PHI 100000000000000001 - 2 11 0

Reds	IP	H	R	ER	BB	SO
Pappas	7	5	1	1	3	3
Abernathy	2	1	0	0	1	2
Queen	2	3	0	0	1	1
McCool	3	0	0	0	1	1
Nottebart	2	1	0	0	2	1
Osteen L (0-1)	1.2	1	1	1	1	2
Totals	**17.1**	**11**	**2**	**2**	**9**	**10**

Phillies	IP	H	R	ER	BB	SO
Short	12	7	1	1	2	8
Hall W (1-2)	6	4	0	0	0	5
Totals	**18**	**11**	**1**	**1**	**2**	**13**

E—Cincinnati Cardenas. DP—Cincinnati 3; Philadelphia 2. 2B—Cincinnati Harper, Pavletich; Philadelphia Rojas 2. 3B—Philadelphia Allen. SF—Philadelphia Briggs. LOB—Cincinnati 8; Philadelphia 12. SB—Cincinnati Harper; Philadelphia Allen. Attendance: 8,641.

May 22, 1952
Phillies 6, Pirates 0

Simmons Matches Deft Pitching, Show of Power

Curt Simmons did it all in this game against the Pirates at Shibe Park. The stylish lefty tossed a complete game shutout and hit the only home run of his 20-year career, an inside-the-park job.

The Phils held a 3–0 lead when he came to bat in the sixth inning. With Jack Mayo on second and Eddie Waitkus on first, Simmons hit a screaming line drive to center.

"I hit it like a two-iron," he recalled. "That ball was rising."

Nineteen-year-old rookie Bobby Del Greco froze as the ball came at him.

"He came in and the ball went over his head," said Simmons. "At Shibe Park, to center field was forever."

As the ball was going over his head, a panicked Del Greco swatted it with his bare hand, which made matters even worse. By the time he ran the ball down and threw it back to the infield, Simmons had crossed the plate.

His three-run homer doubled a lead that the Phillies had built earlier in the game. They scored once in the opening frame when Granny Hamner reached first on a fielder's choice, stole second and went to third after Puddin' Head Jones grounded out. Del Ennis then knocked Hamner in with a single to left. The Phils scored two more in the fifth on four singles.

Simmons, meanwhile, was on top of his game, holding the Pirates to three hits while striking out eight in running his early season record to 3–1.

Simmons was on an amazing run since returning to baseball in late April after missing the entire 1951 season while serving in the military.

At a Glance

WP: Simmons (3–1)

HR: Simmons (1)

Key stat: Simmons CG shutout, 8 Ks, HR, 3 RBIs

"I wasn't in baseball shape but I had been throwing a little bit in the air hangar back in Germany," he rememberd.

Despite missing all of spring training, Simmons picked up a complete game win on April 29, holding the Chicago Cubs to just two runs. It was his first start since Sept. 9, 1950. He lost his next game then came back with a shutout against the Cubs before blanking the Pirates.

Greene's No-Hitter Is 8th in Phils History

In only his second start of the season, 24-year-old Tommy Greene reached the pinnacle of his craft as he became the eighth pitcher in Phillies history to throw a no-hitter.

It wasn't pretty: Greene walked seven Montreal batters. But he also struck out 10, relying heavily on a low- to mid-90s fastball.

The 6-foot-5, 225-pound right-hander came into the game with very little big-league experience. He was making just his 15th career start.

But Greene coasted through each inning. In the ninth, he had to face the heart of the Expos lineup.

Greene struck out Andres Galarraga on high heat. The next batter, Larry Walker, hit a routine grounder to third baseman Rod Booker, who later confessed that he didn't know that his pitcher was throwing a no-hitter.

But everyone else did, including nearly 9,000 Expos fans who were cheering for Greene as he faced Tim Wallach with two outs in the bottom of the ninth.

At a Glance

WP: Greene (3–0)

Key stat: Greene's no-hitter (8th in Phillies history)

The Expos' best chance to break up the no-hitter came on the last pitch of the game when Wallach hit a shot back toward the mound. Greene reached out and snared the ball, then threw his arms up in the air as he ran toward first base and flipped to Ricky Jordan for the final out.

Jordan, who drove in the Phillies' first run with a triple, thought Wallach's smash was going to get through for a base hit.

"I said, 'Grab it. Grab it.'"

In the clubhouse after the game, Greene accepted hugs and beer showers from all around.

"You got one, bubba!" said Mitch Williams, as he embraced Greene.

Catcher Darrin Fletcher said it was an honor to be behind the plate.

"It's the best feeling. The best," said Fletcher. "I was just hoping and praying out there. I really didn't start thinking of it that much until the ninth, when I asked who was up."

Fletcher, who drove in the Phillies' second run with a ninth inning double, said Greene threw fastballs about 85 percent of the time.

"I thought he tired a little bit in the sixth and seventh and he was trying to aim it a little bit," he said. "But in the eighth and ninth, he was throwing as hard as he was in the early innings."

Manager Jim Fregosi said he loved the way Greene went after the hitters.

"It was like, 'If they're going to get a hit off me, they're going to do it off my best, hard stuff.'"

Greene seemed mystified when asked how he did it.

"Adrenaline. Pure adrenaline," said Greene, who improved his record to 3–0.

The North Carolina native was on his way to establishing himself as a solid National League starter, and would become an important member of the '93 starting rotation.

Alexander Guides Phils Past Cubs in Showdown

Led by their ace, Grover Cleveland Alexander, the pennant-bound Phillies jumped back into a tie for first place following this battle between the top two teams in the league.

The 28-year-old Alexander was spectacular as usual, as he limited the Cubs to just two hits.

Alexander was locked in a scoreless duel with Chicago starter Bert Humphries through five innings. Humphries, a 34-year-old side-armer playing in his final season, did not allow a Phillie to advance beyond first base.

But in the sixth, the Phillies broke through for two runs. Third baseman Bobby Byrne lined a one-out single to center and raced to third on a double to the left-field corner by Beals Becker.

With the dangerous Gavvy Cravath now at the plate, Cubs catcher Roger Bresnahan called for a pitchout to intentionally walk the Phillies slugger. But Bresnahan failed to catch the ball, which rolled to the backstop. Byrne dashed home with the game's first run. Cravath then laid down a perfect squeeze bunt to knock in Becker.

At a Glance

WP: Alexander (8–2)

Key Stat: Alexander 9 IP, 0 runs, 9 Ks

The Phils scored their third and final run in the seventh when Alexander singled to bring home Dode Paskert from second.

Chicago had only one decent opportunity to score. That was in the second inning, when Heinie Zimmerman opened with a hard smash to third that Byrne fielded brilliantly. But his throw got by first baseman Fred Luderus, allowing Zimmerman to get to third.

With Vic Saier now at the plate, Phils catcher Bill Killefer called for a pitchout and threw a rocket down to Byrne, who put the tag on a napping Zimmerman for the first out.

Alexander then struck out Saier and retired Cy Williams on a ground-out to end the inning.

"Alex" was in complete control the rest of the way. He finished the game with nine strikeouts.

It was an impressive performance that foreshadowed a season in which the great right-hander would take his game to another level.

Grover Cleveland Alexander

One of the greatest pitchers in baseball history, Grover Cleveland Alexander had his best years with the Phillies.

He broke into the big leagues in 1911 and immediately established himself as one of the top hurlers in the game by posting staggering numbers for a rookie: a record of 28–13, a 2.57 ERA and 227 strikeouts in 367 innings.

In 1915, Alexander led the Phillies to their first National League pennant with a season for the ages. In 49 games he compiled a record of 31–10 with a 1.22 ERA and 241 strikeouts in 376 innings.

Alexander won 33 games in 1916 and 30 more in '17.

He ranks third on the Phillies' career wins list with 190, and is tied for third place with Christy Mathewson on the all-time major league wins list with 373.

Alexander finished the 1915 season with a 31–10 record and a 1.22 ERA. It was the first of three consecutive seasons in which he would win 30 or more games.

Phils Punch Out Pirates, Move into Tie for First

The Phillies moved into a tie for first place after winning a nasty game that featured brushback pitches, a beanball and a wild bench-clearing brawl in front of more than 45,000 fans at Veterans Stadium.

The seeds of trouble were planted in the bottom of the first inning with the Pirates holding a 2–0 lead.

Right-hander Bert Blyleven retired the first two batters then walked Mike Schmidt and Greg Luzinski on several pitches that came dangerously close to their heads.

In the third inning, Blyleven buzzed Schmidt with another high hard one. This time the third baseman took exception and stepped toward the mound. Home-plate umpire Doug Harvey jumped out and prodded Schmidt back to the batter's box. But Schmidt pointed his finger menacingly at Blyleven to let him know, in no uncertain terms, how he felt.

A chorus of boos rained down on Blyleven when he came to the plate in the fourth inning. He grounded out without incident, but in the sixth, when Blyleven batted again, the game took a violent turn.

With two outs, nobody on and the Pirates leading 5–3, lefty reliever Kevin Saucier nailed Blyleven in the hip with the first pitch. An enraged Blyleven picked up the ball and charged the mound. With that, both benches emptied, and the area near the mound quickly turned into a tangle of bodies as players grappled and took swings at one another.

At a Glance

WP: Reed (3–0)

HR: Maddox (3)

Key stat: Maddox 3-for-4, 2 RBIs, 3 runs; Bowa 2-for-5, 2 RBIs

"I don't like to see fights in baseball," said Pete Rose. "I don't know if Sauce did what he did on purpose or not. But if he feels he has to protect his hitters, then hats off to him."

The fight lasted about 15 minutes and ended with Pirates outfielder Lee Lacy and Phillies pitching coach Herm Starette getting ejected.

Lacy later proclaimed his innocence: "I was just trying to be a peacemaker. I had my arms around one of my own players."

Starette also protested. "Hell, I was just trying to break the fight up. He had just tossed Lacy and was looking to toss one of our guys to even the score. I just happened to be there."

Phillies catcher and former University of Texas safety Keith Moreland had a blast.

"I popped Lacy a good one. It's probably one of the best fights anyone's seen around here."

The two teams eventually got back to playing ball and the Pirates quickly increased their lead to 6–3 in the seventh on two singles and Willie Stargell's sacrifice fly.

The Phils got one run back in the bottom of the seventh on an RBI double by Luzinski, and added another one in the eighth. Garry Maddox, who had homered and doubled earlier, led off the inning with a single to right, stole second and came around to score on a base hit by Manny Trillo.

Trailing 6–5 in the bottom of the ninth, Mike Schmidt greeted Pirates closer Kent Tekulve with a leadoff double to left, and Luzinski beat out an infield chopper. With the home crowd now standing for each pitch, catcher Bob Boone slammed a double to tie the game.

Tekulve intentionally walked Maddox to pitch to Bowa, who was punched in the eye during the fight. The fiery shortstop worked the count to 3–1, then punched a game-winning single to right field.

Veteran Taylor, Rookie Bowa the Perfect Combo

A beloved veteran and a feisty rookie provided some badly needed muscle to help the light-hitting Phillies defeat the Expos.

Thirty-four-year-old Tony Taylor, one of the most popular Phillies of all time, slammed a pair of homers, and 24-year-old shortstop Larry Bowa belted a clutch triple in the 11th to seal the win for the Phils, who had to climb back from a 3–0 deficit.

It was a wonder that the defensive-minded Bowa was even in the game at the time.

Manager Frank Lucchesi had the chance to remove him for a pinch-hitter

Tony Taylor, fan favorite from Cuba, smacked two home runs to help the Phils to a 5–3 win over the Expos on May 28, 1970.

in the sixth inning after the Phils scored two runs and had runners on first and second with two outs. But the skipper let Bowa hit. He popped out.

"Maybe I just had a hunch," said Lucchesi. "We're trying to be patient with these youngsters. I've got confidence in Larry. He's helped win a lot of games when the chips were down."

Bowa faced reliever Bill Dillman with one out in the top of the 11th and the Expos outfield playing extremely shallow. He laced a line drive deep into the alley in right-center and raced all the way to third. Bowa scored the go-ahead run on Terry Harmon's sacrifice fly to right.

Taylor then added an important insurance run with his second home run of the game. His first homer in the seventh tied the game at 3.

"This is a good park to hit in," said the native of Cuba, who hit only 75 home runs in his 19-year career.

Starter Grant Jackson was in trouble almost from the first pitch and was taken out at the start of the third after giving up all three Expos runs.

Relievers Lowell Palmer, Joe Hoerner and Dick Selma did a splendid job of shutting down Montreal's offense the rest of the way.

Hoerner threw four scoreless innings to pick up the win. Selma set the Expos down in the 11th to earn the save.

At a Glance

WP: Hoerner (3–2)

HR: Taylor 2 (3)

Key stat: Taylor 2 runs, 2 RBIs

It's a Perfect Game for Halladay

Roy Halladay stepped up to the pedestal alongside Jim Bunning to become just the second pitcher in team history and the 20th in major league history to throw a perfect game.

The 33-year-old right-hander used everything in his arsenal to stymie the Marlins, including fastballs, change-ups, cutters, curves, and splitters. Everything he threw worked with precision. Halladay struck out 11 of the 27 batters he faced, a season high.

"It's something you never think about," he said. "It's hard to explain. There's days when things just kind of click and things happen, and it's something you obviously never go out and try and do. But it's a great feeling."

At a Glance

WP: Halladay (7–3)

Key stat: Halladay perfect game

Halladay was already considered the best pitcher in baseball when he came to the Phillies from Toronto in the off-season. But this performance raised his reputation to new heights.

"It's absolutely amazing," said manager Charlie Manuel. "He did what he had to do. We gave him one run. He made it stand up."

The Phillies scored their lone run in the third, courtesy of a three-base error by Florida center fielder Cameron Maybin, who misjudged Chase Utley's fly ball. Wilson Valdez scored from first as the ball rolled all the way to the wall.

Halladay had thrown 103 pitches as he began the ninth inning at Sun Life Stadium. He got pinch-hitter Mike Lamb to fly to Shane Victorino in center for the first out. Another pinch-hitter, Wes Helms, looked at a called third strike for the second out.

The next batter, Ronny Paulino, fell behind in the count 1–2 then hit a grounder to the left side. Third baseman Juan Castro gloved it, spun around and threw to first for the final out. Twenty-seven batters up, 27 batters down.

Halladay pounded his glove and threw his arms in the air as catcher Carlos Ruiz led the team's charge to the mound.

He was now the 10th pitcher in Phillies history to throw a no-hitter and the first to throw a perfect game since Bunning on June 21, 1964.

Howard's Rise to Slugging Fame Peaks with 8th Grand Slam

It took Ryan Howard just six big-league seasons to become the team's all-time leader in grand slams, and he did it in typical style with a monstrous blast that helped the Phillies beat Washington at Citizens Bank Park.

Howard's slam was the eighth of his career and his second home run of the game, leading manager Charlie Manuel to compare him to the games greatest sluggers.

"I've seen Frank Howard, (Harmon) Killebrew," said Manuel. "Of course, I've seen Hank Aaron and (Willie) Mays and (Carl) Yastrzemski, all the modern day power hitters. Howard is as strong as any of them."

The 29-year-old Howard moved past Mike Schmidt on the grand slam list in the third inning. Carlos Ruiz led off with a walk, moved to second on pitcher Cole Hamels' sacrifice bunt and scored on a single by Jimmy Rollins. After Shane Victorino walked, Chase Utley hit a slow roller that shortstop Alberto Gonzalez was unable to handle.

That brought up Howard, who cleared the bases and sent the sellout crowd into a frenzy with a towering fly ball that landed in the third deck of the right-field stands. The blast gave the Phillies a 6–3 lead.

Howard knew he cranked it as soon as the ball met his bat.

At a Glance

WP: Hamels (3–2)

HR: Howard 2 (13,14)

Key stat: Howard grand slam, 5 RBIs; Victorino 2-for-4, 2 runs

"Sometimes when everything comes together and you get it really good, you never know how far it's going to go," he said. "I saw it in the air and just kind of took off running. I wasn't really sure where it was going to come down."

His first homer wasn't bad either. Howard hit one into the second deck in right in the second inning to cut the Nationals' lead to 3–1.

After Howard's pyrotechnics, the Phillies scored a run in the fourth on back-to-back doubles by Ruiz and Hamels, and two more in the bottom of the sixth.

The bullpen quieted the Nationals the rest of the way to preserve the win for Hamels, who improved his record to 3–2. Brad Lidge picked up the save.

JUNE

Robin Roberts led the National League in complete games five times.
The Hall of Famer once had a streak of 28 consecutive complete games.

Fryman's Mastery Continues with Another Shutout

Not only did Phillies fans get to cheer the most one-sided victory at Connie Mack Stadium in years, they were able to see one of the hottest pitchers in baseball continue his stretch of excellence.

Woodie Fryman gave up only four hits and struck out eight to earn his fourth shutout of the young season.

The 28-year-old left-hander, who was traded by the Pirates to the Phillies in exchange for Jim Bunning, had put together an astonishing streak that began on May 17 when he threw 10 shutout innings to beat the Cardinals and Bob Gibson, 1–0.

Fryman followed that up with a three-hit shutout against the Mets.

His scoreless streak officially ended at 22 $^{2}/_{3}$ innings in his next outing when he gave up three unearned runs against St. Louis.

But if you go strictly by earned runs allowed, the streak continued to 36 innings following this blowout of the Reds.

"It's a lot easier to pitch with all those runs," said Fryman, after the Phillies busted out of a season-long slump and abused six Reds pitchers for 15 hits and 12 runs.

They put up five in the first, two in the second and four more in the third. Every batter in the lineup with the exception of Fryman had at least one hit. Four batters had multiple hits, led by Cookie Rojas and Tony Gonzalez, with three each. Johnny Callison was 2-for-2 with a homer and four RBIs before he was hit by a pitch and had to leave the game. His replacement, Don Lock, went 2-for-2 with an RBI.

The Phils scored their final two runs in the eighth, aided by two Reds errors.

Fryman's earned run streak would end at 37 innings in his next outing on a second-inning home run by Willie Mays. But it would be the only run Fryman would surrender in a 2–1 victory over San Francisco.

At a Glance

WP: Fryman (7–4)

HR: Callison (6), Rojas (5)

Key stat: Callison 2-for-2, 4 RBIs; Rojas 3-for-6, 3 runs; Gonzalez 3-for-4, 3 runs

1 Inning, 5 Home Runs, 10 Runs Scored

The Phillies put on the most impressive one-inning power display in team history in this unforgettable game at Shibe Park.

Trailing 3–2 in the eighth, they bombed five home runs and scored 10 times to turn a tight game into a laugher.

In addition to setting a franchise record, the Phillies tied the major league record for most home runs hit in one inning (set by the New York Giants in 1939), while setting a modern-day record with 26 total bases.

Andy Seminick was the biggest slugger of them all as he hit three homers, including two in that historic eighth inning.

It was a shockingly impressive long ball clinic that came from nowhere.

Reds starter Ken Raffensberger had held the Phils to two runs on four hits through seven innings. But the quiet tone of the game suddenly changed when Del Ennis opened the eighth by lining a first-pitch fastball into the left-field bleachers.

Seminick, who broke a scoreless tie in the second with a solo home run, jumped at another first pitch offering from Raffensberger and hammered it over the left-field roof.

At a Glance

WP: Rowe (2–3)

HR: Seminick 3 (5,6,7), Ennis (7), Jones (3), Rowe (1)

Key stat: Phils set team record with five HRs in one inning

Puddin' Head Jones hit the third homer of the inning off Reds reliever Jess Dobernic. After Eddie Miller popped out, pitcher Schoolboy Rowe hit home run No. 4.

Seminick came up to the plate again with two runners on and belted his second home run of the inning to tie a major league record and set a new team record.

The Phillies nearly hit two more homers in the eighth, which would have shattered the big-league record. Granny Hamner hit a drive that clanked off the railing of the bleachers in left and bounced back in play for a double.

Jones smacked a ball that hit inches below the same railing. It also rebounded back onto the outfield grass as Jones legged out a triple.

Phils owner Bob Carpenter stopped by the locker room after the game to shake hands with each player.

"That was the best game I've ever seen," he said.

Johnson in Unchartered Waters with 2nd Pinch Grand Slam

Davey Johnson won a ballgame and set a major league record in this game with one swing of the bat.

The veteran second baseman bashed a pinch-hit walk-off home run with the bases loaded in the ninth inning to give the Phillies a shocking victory over the Dodgers at Veterans Stadium.

It was Johnson's second pinch-hit grand slam of the season, a feat that no other player in big league history had ever accomplished.

His astounding blast abruptly ended what had been a fine pitchers' duel between two tough right-handers.

Bob Boone broke a scoreless tie in the bottom of the fifth when he walloped a home run off Don Sutton. But the Dodgers responded with a run of their own in the sixth.

Larry Christenson walked Billy North, then made a wild pickoff throw to first. North took second, went to third on a bunt and scored on a sacrifice fly.

The two teams were still tied heading into the ninth. Garry Maddox singled to lead off the inning and darted to second after Dodgers reliever Terry Forster made the same mistake as Christenson. But Forster's throw over to first sailed so far past first baseman Steve Garvey that Maddox was able to make it all the way to third.

At a Glance

WP: McGraw (4–3)

HR: Boone (5), Johnson (2)

Key stat: Johnson grand slam, 4 RBIs; Maddox 2-for-4, run; Boone 2-for-3, RBI.

Tommy Lasorda now did what any desperate manager would do: he brought the infield up, his outfielders into shallow territory and ordered intentional walks to the next two batters to load the bases and setting up a force at home.

The wheels were also turning in the Phillies' dugout. Manager Danny Ozark called on-deck hitter Jay Johnstone back and told Johnson to grab a bat.

"I was looking for a fly ball," Ozark said.

Johnson swung at an inside slider and pulled it high and deep down the left-field line. It was more than enough to bring home the winning run.

"I was just hoping it would stay fair," said Johnson.

His wish came true. The ball cleared the 330 sign, touching off a thunderous ovation from the crowd of more than 31,000.

Johnson's blow overshadowed a tremendous effort from Christenson, who held the Dodgers to two hits and one unearned run over eight innings.

"I thought I pitched pretty good," said LC, who didn't get the decision. "But the team got the win and that's what's important. I kept us in the game for eight innings so I feel I did my job."

It was a big win for the two-time defending Eastern Division champs, who were trying to keep up with the first-place Chicago Cubs. The Phils would catch them later in June and go on to capture their third straight Division flag.

Bob Boone

A third baseman in college, Bob Boone was converted to a catcher after he was signed by the Phillies in 1969 and became one of the most durable and consistent backstops in team history.

He spent nearly a decade behind the plate for the Phillies beginning in 1973, developing into a three-time All-Star and two-time Gold Glove winner.

Boone was also a pretty good hitter, compiling a batting average of .259 with 65 homers and 456 RBIs during his Phillies career.

His best years with the bat were from 1977-79, when he .280 or better each year.

Roberts Ekes Out a Win, Ends Seven-Game Skid

A poignant scene played out in the Phillies locker room after they had beaten the Giants 3–2 at Candlestick Park. Thirty-four-year-old Robin Roberts, now in his 14th season, sat in front of his locker, exhausted and fighting back tears after picking up his first win of the year, and what would turn out to be his last in a Phillies uniform.

The great right-hander called it "an emotional binge" and admitted he never worked harder in any ballgame.

"That was the one I had to win," he said. "Now, I've just got to keep going."

The victory broke a humiliating seven-game losing streak for Roberts, who was suffering through the worst season of his career. Injuries and age had taken their toll. But Roberts was determined to play on and find success again.

Things did not look good early in the game when Giants rookie Chuck Hiller hit a second-inning two-run homer.

But in the top of the third, Robbie got some help from his teammates and the Giants. Lee Walls started a rally with a one-out single to left. Ken Walters hit a grounder to third that appeared to be an easy double-play ball. But Hiller, moving to second for the force, dropped the throw from third baseman Harvey Kuenn as he rushed to make his relay throw to first.

The miscue came back to bite the Giants when the next batter, first baseman Pancho Herrera, ripped a 1–2 fastball high over the fence in left field for a three-run homer.

At a Glance

WP: Roberts (1–7)

HR: Herrera (6)

Key stat: Roberts earns last win as a Phillie; Herrera 3 RBIs.

Roberts flirted with disaster several times but managed to escape when the Giants hit a number of line drives right at Phillies fielders. He also got help from the swirling winds at Candlestick Park when Willie McCovey and Ed Bailey hit mammoth blasts that blew foul at the last second.

In the ninth, Roberts faced his biggest challenge. McCovey hit a one-out bloop single into center field and moved to second when Matty Alou grounded out to Herrera. After Bailey walked, Kuenn hit a tapper that rolled up the middle past Roberts. But shortstop Ruben Amaro alertly moved over, gobbled it up and stomped on the bag to end the game.

"I wanted to be sure the umpire saw what I was doing," said Amaro.

Roberts was relieved that he didn't attempt to make a play on the ball.

"I would have messed up the whole thing," he said.

His gutsy performance earned the admiration of everyone in the Phillies' clubhouse.

Manager Gene Mauch said, "I'm so proud of Robbie I could bust a gut."

"I never saw so many pleased ballgamers in one place," said reliever Ken Lehman.

Pancho Herrera probably put it best when he pounded his chest and declared, "I am so happy because I hit one for my very good friend, Robin Roberts."

Robin Roberts

The premier right-hander of the 1950s and one of the top three pitchers in team history, Robin Roberts compiled 234 of his 286 career wins with the Phillies.

Robbie broke in with the team as a raw, talented 21-year-old fresh out of Michigan State in 1948. Two years later, he led the Whiz Kids to the National League pennant and kicked off a string of six straight 20-win seasons.

His best year was 1952, when he went 28–7 with a 2.59 ERA and was named Major League Player of the Year.

Consistency and control best defined the right-hander. Roberts was a workhorse who often finished what he started. Five times he led the National League in complete games, with a career high of 33 in 1953. At one point he completed 28 consecutive games.

Roberts also threw at least 300 innings while keeping his walk count in double digits for six straight years.

Robin Roberts was selected into the Hall of Fame in 1976.

June 6, 1965
Phillies 2, Cubs 1 (Game 1); Phillies 10, Cubs 9 (Game 2)

Callison Gives Fans Even More Reasons to Love Him in Doubleheader

Johnny Callison was at the top of his game and the peak of his career in this doubleheader sweep at Wrigley Field.

The All-Star right fielder displayed all the power and defensive wizardry that made him one of the most popular players to ever wear a Phillies uniform.

Tony Gonzalez was the hitting star and Ray Culp was brilliant on the mound, but it was Callison's marvelous catch in the bottom of the ninth that preserved the 2–1 victory in Game 1.

Gonzalez went 4-for-5 out of the leadoff spot and knocked in both runs with an infield single in the third inning and a base hit to center in the seventh.

Culp held the Cubs to five hits in going the distance, but he needed help from his right fielder to finish the game a winner.

The bases were loaded with two outs in the ninth when Jim Stewart hit a pop fly to shallow right. On a normal day the ball would have fallen in for a hit, but the wind, blowing in from Lake Michigan, held it up just long enough for Callison to have a chance.

He sprinted as hard as he could, lunged and caught the ball inches from the grass to end the game.

"I was ready to dive," he said.

Culp was grateful for his teammate's hustle and the brisk Wrigley Field breeze.

"It kept the ball in the air just long enough for Callison to catch it," said Culp.

In Game 2, Callison stole the show with a barrage of home runs. His solo shot in the first inning set off a five-run rally that featured five hits, including a three-run homer from Cookie Rojas

In the third, Callison broke his bat on an inside pitch yet still managed to hammer the ball over the wall in right field, something that few hitters have done.

At a Glance

Game 1

WP: Culp (3–2)

Key stat: Gonzalez 4-for-5, 2 RBIs

Game 2

WP: Wagner (1–1)

HR: Callison 3 (10,11,12), Rojas (1), Stuart (6)

Key stat: Callison 4-for-5, 4 RBIs; Rojas 2-for-4, 4 RBIs

"I'll take it," he said. "I hit the ball good."

The Phillies were winning 8–6 in the ninth when Callison belted a two-run blast, which proved to be the game-winner after the Cubs scored three in the home half of the inning.

This was the second time in as many seasons that Callison hit three home runs in a game. He banged three in a losing cause against Milwaukee during the Phillies' infamous 10-game losing streak that cost them the pennant in September 1964.

Did You Know?

Richie Ashburn hit two home runs in a game three different times. The first was on June 21, 1955. Ashburn was on his way to winning his first batting title but took one day to flex his muscles against the Cardinals at Sportsman's Park in St. Louis.

He turned the trick again the following year at the Polo Grounds, and once more in 1962 as a New York Met, when he belted a pair against the Houston Colt .45s at the Polo Grounds.

June 7, 1957
Phillies 1, Cubs 0

Sanford's Dream Comes True on Way to Top Rookie Honors

Jack Sanford, on his way to becoming the first National League Rookie of the Year in Phillies history, threw his second straight shutout and tied the team's all-time single game strikeout record in a virtuoso performance against the Chicago Cubs.

The 28-year-old Sanford fanned 13 to put his name alongside Ray Benge and Robin Roberts for most strikeouts in a nine-inning game.

"It's like a dream," Sanford said. "The kind of dream you wouldn't expect to come true."

Indeed, Sanford was living the dream after toiling for many years in the minors.

In his previous start, the right-hander pitched a two-hit shutout against the Brooklyn Dodgers and was now leading the league in wins and strikeouts.

Facing the Cubs, Sanford was even more dominating.

"He was fast, plenty fast," said catcher Stan Lopata.

At a Glance

WP: Sanford (7–1)

Key stat: Sanford 13 Ks, shutout

The Phillies scored their lone run in the fourth inning. Ed Bouchee opened with a double, but was thrown out at third on Willie Jones' grounder back to pitcher Dave Hillman. Rip Repulski doubled but Jones held at third.

Hillman then walked Bob Bowman to load the bases. Chico Fernandez stepped in and looked at strike one, then unloaded a long fly ball into the wind to deep left, allowing Jones to score easily from third.

Sanford, meanwhile, was virtually unhittable. Early in the game he struck out five Cubs in a row. In the fifth, Sanford struck out the side again, and in the eighth inning, he blew away two pinch-hitters on six pitches.

After giving up two hits in the first two innings, Sanford limited the Cubs to a single walk through the eighth.

Jack Sanford became the Phillies' first National League Rookie of the Year in 1957. On June 7, he fanned 13 batters to earn a spot in the Phillies' record book for strikeouts in a nine-inning game.

His only tight spot came in the ninth inning when Bob Speake singled to right and Ernie Banks walked to put runners on first and second.

But Walt Moryn's attempt to bunt the runners over backfired when Sanford broke quickly for the ball, turned and threw Speake out at third.

Dale Long then popped out to second and Sanford struck out Lee Walls to end the game.

Sanford was an easy choice for National League Rookie of the Year honors. His '57 season included a record of 19–7, a league-leading 188 strikeouts and a 3.08 ERA.

Did You Know?

Jack Sanford is among four Phillies who have been honored as National League Rookie of the Year.

Dick Allen won it in 1964, Scott Rolen broke a 33-year drought when he was named the winner in 1997, and Ryan Howard won the award in 2005.

Down 10 Runs After One? No Problem for Phils against Pirates

Fueled by a number of astonishing individual performances, the Phillies pulled off one of the great comebacks in franchise history after spotting the Pirates 10 runs in the first inning.

The Pirates buried Phillies lefty Larry McWilliams under a blizzard of hits that produced six runs before late-arriving fans had even made it to their seats. McWilliams was taken out and replaced by Steve Ontiveros, who was torched for four more runs.

But Ontiveros steadied himself and shut down the Pirates over the next three innings.

The Phillies began to chip away at the enormous deficit in the bottom of the first when Von Hayes hammered a two-run homer. Hayes struck again in the third with another two-run shot to reduce the lead to 10–4.

"When I hit the first one, I felt it gave us a little left, because at least we got right back on the board," said Hayes. "Then the second one got us a little closer, and then it was the Jet's turn."

"The Jet" was light-hitting switch-hitter Steve Jeltz, who made it a 10–6 game with a two-run homer from the left side in the bottom of the fourth, causing the Veterans Stadium crowd of 18,511 to stir.

Jeltz wasn't even supposed to play. He entered the game in the second for Tommy Herr, who was nursing a sore foot.

Manager Nick Leyva decided that with the Phillies down by so many runs he'd give Herr a blow.

"I look like a genius on that one, don't I?" laughed Leyva.

Jeltz hit another homer, this one as a right-hander, in the sixth inning.

"I didn't think either one of them was going to get out," said Jeltz, whose three-run blast made the score 11–9.

It soon became 11–10 when John Kruk doubled to left, then scored on Ricky Jordan's two-out single.

In the eighth, the Phillies completed their improbable comeback. Kruk started it with a one-out single, his fourth hit of the night. Juan Samuel and pinch-hitter Bob Dernier both drew walks. With the bases now loaded, the

June 8, 1989
Phillies 15, Pirates 11

Pirates' rattled reliever, Don Robinson, threw a wild pitch, allowing Kruk to score the tying run.

Pirates	AB	R	H	RBI
Bonds lf	3	2	1	3
Lind 2b	5	1	1	0
Van Slyke cf	5	2	3	2
Bonilla 3b	4	1	1	0
Redus rf-1b	5	1	3	2
Robinson p	0	0	0	0
Samuels p	0	0	0	0
King 1b	2	1	0	0
Landrum p	0	0	0	0
Distefano 1b	1	0	0	0
Quinones ss	5	1	2	2
Ortiz c	3	1	1	0
Reynolds ph	1	0	0	0
Walk p	2	1	1	2
Kipper p	1	0	0	0
Cangelosi rf	2	0	1	0
Totals	**39**	**11**	**14**	**11**

Phillies	AB	R	H	RBI
Ready 3b	4	3	3	0
Herr 2b	1	0	0	0
Jeltz 2b	4	3	2	5
Hayes 1b-rf-1b	5	2	2	4
Kruk lf	5	2	4	0
Samuel cf	4	1	1	0
Murphy rf	1	0	0	0
Jordan ph-1b	2	0	1	1
Carman p	0	0	0	0
Dernier ph-rf	0	1	0	0
Thon ss	3	1	0	0
Daulton c	4	2	1	2
McWilliams p	0	0	0	0
Ontiveros p	1	0	0	0
Ryal ph	1	0	0	0
Harris p	0	0	0	0
Ford rf	2	0	1	2
Bedrosian p	0	0	0	0
Totals	**37**	**15**	**15**	**14**

PIT 10 0 0 0 1 0 0 0 0 - 11 14 0
PHI 2 0 2 2 0 4 0 5 X - 15 15 0

Pirates	IP	H	R	ER	BB	SO
Walk	3.2	5	6	6	4	2
Kipper	2	3	4	4	2	3
Landrum	1.1	3	0	0	0	2
Robinson L (2-4)	0.1	1	4	4	3	0
Samuels	0.2	3	1	1	0	0
Totals	**8**	**15**	**15**	**15**	**9**	**7**

Phillies	IP	H	R	ER	BB	SO
McWilliams	0.1	4	6	6	2	0
Ontiveros	3.2	6	4	4	3	1
Harris	2.2	3	1	1	0	1
Carman W (2-9)	1.1	0	0	0	1	0
Bedrosian	1	1	0	0	0	2
Totals	**9**	**14**	**11**	**11**	**6**	**4**

DP—Philadelphia. 2B—Pittsburgh Quinones, Van Slyke; Philadelphia Kruk 2, Ready. 3B—Philadelphia Ford. HR—Pittsburgh Bonds (10); Philadelphia Jeltz 2 (2,3), Hayes 2 (11,12). LOB—Pittsburgh 7; Philadelphia 8. SB—Pittsburgh Redus. Attendance: 18,511.

After Dickie Thon was intentionally walked to reload the bases, Darren Daulton, batting .188, lined a single to center to score two more runs and give the Phillies their first lead of the night.

"I've been struggling for how long now," Daulton said. "But I like to think that hits like this can turn things around. And games like this can turn teams around."

Curt Ford provided the finishing touch with a two-run triple.

In the giddy postgame locker room, Jeltz called the victory "a great thrill. And this game is a thrill for the whole team. It just shows that you can never give up in any game."

Lefty Outdoes Himself with Record 16 Strikeouts vs. Cubs

He was 37 years old, but Steve Carlton showed that he still had plenty of gas left in the tank as he fanned 16 Cubs to break his own team record for strikeouts by a left-hander in a single game.

Armed with his devastating slider, Lefty was particularly dominant early in the game, whiffing seven of the first 10 batters he faced. By the sixth inning, Carlton had struck out 11.

One of his victims was former teammate Larry Bowa.

"When you play behind him, you watch him and you wonder how many guys can swing at pitches down and in," he said. "But after you face him you know why.

"His breaking ball is just unbelievable. His stuff just explodes right at home. And I'm talking about literally exploding."

Bowa struck out once, which was better than most of his teammates. Carlton fanned Ryne Sandberg four times, and Junior Kennedy and Steve Henderson three times.

He struck out two batters in one inning six times, including the eighth and ninth.

At a Glance

WP: Carlton (7–6)

HR: Schmidt (5), Diaz (10)

Key stat: Carlton 16 strikeouts (sets record for a Phillies lefty)

His teammates and manager Pat Corrales were amazed but not surprised.

"He's in such great physical condition," said Corrales. "He works at it every day. That's why he's been this great this long."

Though dominant, Lefty had moments when he struggled. He gave up 10 hits, including a game-tying homer to Gary Woods in the second.

In the sixth, Carlton surrendered a double to Bill Buckner, a single to Woods and a run-scoring sacrifice fly to Henderson.

That tightened the scored to 3–2. But Corrales was never concerned about the outcome.

"He can be cruising along and get himself out of trouble faster than any human being I've ever seen," said Corrales.

Another reason the Cubs managed to stay close was the guy they had on the mound. Ferguson Jenkins, a former Phillie and, like Carlton, a future Hall of Famer, was also getting up in years but still knew how to get batters out.

Jenkins battled for six innings, holding the Phils to three runs on six hits. He made only two mistakes, giving up home runs to Bo Diaz in the second and Mike Schmidt in the fourth.

The Phillies scratched out their first run in the first inning on a couple of singles and a sacrifice fly RBI by Gary Matthews.

They scored an insurance run in the eighth inning when Garry Maddox singled home Matthews from second.

With the win, Carlton improved to 7–6. He would eventually demonstrate that age was no barrier by winning his fourth Cy Young Award with a record of 23–11 and 286 strikeouts in more than 295 innings.

Loudspeaker Limits Schmidt's Homer Total

Mike Schmidt hit 548 home runs in his illustrious career and would have had one more were it not for his enormous power and a misplaced loudspeaker suspended from the top of the Astrodome.

The young third baseman had a Roy Hobbs moment in the first inning as he faced Astros lefty Claude Osteen.

With two runners on, Schmidt hit a booming blast straight up and deep toward center field, clearly on its way out. But the ball suddenly hit the public address speaker 117 feet above the field and 300 feet from home plate. The ball came down in center field, causing confusion all around.

"I took one look and knew it was gone," said Dave Cash, who was on second base at the time. "Then I took another look and there it is coming down.... I figured it had to be something weird."

The umpires ruled that the ball was in play. Schmidt stopped at first, Larry Bowa went to second and Cash advanced to third. Team members and fans were awestruck.

"I didn't think anyone thought they'd see a ball hit that far and that high," said Phillies third base coach Billy DeMars.

Astros manager Preston Gomez summed it up in three words: "It was awesome."

Schmidt eventually scored as the Phillies put three runs on the board in the first inning. They added five more in the second to increase their lead to 8–0, making life easy for Jim Lonborg, who threw his second shutout of the year.

At a Glance

WP: Lonborg (7–5)

Key stat: Schmidt 3-for-4, 3 RBIs (fly ball hits speaker 117 feet above field in center field); Robinson 3-for-5, 2 RBIs; Anderson 2-for-4, 2 RBIs

"It would have been nice to see where it landed," said Schmidt.

No one would ever know. But everyone who witnessed the prodigious shot was eager to speculate.

"It was over everything," marveled Astros center fielder Cesar Cedeno. "I never saw a ball hit so hard. I've seen some real line shots by Richie Allen and guys like that but nothing like this."

June 11, 1985
Phillies 26, Mets 7

Hayes Puts Phils on Their Way to Run-Scoring History

The Phillies shattered a slew of team records in recording one of the most one-sided victories in baseball history.

A crowd of 22,591 at Veterans Stadium knew very quickly that they were in for a special night when Von Hayes became the only player ever to hit two home runs in the first inning of a game.

Hayes led off with a high drive that cleared the fence in right-center and landed at the base of the scoreboard.

He came around to bat again a few minutes later, this time with the bases loaded, and slammed a 2–2 pitch over the right-field fence. Hayes' grand slam was the highlight of a memorable nine-run first inning.

At the end of two, the Phils were ahead 16–0 but they continued to swing away, scoring five in the fifth, another in the sixth, and four more runs in the seventh.

"It was the funniest game I've ever been in. It was unbelievable," said Hayes, who had six RBIs and scored four runs. "I'm sure I'll wake up tomorrow and pat myself on the back, but right now I'm patting everybody on the team.

"I mean, guys went out and got four, five hits all over the place. All the fireworks came after the two homers, really."

Every starter in the lineup had at least one hit and one RBI. Second baseman Juan Samuel and third baseman Rick Schu set a club record with seven at-bats. Sammy had a career-high five hits while Schu recorded the first four-hit game of his career.

Also adding to the onslaught was Bo Diaz with three doubles. Glenn Wilson had three hits and three RBIs and Garry Maddox knocked in a pair with a triple and a single.

The Phillies set team records for runs scored (26); hits (27); doubles (10); total bases (47); and extra-base hits (14).

In addition, the 26 runs were the most scored in the major leagues in 41 years.

The Phillies of '85 were one of the least likely clubs to roll out that kind of attack. They had an overall batting average of .230 and scored just 25 runs in the first nine games of June. Batting coach Del Unser watched with pride as the hits kept coming.

"The one word that kept going through my mind was confidence," said Unser. "It's something our hitters have needed more than anything else."

Mets manager Dave Johnson wanted to know the license plate of the truck that had just run his team over.

"It was kind of like being in a fight and laying on the ground and they keep beating on you," he said. "If you recover, it's something you don't forget."

Mets	AB	R	H	RBI
Backman 2b	4	1	3	1
Johnson 3b	5	0	2	1
Hernandez 1b	2	0	1	0
Christensen cf	2	0	0	0
Carter c	2	0	1	1
Reynolds c	3	1	1	0
Heep cf-1b	5	1	1	0
Foster lf	5	1	1	1
Hurdle rf	4	1	1	0
Santana ss	2	1	2	2
Gorman p	0	0	0	0
Schiraldi p	0	0	0	0
Sisk p	2	1	0	1
Staub ph	1	0	0	0
Sambito p	0	0	0	0
Knight ph	1	0	0	0
Orosco p	0	0	0	0
Totals	**36**	**7**	**13**	**7**

Phillies	AB	R	H	RBI
Hayes lf	6	4	3	6
Schu 3b	7	2	4	2
Samuel 2b	7	3	5	2
Schmidt 1b	2	2	2	2
Jeltz ss	4	1	1	1
Wilson rf	6	4	3	3
Diaz c	4	3	3	3
Rucker p	2	1	2	0
Andersen p	0	0	0	0
Maddox cf	4	3	2	2
Thomas cf	1	0	0	0
Aguayo ss	1	1	0	1
Gross 1b	2	1	1	2
Hudson p	3	1	1	1
Wockenfuss ph-c	1	0	0	0
Totals	**50**	**26**	**27**	**25**

NYM	0	0	3	2	2	0	0	0	0	-	7	13	2
PHI	9	7	0	0	5	1	4	0	X	-	26	27	1

Mets	IP	H	R	ER	BB	SO
Gorman L (3-3)	0.1	4	6	6	2	0
Schiraldi	1.1	10	10	10	0	1
Sisk	2.1	2	0	0	0	1
Sambito	3	9	10	8	5	0
Orosco	1	2	0	0	0	1
Totals	**8**	**27**	**26**	**24**	**7**	**3**

Phillies	IP	H	R	ER	BB	SO
Hudson W (2-6)	5	13	7	6	0	3
Rucker	3	0	0	0	2	2
Andersen	1	0	0	0	1	1
Totals	**9**	**13**	**7**	**6**	**3**	**6**

E—New York Santana, Johnson; Philadelphia Hayes. DP—New York 2; Philadelphia. 2B—New York Foster, Santana, Johnson; Philadelphia Jeltz, Schmidt, Wilson 2, Samuel, Schu, Rucker, Diaz 3. 3B—Philadelphia Maddox, Schu. HR—Philadelphia Hayes 2 (4,5). SF—New York Foster, Santana; Philadelphia Gross. HBP—Philadelphia Aguayo. LOB—New York 7; Philadelphia 9. SB—Philadelphia Samuel 2. Attendance: 22,591.

The Balls Kept Coming to Harmon at Second

He wasn't a spectacular fielder, but Terry Harmon was rock steady, and in this win over the Padres, the third-year utility player showed a steadiness that baseball had never seen.

Harmon set a modern-day record for second baseman by handling 18 chances to help Jim Bunning nail down the win.

Harmon's flawless night included seven putouts and 11 assists. He smashed the old National League record of 16 held by three players—Miller Huggins of the Cardinals in 1911, Jay Partridge of the Brooklyn Dodgers in 1927, and the Cardinals' Frankie Frisch in 1930. Jimmy Dykes of the Philadelphia Athletics and Nellie Fox of the Chicago White Sox shared the American League record with 17 chances.

Harmon took his busy night in stride.

"There wasn't a hard chance in the lot," he said. "Dave Campbell got some wood on a ball through the middle but it was right at me."

A big reason Harmon was so active was the way his pitcher was throwing. Bunning, in the final year of a Hall of Fame career, kept the Padres off balance all night with sliders and change-ups. The result was plenty of ground balls.

The Phillies were limited to four hits by Padres starter Steve Arlin. But they used two of them to score all three of their runs in the first inning.

At a Glance

WP: Bunning (4–8)

Key stat: Harmon 18 chances (sets record); Gamble 1-for-3, 2 RBIs

Harmon led off the game by striking out. But Arlin's pitch seemed to cross up catcher Bob Barton. The ball sailed to the screen and Harmon raced to first base. The next batter, Tim McCarver, hit a fly ball that was dropped by left fielder Leron Lee.

With runners on first and second, Willie Montanez ripped a single to center to score Harmon. McCarver and Montanez tagged up and moved to third on Deron Johnson's lineout to center field. Both runners scored on Oscar Gamble's double.

From there, it was Bunning and Harmon, one ground ball at a time.

Bunning ran into trouble only once but escaped with help from the hapless Padres.

Nate Colbert led off the seventh inning with a single. Ollie Brown then hit a chopper that bounced so high that Bunning had no chance to make a play. But when Colbert made too big a turn at second base, Bunning wheeled and alertly threw to second, where Harmon was waiting to make the putout.

It was a huge play because Lee doubled to left to put runners on second and third. Ed Spiezio was hit by a pitch, but Barton hit into an inning-ending double play.

Manager Frank Lucchesi replaced Bunning in the eighth with Darrell Brandon, who threw two scoreless innings, thanks to a lot of help from his second baseman.

Harmon had four assists in the final two frames. He broke the record in the ninth by throwing out the last three Padre batters.

It's Beatdown Time After 3 Homers in a Row

You knew that something special was in the air when Chase Utley, Ryan Howard and Pat Burrell homered in succession in the first inning of this game against St. Louis. What transpired was one of the most unforgettable beatdowns in team history.

The Phillies scored 20 runs on a season-high 21 hits in routing the Cardinals at Busch Stadium. It was the second time in '08 that the Phils scored 20 runs in a game.

"This is one of the most dangerous lineups in baseball when guys are clicking," said Howard, who led the assault with two home runs and five RBIs. Carlos Ruiz went 4-for-6 with four RBIs.

The Phillies were ahead 4–1 when they exploded for nine runs in the fourth. Fifteen batters went to the plate. Seven got hits, five drew walks.

"I'm glad I'm on this side," said winning pitcher Kyle Kendrick. "We have a great offense."

The Phils scored another run in the fifth, and then, in the top of the sixth, Howard hit a three-run bomb to expand the lead to 17–1.

Things got testy in the eighth when Howard was drilled by a pitch thrown by Russ Springer. Home-plate umpire Larry Vanover immediately ejected the Cardinals' reliever. Manager Tony La Russa burst out of the dugout to argue the call and was also tossed.

"I don't know if it was intentional or not," said Howard. "If it was, it was. It's over. We'll go out and play tomorrow.

With Howard on first and two outs, the Phils mounted one final rally against the humiliated Redbirds.

At a Glance

WP: Kendrick (6–2)

HR: Burrell (17), Howard 2 (16,17), Utley (22)

Key stat: Phils post 20 runs on 21 hits; Utley, Howard, and Burrell hit consecutive homers

So Taguchi singled to center and came around to score behind Howard after Geoff Jenkins doubled to left-center. Jenkins scored the 20th run on a single by Ruiz. The Cardinals' pitching staff was so battered that second baseman Aaron Miles was brought in to finish up.

Kendrick pitched seven strong innings to get the win for the Phils, who expanded their lead to four games over the second-place Florida Marlins in the National League East.

Shock Follows Win When Waitkus Gets Shot

The Phillies' season, and Eddie Waitkus' life, took a fateful turn after the Phils beat up on Chicago in an afternoon game at Wrigley Field.

That evening, Waitkus was shot in a hotel room by Ruth Ann Steinhagen, a psychotic 19-year-old who harbored an unhealthy obsession for the star first baseman from the moment Waitkus broke in with the Cubs in 1941.

The 29-year-old Waitkus was batting .300 and leading the National League's All-Star balloting when the Phillies pulled into the Windy City.

In the first of a three-game series, the Phils had their way with the Cubs, scoring five runs in the top of the third inning off starter Bob Muncrief.

Russ Meyer, Philadelphia's starting pitcher, got the rally rolling with a lead-off double and scored on Richie Ashburn's single. Base hits by Waitkus and Del Ennis, a Cubs error and a double off the bat of Willie Jones accounted for the four other runs.

In the sixth inning, Waitkus and Ennis walked. Andy Seminick then sealed the win with a three-run homer.

Meyer went all nine innings, scattering 10 hits and striking out three. Waitkus went 1-for-4 and scored two runs. After the game, he and his teammates went back to the Edgewater Beach Hotel, where Steinhagen was waiting in ambush.

At a Glance

WP: Meyer (5–4)

HR: Seminick (12)

Key stat: Seminick 1-for-4, HR, 2 runs, 4 RBIs; Meyer 2-for-4, CG

She had made her reservation a month earlier and traveled lightly, bringing along just a change of clothes. Steinhagen was also carrying a knife and a .22 caliber rifle when she checked in.

Steinhagen's rage had been growing almost daily since the popular Waitkus was traded by the Cubs to the Phillies after the 1948 season. By that time she had collected a thick scrapbook of photos and press clippings of him going back to when she was 11 years old.

When Eddie made it back to the hotel, there was a note waiting for him from a "Ruth Ann Burns," saying that she was staying in room 1297. Recognizing the name as that of a woman he was dating, Waitkus rushed to the room and knocked on the door.

Steinhagen answered and told Waitkus she was a friend of Burns. He was sitting in a chair when Steinhagen opened a closet door, pulled out her rifle and told him, "If I can't have you, nobody can."

She fired once, right into his chest. As Waitkus dropped to the floor, Steinhagen called the front desk and told the receptionist what she had done.

Waitkus survived the shooting but he would miss the rest of the '49 season. At the time of the incident, the Phillies were 29–25, just 4.5 games out of first place. Without his big bat and sure hands at first, the Phils finished in third place, a distant 16 games behind the first-place Dodgers.

Waitkus returned in 1950 and helped the Phillies win the National League pennant.

Steinhagen was tried for attempted murder and was found legally insane. After spending some time in a mental institution she underwent electroshock therapy, was declared sane and released in 1952.

Eddie Waitkus rests in a hospital while recovering from a near-fatal shooting in Chicago by a psychotic fan.

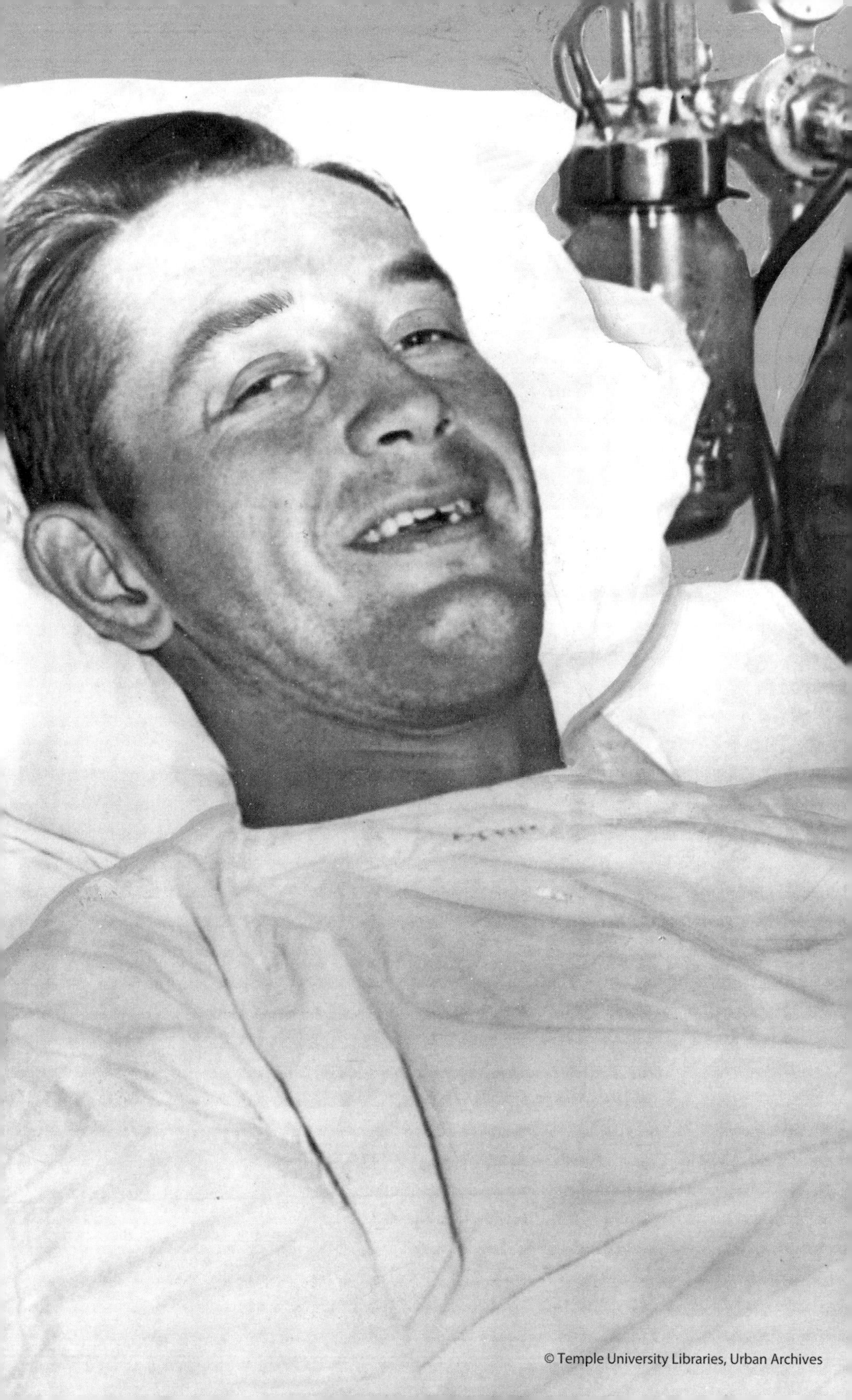

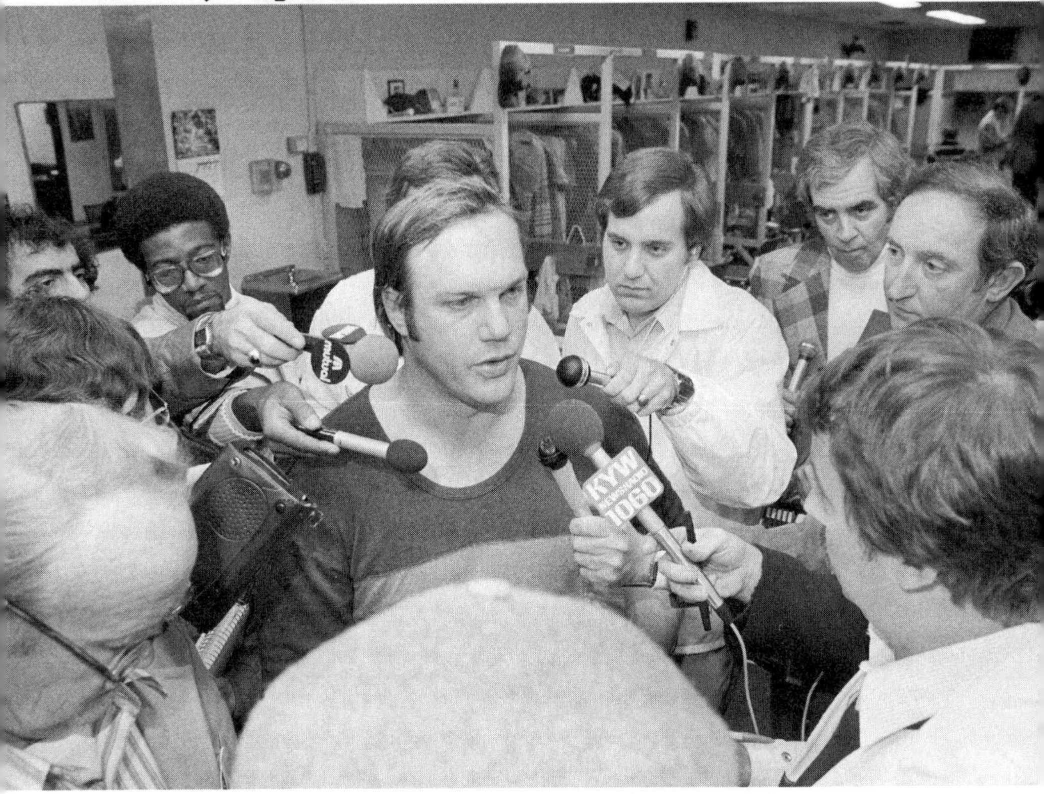

Bull's Blast Part of a Power-Packed Season

Greg Luzinski drilled a game-winning home run off 1974 Cy Young Award winner Mike Marshall as the up-and-coming Phillies sent the defending National League champion Dodgers to their fifth loss in six games.

The Bull's blast in the top of the eighth broke a 3–3 tie and silenced the crowd of nearly 41,000 fans who packed Dodger Stadium.

It was a moment of supreme redemption for the young slugger, who came up short in a big spot the night before. With two outs, runners at the corners, and the Phils trailing the Dodgers by a run, Luzinski hit a tapper back to the mound. Marshall flipped the ball to first the end the game.

At a Glance

WP: Garber (5–3)

HR: Luzinski (13), Cash (2)

Key stat: Allen 3-for-4, RBI; Luzinski 2-for-4, 2 runs, RBI; Cash 3-for-4, 2 runs, RBI

Slugger Greg Luzinski eventually gained fame in the playoffs, but he also made his mark on June 15, 1975, when "The Bull" hit the game-winning home run against the Dodgers. Luzinski set career highs in 1975 with 34 home runs and 120 RBIs.

This time, Luzinski dug in, determined to make amends.

"I know he's going to try and keep the ball away from me," he explained. "So, when he missed with two screwballs, I was looking for a pitch low and away. And I got it. A fastball."

He went with the pitch and sent the ball soaring over the fence in right-center field.

"You've got to be some kind of strong to do that," said Dodgers outfielder Jimmy Wynn.

It was the 13th homer of the season for The Bull, who would set career highs in '75 with 34 homers and a league-leading 120 RBIs.

But Luzinksi pointed to teammate Ollie Brown as the biggest hero for making a circus catch that saved the game in the ninth inning.

Pinch-hitter Henry Cruz, facing reliever Gene Garber with one out and nobody on, smashed a liner to deep right field. Brown hustled back, and at the last instant, leaped up, backhanded the ball and slammed into the wall.

The violent impact threw Brown back to the ground. But somehow, he held on to the ball. As he lay on his back, aching and groggy, center fielder Jerry Martin ran over and plucked the ball out of Brown's glove.

"Ollie's been doing the job for us all season without getting nearly enough credit," said Luzinski. "I picked the right time with the bat and Ollie picked the right time with the glove."

Greg Luzinski

The Bull was one of the most feared sluggers of his era.

A first-round draft pick in 1968, Luzinski made his debut at the age of 19 in 1970, then hit 18 home runs and knocked in 68 runs in 1972, his first full season.

In '73, he broke out with 29 homers and soon combined with Mike Schmidt to form one of the deadliest one-two power punches in the league.

Luzinski's best season was 1977, when he hit .309 with 39 homers and 130 RBIs, finishing as the runner-up to Cincinnati's George Foster in the MVP balloting.

The Bull came back with 35 homers in '78, but injuries began to take their toll after that. Luzinski left Philadelphia after the Phillies sold him to the Chicago White Sox at the end of the 1980 season. He hit 223 home runs for the Phillies.

Lieberthal's Pinch-Hit Homer Caps Comeback

After sleepwalking through eight innings, the Phillies suddenly awoke and stunned Pittsburgh with a seven-run ninth inning capped off by Mike Lieberthal's three-run walk-off home run.

"I don't believe it," said shortstop Desi Relaford. "There weren't many fans left but they were sure into it. ... That was unbelievable."

Most of the 24, 615 fans had left when the rains came in the seventh inning, choosing not to sit through what turned out to be a 63-minute delay. The die-hards who remained witnessed the greatest Phillies' comeback in 10 years.

The Pirates abused Tyler Green early in the game, scoring all seven of their runs off the right-hander in five innings. Six of those runs were the product of three-run homers by Aramis Ramirez and Al Martin.

Aside from a Gregg Jefferies home run in the sixth inning, the Phils offered no resistance until the final frame.

Mark Lewis led off the inning with a single and scored when Bobby Abreu roped a triple.

After Mark Parent and Relaford drew walks to load the bases, Alex Arias hit a grounder that shortstop Lou Collier mishandled, allowing two runs to score.

Doug Glanville stepped up next and hit a fly ball to right, deep enough to score Relaford.

At a Glance

WP: Dodd

HR: Jefferies (5), Lieberthal (7)

Key Stat: Lieberthal 3-run walk-off homer

Lieberthal had been given the night off. But with his team now showing a rapid pulse, he was told to hit for reliever Robert Dodd, who had thrown a scoreless ninth.

Facing closer Rich Loiselle, the Phillies' catcher swung at a 2–2 fastball and drove it over the fence in left field for his seventh home run of the season.

"It was the highlight of my life," said Lieberthal. "That's the most excited I've ever been on a baseball field. It was so amazing."

Manager Terry Francona shook his head in wonder after the game.

"This goes to show if you play the game hard all the way, you'll sometimes win a game you're not supposed to."

Klein Sets Franchise Record with 26-Game Hitting Streak

Chuck Klein set a modern-day franchise record by running his hitting streak to 26 games while helping the Phillies beat Pittsburgh in 10 innings at Baker Bowl.

The Hall of Famer began his historic run on May 18 in Brooklyn as the Phils were getting swept by the Robins in a doubleheader.

After going hitless in the first game, Klein went 2-for-4 with a home run and two RBIs in the nightcap.

After that, Klein caught fire. During the streak, he collected 17 multi-hit games, including one four-hit effort, and was leading the league in hitting by the time Game 26 rolled around.

Left-hander Larry French held Klein in check most of the afternoon. French had much more trouble with the first two batters, Denny Sothern and Monk Sherlock.

At a Glance

WP: Nichols (1–0)

Key stat: Klein extends hitting streak to 26 games; Sothern 3-for-5, RBI, 2 runs; Sherlock 2-for-5

In the second inning, the Phils got their first two runners on base thanks to some shoddy glove work by the Pirates' infield.

Catcher Spud Davis then hit a liner to left to knock in Bernie Friberg. Pitcher Chet Nichols' groundout brought in the second run. Sothern was up next and belted a two-out double to left to score Davis.

Sothern set up the Phillies' fourth run in the bottom of the fifth with a one-out single. After motoring to third on Sherlock's base hit, Sothern hustled in to score on Paul Waners' wild throw back to the infield.

Nichols was untouchable on the mound through five innings, using an effective mixture of lively fastballs and slow curves. But in the sixth, Nichols fell apart as the Cubs strung together six hits to tie the score.

Klein was 0-for-3 when he came to bat in the bottom of the eighth. But this time the right fielder rapped a clean hit up the middle to keep the streak alive.

Both starting pitchers were still around in the 10th. After Nichols sat down the Pirates in the top of the inning, the Phils mounted their game-winning rally, and once again, Sothern was right in the thick of it.

The fleet-footed center fielder led off with his third single of the day. Sherlock moved his teammate to second after hitting a slow roller back to the mound.

That brought up Lefty O'Doul, who was having an uncharacteristically quiet day at the plate. One of the most feared hitters in the game, O'Doul led the National League in 1929 with a .398 batting average. Like Klein, he went hitless his first three trips to the plate. But this time, the left-handed hitting O'Doul hit a missile off the right-field fence to bring Sothern home with the winning run.

Klein's hitting streak ended after this game. But he started another one on July 12. It, too, went 26 games.

Chuck Klein

One of the great left-handed hitters of the late 1920s and early 30s, Chuck Klein arrived in Philadelphia midway through the 1928 season and immediately became a fixture in the Phillies' lineup. His smooth left-handed swing produced 11 home runs and a .360 batting average in 253 at-bats his rookie year.

In 1929, Klein led the league with 43 homers while driving in 145 and batting .356. He topped that with one of the greatest seasons ever in 1930, when he hit .386 with 40 home runs and 170 RBIs.

Klein led the National League in homers four times, including 1932 when he was voted MVP, and 1933, when he won the Triple Crown with a .368 batting average, 28 home runs and 120 RBIs.

Klein was also an excellent outfielder with a powerful arm. He holds the single-season National League record with 44 assists.

Klein retired in 1944 with 300 home runs, 1,201 RBIs, and a .320 batting average.

He was selected to the Hall of Fame in 1980.

Brett Shows That Pitchers Dig the Long Ball, Too

As George Brett was launching his Hall of Fame career in Kansas City, his brother, Ken, was making headlines in Philadelphia as one of the best hitting pitchers in the game.

Facing the Mets, the veteran southpaw tied a major league record for pitchers by hitting a home run in his third consecutive game.

Brett started his streak at Veterans Stadium on June 9, when he hit his first home run of the season off Bill Greif in a winning effort against the San Diego

Ken Brett shows his swing that helped him tie a major league record for pitchers by hitting a home run in three consecutive games.

Padres. On June 19, he hit a solo home run off Charlie Hough in the fifth inning as the Phillies blew out the Dodgers, 16–3. Brett also threw a complete game to improve his record to 5–2.

Now, the eyes of 13,190 fans were on the 24-year-old Brett as he stepped onto the Veterans Stadium field to face the New York Mets.

He got off to a rough start on the mound, giving up a three-run homer to Rusty Staub in the first inning. But the Phils tied the game in the bottom of the first.

Brett batted for the first time in the home half of the second inning, lifting a fly ball to left that was deep enough to score Larry Bowa from third.

In the bottom of the fourth, with the Phillies holding a 5–4 lead, Brett tied the record when he stroked a 3–2 pitch off Mets reliever Ray Sadecki into the right-field stands. He arrived at home plate to a thunderous standing ovation. The Phillies went on to win, 9–6.

Years later, Brett liked to point out that he technically beat the home run record in this game. On June 3, at Candlestick Park in San Francisco, he crushed a ball to center field that cleared the fence on one hop, according to second-base umpire Dick Stello, who ruled it a ground-rule double. But replays showed that Stello was wrong; the ball went over the fence on the fly.

In his next start, in Montreal on June 23, Brett hit his fourth consecutive homer to break the record.

It would be the last one he would hit in '73. Brett finished the season with 16 RBIs and a batting average of .250, outstanding numbers for a pitcher.

He was solid on the mound as well, posting a career-high 13 wins against nine losses and a 3.44 ERA.

At a Glance

WP: Brett (6–2)

HR: Brett (3), Schmidt (4)

Key Stat: Brett ties record for pitchers with HR in third consecutive game

Despite those numbers, the Phillies traded Brett the following December to the Pirates for a talented and energetic second baseman named Dave Cash.

Bake Makes an Immediate Impact

Appearing in the starting lineup for the first time, Bake McBride immediately injected life into a team that was floundering in third place.

The speedy outfielder had been picked up from the St. Louis Cardinals four days earlier in a trade for pitcher Tom Underwood, first baseman Dane Iorg and outfielder Rick Bosetti.

It was a deal that sent a jolt of optimism through the team's knowledgeable and passionate fan base. McBride got his first taste of that passion the night before when he appeared for the first time as a pinch-hitter and got a standing ovation.

"It's something that never happened to me before," said McBride. "I didn't know what to do, whether to tip my hat or what. It sent chills through me."

McBride, batting second, flied out his first time up and could only watch his new teammates score a run in the first and two more in the second.

In the bottom of the third, McBride gave fans their first look at his blazing speed when he led off with a single and stole second.

Pitcher Steve Hargan was so distracted by McBride's presence that he unleashed a wild pitch. Bake glided into third and scored the fourth run on a single by Greg Luzinski.

At a Glance

WP: Carlton (9–3)

Key stat: McBride 1-for-4, SB, run; Schmidt 3B

It was more than enough for Steve Carlton, who threw a six-hitter to pick up his 100th win as a Phillie.

Lefty was in a groove for much of the night as he retired the first 14 batters he faced. Carlton lost his perfect game when he walked Vic Correll with two outs in the fifth, then lost his no-hitter the next inning to pinch-hitter Tom Paciorek, who singled to center.

"Give him credit," said Carlton. "I made a good pitch on him and he fought it off."

Carlton tired in the later innings but still finished the game, giving up two runs while striking out nine.

The addition of McBride would have a profound impact on the Phillies, who would go on to win 101 games and repeat as division champs. McBride was the catalyst, batting .339 for one of the most talented teams in Phillies history.

June 20, 1971
Phillies 9, Mets 7 (Game 2) (11 innings)

Johnson Pops a Grand Slam for the First Time of His Life

Deron Johnson's first career grand slam could not have come at a better time. The veteran slugger unloaded in the top of the 11th to break a 5–5 tie and beat the Mets in the second game of a doubleheader at Shea Stadium.

Johnson had never hit a grand slam in his life, not even in high school.

"You'd think it would have happened to me at least once before—if only by accident. I never thought too much about it, but it's a dandy way to get RBIs in bunches," said Johnson, who had knocked in a pair of runs in the fifth after belting a double.

Johnson was certain his long fly was going to score at least the go-ahead run, but he didn't think it was going to leave the yard.

"Ron Taylor threw me a good fastball. It was high and tight. I hit it hard but not nearly as hard as the one the other night that was caught out near the wall," he said.

The Phillies ended up needing all four of those runs because in the bottom of the 11th, the Mets mounted a comeback.

Woodie Fryman gave up a leadoff walk to Al Weis and a single to Don Hahn, but seemed to regain control after getting Jerry Grote to ground into a double play.

At a Glance

WP: Fryman (1–3)

HR: Johnson (9)

Key stat: Johnson 3-for-5, grand slam, 6 RBIs; Montanez 1-for-3, 2 RBIs, 2 runs

But Donn Clendenon doubled to knock in Weis, and Ken Singleton singled to bring in Hahn and make it a 9–7 game.

With more than 52,000 screaming Mets fans now on their feet, Fryman induced Bob Aspromonte to hit a grounder to shortstop. Larry Bowa flipped the ball over to second baseman Terry Harmon for a game-ending force out.

Father's Day Perfection for Bunning

Jim Bunning, a father of seven, spent his Father's Day making history on the mound at steamy Shea Stadium as he became the first National League pitcher in the 20th century to throw a perfect game.

His virtuoso performance came in the first game of a doubleheader sweep of the Mets. In the nightcap, 18-year-old Rick Wise won his first major league game.

The 32-year-old right-hander defied superstition by talking about the unfolding event throughout the afternoon and counting down the outs.

"Sure I knew I had it going," said Bunning, who remembered blowing a perfect game against Houston three weeks earlier while taking the silent route. "So when this one came up I said, 'The heck with that . . . I'm gonna talk,' and that's what I did."

At a Glance

Game 1

WP: Bunning (7–2)

HR: Callison (9)

Key stat: Bunning perfect game, 10 Ks

Game 2

WP: Wise (1–0)

HR: Callison 10, Briggs 1

Key stat: Wise 6 IP, 0 ER

He also spit in the face of the weather. Despite the 91-degree heat and oppressive humidity, Bunning got stronger in the later innings.

"I really felt good," said Bunning, who threw just 87 pitches and struck 10, including six in the last three innings. "Everything was working. It has to be to get everyone out."

Only four batters hit the ball to the outfield, but the Mets did come close to breaking up Bunning's masterpiece several times.

In the fourth inning, Ron Hunt hit a humpback liner down the right-field line that curved foul at the last second.

In the fifth, Jesse Gonder smacked a ball that appeared to be going through the right side for a hit. But second baseman Tony Taylor made a diving stop and threw him out.

And in the seventh inning, Hunt smashed a grounder to the left side that Dick Allen snagged.

The Phils had a 2–0 lead through five then broke out for four runs in the sixth. Bunning helped himself by knocking in two of those runs with a double to center. By the ninth inning, the crowd of 32,026 switched sides and began cheering for Bunning. After retiring the 25th batter, Charley Smith, on a popup, Bunning called catcher Gus Triandos out to the mound.

"He got downright silly out there . . . says I should tell him a joke, just to give him a breather," said Triandos. "I couldn't think of any so I just laughed at him and walked back."

Bunning went back to work and finished with a flourish. He struck out pinch-hitter George Altman on three pitches, then faced another pinch-hitter, left-handed hitting Johnny Stephenson.

"I figured I could get him if I could get three curves over the plate," said Bunning, who retired Stephenson on a 2–2 curveball.

After Stephenson waved at strike three, a joyful Bunning pounded his glove as his teammates rushed in from the field and out from the dugout to congratulate him.

Bunning had been down this road before, having thrown a no-hitter in 1958 as a member of the Detroit Tigers. But this was different.

It was the first perfect game thrown by a National League pitcher since 1880, and only the seventh perfect game in the history of baseball.

Bunning's perfecto virtually obliterated any memory of the second game of that doubleheader. The pitching mastery continued with Wise and reliever Johnny Klipstein teaming up to limit the Mets to three hits in an 8-2 win.

Wise, a bonus baby barely out of high school, was making only his second big league start. But he showed no signs of nervousness, thanks in large part to his teammates, who staked him to a three-run lead in the first inning. One of those runs came off the bat of 20-year-old John Briggs, another rookie, who hit his first big-league homer.

Jim Bunning

He was 32 years old and coming off a losing season when the Phillies acquired him from the Detroit Tigers on Dec. 5, 1963. But it turned out Jim Bunning was just entering his prime and would become one of the all-time great pitchers in Phillies history.

Bunning won 19 games three years in a row, beginning in 1964. Throughout the mid 1960s he consistently ranked among the leaders in wins, strikeouts and earned-run average.

The Phillies traded Bunning to the Pirates after the 1967 season, but got him back in 1970. He hung around long enough to become the first pitcher since Cy Young to win 100 games in both leagues.

Bunning is also among the famous few to pitch a no-hitter in the National and American Leagues.

He was inducted into the Hall of Fame in 1996.

June 23, 1971
Phillies 4, Reds 0

'A No-Hitter and Two Home Runs, That's NEVER Been Done!'

On a hot, sultry night at Cincinnati's Riverfront Stadium, Rick Wise gave what was arguably the single most dominating all-around performance by a pitcher in big-league history. The 25-year-old right-hander not only threw a no-hitter, but socked two home runs to single-handedly beat the Reds.

Wise had been suffering from the flu and didn't feel like he had much to offer that night.

"Warming up, I said, 'Boy I better locate my pitches well or I won't be around long,'" said Wise. "I didn't feel I had the strength to attack but I had to make sure that I located my pitches because I felt weak."

But by the fourth inning, the heat and humidity at Riverfront Stadium seemed to revive the young veteran.

"I must have sweated it out by then," he said. "I remember there was a good tempo to the game. Things were happening within three or four pitches to every batter, and as it turned out they were all outs."

Wise was also helped out by a defensive shift that placed three infielders on the left side whenever the Reds' right-handed sluggers—Lee May, Johnny Bench and Tony Perez—came to the plate.

The Phillies scratched out a run in the second to take the lead. By the middle innings, Wise had completely taken over the game.

With one out and Roger Freed on second in the top of the fifth, he hit a high slider off Reds starter Ross Grimsley that cleared the wall in left field with plenty of room to spare.

After retiring the Reds in order in the bottom of the inning, Wise began to realize that something

Phillies	AB	R	H	RBI
Harmon 2b	4	0	0	0
Bowa ss	4	0	0	0
McCarver c	3	0	2	0
Johnson 1b	2	0	0	0
Lis lf	2	1	0	0
Stone lf	1	0	0	0
Montanez cf	4	0	1	0
Freed rf	4	1	1	1
Vukovich 3b	4	0	1	0
Wise p	4	2	2	3
Totals	32	4	7	4

Reds	AB	R	H	RBI
Rose rf	4	0	0	0
Foster cf	3	0	0	0
May 1b	3	0	0	0
Bench c	3	0	0	0
Perez 3b	3	0	0	0
McRae lf	3	0	0	0
Granger p	0	0	0	0
Helms 2b	3	0	0	0
Concepcion ss	1	0	0	0
Stewart ph	1	0	0	0
Grimsley p	1	0	0	0
Carbo ph	1	0	0	0
Carroll p	0	0	0	0
Cline lf	1	0	0	0
Totals	27	0	0	0

PHI	0	1	0	0	2	0	0	1	0	-	4	7	0
CIN	0	0	0	0	0	0	0	0	0	-	0	0	0

Phillies	IP	H	R	ER	BB	SO
Wise W (8-4)	9	0	0	0	1	3
Totals	9	0	0	0	1	3

Reds	IP	H	R	ER	BB	SO
Grimsley L (4-3)	6	4	3	3	2	1
Carroll	2	2	1	1	1	1
Granger	1	1	0	0	0	1
Totals	9	7	4	4	3	3

DP—Cincinnati 2. 2B—Philadelphia Freed, Montanez. HR—Philadelphia Wise 2 (3,4). HBP—Philadelphia Lis. LOB—Philadelphia 5; Cincinnati 1. Attendance: 13,329.

special was happening.

"You know, you're sitting there in the dugout, lookin' up at the scoreboard and you can see no hits and I don't remember anybody being on," said Wise.

He lost his perfect game in the bottom of the sixth after walking Dave Concepcion with one out. But Wise continued to mow down the Reds.

"Every time there was an out it was just one more down," Wise recalled. "After seven innings I thought I had a real shot at it."

Wise struck again at the plate in the top of the eighth with a leadoff homer against Reds reliever Clay Carroll.

"It was a ball two cripple pitch," he recalled. "I looked down at third base and (coach) George Myatt turned his back on me so I knew I had the green light. So he (Carroll) put one right down the middle and I hit it good, to left-center."

By this time, Wise's teammates were abiding by the old superstition of silence. Manager Frank Lucchesi went a step further by spending the last five innings standing in the same position in the dugout, afraid to move.

"I didn't want to put the whammy on Rick," said Lucchesi.

In the ninth, the first batter Wise faced was pinch-hitter Jimmy Stewart. He struck him out on a 3–2 curveball.

Ty Cline was next and hit a slow roller to second. Terry Harmon gobbled it up and flipped to Wise covering first for the second out.

Wise now faced Pete Rose, one of the toughest outs in baseball. On a 3–2 count, Rose punched a soft liner to third that John Vukovich squeezed for the final out. Wise threw up his arms in triumph and was soon swallowed up by his teammates. He called it his biggest thrill.

After the game, Wise and some other players went out to celebrate.

"We walked back to the hotel from the ballpark and Mike Ryan kept saying, 'Do you know what you've just done, do you KNOW what you've DONE!? A no-hitter and two home runs, that's NEVER been done!' And Mike talked to the guy in the hotel lounge, told him, 'He just threw a no-hitter, get the champagne out.' And they started pouring champagne. I didn't get to sleep 'til late that night."

Morandini Shines as Dykstra Returns

With the Phillies riding high atop the National League East, leadoff batter Lenny Dykstra returned from an injury that sidelined him for three weeks, a development that paid immediate dividends for Mickey Morandini.

The Phils' second baseman was a classic number two hitter who struggled in the leadoff slot, batting just .208 after Dykstra went down with a back injury.

But with the centerfielder now back, Morandini returned to his familiar role and turned in the best game of his career, going 5-for-6 with three RBIs as the Phils hung on to beat the Cardinals at Busch Stadium.

"I've hit there for four or five years," said Morandini. "Plus, Lenny's always on base and I get a lot of good pitches to hit."

Morandini wasn't the only one to get in the swing of things. The Phillies tallied 17 hits, including four from Jim Eisenreich, the league's leading hitter at the time, and three by Charlie Hayes. They built a commanding 9–1 lead, only to watch it disappear through a combination of errors and timely hitting by the Cardinals, who scored five runs off Paul Quantrill in the fifth.

At a Glance

WP: Quantrill (7–2)

Key stat: Morandini 5-for-6, 3 RBIs, 2 runs; Hayes 3-for-5, 3 RBIs; Eisenreich 4-for-6, 2 RBIs, 2 runs

Morandini's run-scoring single in the top of the sixth made it 10–6, but the Cardinals continued to chip away, adding a run in the bottom of the sixth and two more in the seventh.

"It looked like Paul ran out of gas," said Eisenreich. "I thought it was going to be one of those easy days."

In the eighth, Cardinals catcher Danny Sheaffer led off with a single and moved to second on a sacrifice bunt. But Phils reliever Ricky Bottalico blew away Darnell Coles with a 3–2 heater, then retired Bernard Gilkey on a grounder to shortstop Kevin Stocker.

Manager Jim Fregosi never felt comfortable, once the Cardinals started to roll. "There was no doubt in my mind that they were going to find a way to get the tying run to the plate in the bottom of the ninth," said Fregosi.

Shortstop Tripp Cromer got a leadoff single, but Heathcliff Slocumb retired the next three batters in order to post his 18th save.

It was the high point of the season for the Phillies, who sagged badly after this game and finished in third place, a distant 21 games behind first place Atlanta.

June 25, 1969

Phillies 6, Mets 5 (10 innings)

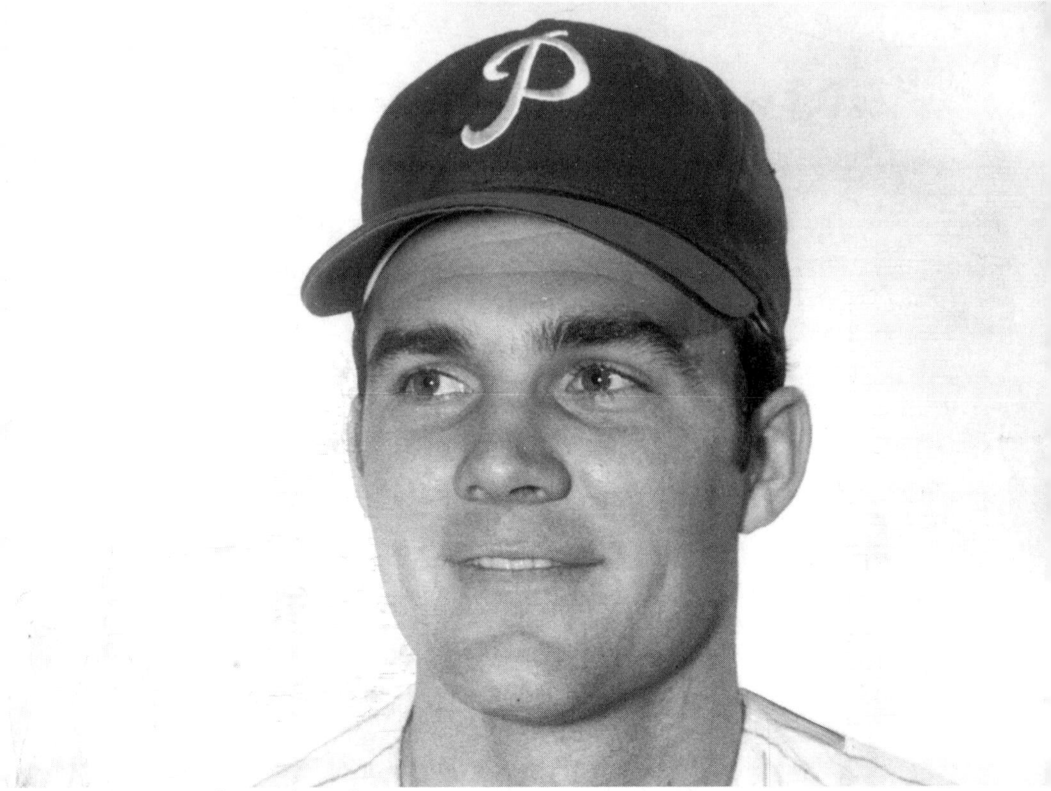

Unlikely Hero Posts the Game of His Life

The unlikeliest of heroes emerged to help the Phillies defeat the Mets in 10 thrilling innings at Shea Stadium.

Rookie Dave Watkins, a seldom-used backup catcher, was pressed into emergency service as a third baseman, and responded with the biggest day of his short career.

Watkins belted his first major league homer to tie the game in the eighth, then scored the winning run in the 10th after swatting a triple.

He entered the game in the fifth inning after Cookie Rojas was ejected during an argument with umpire Ken

At a Glance

WP: Wilson (2–2)

HR: Watkins (1)

Key stat: Watkins 2-for-3, RBI, 2 runs; R. Stone 2-for-4, 2 RBIs

Rookie Dave Watkins had the game of his life on June 25, 1969, when he hit a home run and a triple to guide the Phillies past the Mets, 6–5.

Burkhart. The Phils were already undermanned with several regulars injured, so manager Bob Skinner called on the rookie to do the best he could at a position he hadn't played since ninth grade.

"My heart started beating fast," said Watkins, who decided not to take any chances and removed a denture plate before taking the field.

At the time, the Mets were leading 4–0 behind young flamethrower Nolan Ryan, who was working on a perfect game.

Shortly after Watkins came in, the Mets padded their lead to 5–0 on an RBI single by Cleon Jones.

Ryan lost his perfect game in the sixth after hitting Terry Harmon on the elbow with a fastball. Two batters later he lost his no-hitter and shutout when Larry Hisle tripled. In the seventh, an error and a wild pitch led to three more runs and the end of Ryan's day.

Watkins took center stage in the top of the eighth. Facing veteran reliever Cal Koonce, he tore into a fastball, sending it over the 396 sign in left-center to tie the game.

The next time up, with two outs in the top of the 10th, Watkins hit a bomb off the centerfield fence for a triple. Briggs then drove in Watkins with the go-ahead run.

Did You Know?

In their game on June 25, 1969, the Phillies and Mets set a National League record for futililty by striking out 27 times.

Larry Hisle and Gene Stone were the leading offenders for the Phillies. They struck out three times apiece.

For the Mets, Tommie Agee went down on strikes four times, while Ken Boswell, Cleon Jones, J. C. Martin, and Nolan Ryan all struck out twice.

Nolan Ryan fanned 10 batters in 6 ⅓ innings. Phillies starter Lowell Palmer struck out nine in just 4 ⅓ innings. Phils reliever Billy Wilson mowed down five and the Mets' Cal Koonce came out of the bullpen to strike out three batters.

Nip-and-Tuck Affair Goes to Phillies at Long, Long Last

It took 17 innings for the Phillies to beat the St. Louis Cardinals in a game that featured terrific pitching and numerous blown opportunities.

The starters for both teams were outstanding. Lefty Shane Rawley, enjoying an All-Star season for the Phillies, surrendered only one run over nine innings while giving up five hits and striking out five.

The Cardinals' Bob Forsch was equally effective. The Phils got their only run off him in the third when Rawley hit a one-out double and scored on a single by Jeff Stone.

The Phillies had a great chance to win the game in the top of the 15th. Juan Samuel made it to first after grounding into a force. After Sammy stole second, Ron Roenicke drilled a single to left. But Vince Coleman closed on the ball in a hurry and gunned it to the plate in time for catcher Mike LaValliere to put the tag on Samuel.

St. Louis threatened in the 12th. Coleman hit a two-out single and stole second. Reliever Steve Bedrosian intentionally walked Ozzie Smith, then committed a balk, allowing both runners to move up. But Bedrosian rebounded by striking out Tommy Herr to end the inning.

Willie McGee led off the Cardinals' 13th with a double, but his teammates left him stranded.

At a Glance

WP: Tekulve (2–1)

Save: Hume (1)

Key stat: Thompson 2-for-3, RBI; Stone 2-for-4, RBI

The two teams continued to put up goose eggs until the 17th inning, when John Russell led off with an infield single, moved to second on a sacrifice bunt and scored on Milt Thompson's single to center.

Tom Hume retired the Cardinals in the bottom half of the inning to get the save. The win went to submariner Kent Tekulve, who pitched three scoreless innings.

Hitting for the Cycle a Family Affair for Bell

Hitting for the cycle is one of the rarest of feats, but when David Bell became the seventh player in Phillies history to do it, he also worked his way into the major league record books as part of the only grandfather-grandson tag-team to hit for the cycle.

Bell's grandfather, Gus, turned the trick as a member of the Pittsburgh Pirates on June 4, 1951. Ironically, Gus Bell got his cycle in a game against the Phillies at Shibe Park.

David, a third generation big-leaguer (his father, Buddy, was a third baseman and manager), completed his cycle with a triple in the seventh inning off Expos reliever Rocky Biddle.

"I didn't realize what happened after I got to third base," said Bell. "I probably would have thought of it if I had a triple earlier in the game. This is special because it doesn't happen very often."

As he was congratulated by third-base coach John Vukovich, Bell got a standing ovation from the crowd at Citizens Bank Park and noticed his teammates clapping and hollering in the dugout.

"That was nice to see," he said. "It meant a lot to me."

But he had to wait a few minutes to make sure the call would stand. Center fielder Brad Wilkerson and Expos manager Frank Robinson argued that a fan had interfered with the ball as it bounced off the stands in center field, and that Bell should have been awarded only a double. But umpire crew chief Ed Montague held his ground.

At a Glance

WP: Millwood (6–5)

HR: Bell (9), Burrell (14), Utley (6)

Key stat: Bell hits for cycle, 4-for-4, 6 RBIs; Burrell 3-for-5, 3 RBIs

Phils manager Larry Bowa said that he would have gone out to argue had the call gone the other way. "With the way David runs, he doesn't get many triples," Bowa chuckled.

The 31-year-old third baseman started his big night with a double in the second inning. He belted a three-run homer in the fourth as part of a six-run inning, and singled in another run in the sixth. His seventh-inning triple plated two more runs.

For the night, Bell was 4-for-4 with a career-high six RBIs, part of a relentless offense that pounded Expos pitching the entire game.

June 29, 2004
Phillies 17, Expos 7

Phils Reach New Heights in Homer-Filled Month

The powerful Phillies slugged four more homers in their blowout of Montreal to break the club record of 43 home runs in a month.

Placido Polanco was the first to clear the fence at Citizens Bank Park with a solo home run to lead off the third inning. The Phils added five more runs on five hits to take an 8–3 lead and drive rookie right-hander Shawn Hill from the game.

But the Expos continued to have their way with Phillies lefty Eric Milton. They scored four in the top of the fifth to make it a one-run game.

In the bottom of the fifth, the Phillies put their offense into overdrive and sped away from their neighbors to the north.

Bobby Abreu highlighted a five-run inning with a three-run moonshot that landed in the visitors' bullpen beyond center field.

In the sixth, Milton was replaced by rookie right-hander Ryan Madson, who calmed down the Expos' bats with three innings of scoreless relief.

David Bell's two-run homer to left in the eighth tied the franchise record for homers in a month, set in June 1977. Tomas Perez broke it later that inning with a pinch-hit, two-run swat.

At a Glance

WP: Milton (10–2)

HR: Polanco (4), Abreu (16), Bell (10), Perez (5)

Key stat: Bell 2-for-4, 3 RBIs; Polanco 2-for-6, 2 RBIs; Rollins 3-for-6, 3 RBIs

"We know we've got a small park," Perez said. "But we've got good hitters, too."

The 17 runs scored was a season high for the Phillies, who scored 14 the night before.

"We're not done, either," said leftfielder Pat Burrell.

And he was right. The next night Jim Thome hit his league-leading 27th home run to raise the record to 44.

JULY

Deron Johnson had a July to remember in 1971,
when he hit home runs in four consecutive at-bats on July 10-11.

This Game Had It All, From Runs to Hits to a Cycle for Chuck Klein

Phillies fans witnessed an action-packed game that included a little bit of everything, including at least one run scored in every inning, 27 hits combined, a future Hall of Famer hitting for the cycle, and a triple play.

Chuck Klein began working on the first of his two career cycle days in the bottom of the first when he roped a two-run triple as the Phils took a 3–1 lead.

Chicago picked up a run in the second and tied the game in the third after Hack Wilson homered. The Cubs were threatening in the top of the fourth when the Phillies pulled off the first triple play of the 1931 season.

Kiki Cuyler was on second and Woody English on first when Danny Taylor scalded a line drive toward right field. As the runners took off, second baseman

Chuck Klein hit for the cycle twice in his career. On July 1, 1931, he did it by going 4-for-5 to take over the National League batting lead.

Les Mallon jumped up, caught the ball with his outstretched glove and flipped it to first baseman Barney Friberg to double up English. Friberg then whipped the ball over to second, where shortstop Dick Bartell was waiting to put the tag on an astonished Cuyler.

The Phillies' amazing glove work seemed to take the fight out of the Cubs and reinvigorate pitcher Jumbo Elliot, who was in trouble every inning. The big lefty settled down and breezed through the next four innings. He also chipped in at the plate with a pair of singles and an RBI.

In the fifth, Klein got his second hit, a single, then came around to score on Pinky Whitney's double to make it a 5–3 game.

After doubling in the sixth, he completed the cycle, one of the rarest feats in baseball, by launching a two-run homer in the eighth.

At a Glance

WP: Elliot (10–7)

HR: Klein (21)

Key stat: Klein 4-for-5, cycle, 5 RBIs, 3 runs; Bartell 3-for-5; Elliot 2-for-4, RBI

Klein finished 4-for-5 with five RBIs and three runs scored. He also vaulted into the lead in the National League batting race with a .375 average, just ahead of teammate Spuds Davis.

Elliot sputtered in the ninth after giving up three runs, but was bailed out by reliever Phil Collins, who got the final out to end the game. Jumbo, who was picked up in an off-season trade with Brooklyn, earned his 10th victory, matching his total output from the year before. He would go on to enjoy the best season of his career with a record of 19–14.

July 2, 1993

Phillies 6, Padres 5 (10 innings) (Game 2)

All-Time All-Nighter Ends at 4:45 AM

As most of the Delaware Valley slept, the Phillies and Padres pulled the all-time all-nighter. The two teams slogged through the longest and perhaps strangest doubleheader in Phillies history. Due to numerous rain delays, Game 2 didn't begin until 1:29 in the morning. When it ended at 4:45 AM, about 6,000 of the original 54,617 fans were still around to see the dramatic finish. And what a finish!

The long night featured three rain delays totaling five hours and 54 minutes, a franchise record. The Phils and Padres also set a major league record for the latest finish to a game. A fireworks show that was supposed to go on after the twinbill ended was postponed. And the second game was won on a hit by a relief pitcher who hadn't batted all season.

After losing the first game 5–2, the Phils fell behind 5–0 in the nightcap before mounting a comeback.

The Phillies finally tied the game in the eighth. With two outs and runners on first and second, manager Jim Fregosi sent Darren Daulton out to pinch hit for catcher Todd Pratt. Dutch delivered a clutch single to knock in Dave Hollins.

In the 10th, Pete Incaviglia led off with a walk against Trevor Hoffman and Jim Eisenreich followed with a single to right. But Daulton struck out. Now the batter was reliever Mitch Williams.

The last time he batted in a game was on Sept. 28, 1992. But Fregosi was out of options. He had no pinch-hitters left.

At a Glance

WP: Williams (2–3)

HR: Jordan (3)

Key stat: Williams game-winning hit; Jordan 2-for-5, 3 RBIs; Eisenreich 2-for-5, RBI

So "Wild Thing," with two career hits and three RBIs under his belt, walked to the batter's box to face the future all-time saves leader—and smashed a line drive into left-center to knock in the winning run.

The sun would soon be up. But all of a sudden, the Phillies and those who remained in the stands were wide awake with a fresh jolt of adrenaline. The pre-dawn celebration featured fans chanting Williams' name until he came back out from the clubhouse to tip his cap and wave.

"I've never been through anything like this," he said. "I stayed because I had to."

It's Fireworks Night on the Field, in the Sky

The 58,000 people who showed up at Veterans Stadium for Fireworks Night also got to see the Phillies light up the scoreboard as they pounded seven Cubs pitchers for 21 runs and 21 hits.

The massacre began immediately with the Phillies sending 12 batters to the plate during a first inning that produced eight runs on eight hits. Three of those runs scored on back-to-back homers by Rico Brogna and Mike Lieberthal.

The inning also featured two hits by Ron Gant—an RBI double and a triple to center that knocked in two more.

For about 30 minutes the Phillies battered Chicago starter Kyle Farnsworth, who got only one batter out before he was replaced by lefty Dan Serafini.

"It was like a rain delay," said manager Terry Francona.

Ironically, the lengthy inning had a negative impact on Phillies starter Paul Byrd.

After a scoreless first, the right-hander gave up one run in the second and three more in the third on a bases-clearing double by Henry Rordriguez.

"With the big lead, I probably threw too many fastballs," said Byrd. "It was a strange night, but I'm just glad to get the win."

Rookie Marlon Anderson collected five hits for the first time in his career. Scott Rolen hit a grand slam for the Phillies as well.

Cubs	AB	R	H	RBI
Morandini 2b	4	1	1	0
Hernandez ss-rf-ss	3	2	0	0
Grace 1b	4	2	2	0
Heredia p	0	0	0	0
Karchner p	0	0	0	0
Hill ph-rf	1	1	1	1
Sosa rf	4	2	2	3
Alexander ss-3b	1	0	0	0
Rodriguez lf	5	0	3	3
Houston c-1b	4	0	0	0
Gaetti 3b-p	4	0	1	0
Goodwin cf	3	0	1	1
Farnsworth p	0	0	0	0
Serafini p	2	0	0	0
Sanders p	0	0	0	0
King p	0	0	0	0
Blauser ph	1	0	0	0
Martinez c	1	0	0	0
Totals	37	8	11	8

Phillies	AB	R	H	RBI
Glanville cf	5	2	3	2
Poole p	0	0	0	0
Gant lf	4	2	2	4
Grahe p	0	0	0	0
Doster ph-3b	2	0	0	0
Abreu rf	4	2	1	2
Rolen 3b	3	3	1	4
Jordan 3b-1b	1	0	1	0
Brogna 1b	4	2	2	2
Bennett ph-c	1	0	0	0
Lieberthal c	4	1	2	2
Schrenk p	0	0	0	0
Ducey ph-cf	1	0	0	0
Anderson 2b	6	4	5	2
Arias ss	5	3	3	2
Byrd p	3	2	1	1
Sefcik ph-lf	3	0	0	0
Totals	46	21	21	21

CHI	0	1	3	0	3	0	0	1	0	-	8	11	1
PHI	0	1	0	7	1	2	0	2	X	-	21	21	0

Cubs	IP	H	R	ER	BB	SO
Farnsworth L (2-3)	0.1	7	8	6	0	1
Serafini	3.1	5	5	5	4	0
Sanders	0.1	2	3	3	2	0
King	1	2	1	1	0	0
Heredia	1	2	2	2	2	0
Karchner	1	1	0	0	0	1
Gaetti	1	2	2	2	1	1
Totals	8	21	21	19	9	3

Phillies	IP	H	R	ER	BB	SO
Byrd W (11-4)	5	9	7	7	2	2
Grahe	2	1	0	0	3	3
Schrenk	1	1	1	1	0	1
Poole	1	0	0	0	0	0
Totals	9	11	8	8	5	6

E—Chicago Farnsworth. 2B—Chicago Rodriguez; Philadelphia Brogna, Gant, Abreu, Anderson. 3B—Philadelphia Gant, Glanville. HR—Chicago Hill (13), Sosa (31); Philadelphia Brogna (11), Anderson (4), Rolen (18), Lieberthal (18). HBP—Chicago Hernandez; Philadelphia Glanville. LOB—Chicago 8; Philadelphia 11. SB—Philadelphia Abreu, Anderson, Glanville. Attendance: 58,086.

Phillies 10, Boston Bees 2 (Game 2)

© Temple University Libraries, Urban Archives

Shibe Park Hosts a Celebration for All

The Phillies celebrated Independence Day by winning their first game in their new home.

Shibe Park was just seven blocks from Baker Bowl in North Philadelphia. But it was a world away in terms of spaciousness and comfort.

Baker Bowl, built in 1887, had become a dilapidated dungeon for ballplayers and fans by the 1930s. So management made the move to Connie Mack's concrete and steel palace at 21st and Lehigh midway through the 1938 season.

Team president Gerald Nugent and his wife, Mae, were presented with flowers in a pre-game ceremony, and a band entertained the crowd of 12,000 between innings of the park's inaugural doubleheader.

The Phillies lost the first game but came back to win the second behind Claude Passeau, who held the Bees to two runs on seven hits.

The Baker Bowl, pictured, was the Phillies' home before they moved into Shibe Park on July 4, 1938.

"Shibe Park is a swell place to pitch," said Passeau. "Before the game, (manager) Jimmy Wilson told me to use a knee-high fastball as much as I wanted to. In Baker Bowl that toss was usually good for a whack against the right-field wall by left-handed hitters. Today when I let the number one go I had no fear."

Infielders also had less to fear chasing grounders on Shibe's emerald grass and smooth infield mixture of dirt and sand.

At a Glance

WP: Passeau (6–8)

Key stat: Jordan 4-for-6, 3 runs; Arnovich 3-for-4, 4 RBIs

"I never knew when a ground ball was going to bounce off a pebble and go for a hit or hit me in the chin," said third baseman Pinky Whitney. "Here, the ball zips along like on a billiards table. You can't miss 'em."

While Passeau silenced Boston's bats, the Phillies went right after starter Dick Errickson, scoring three times in the first.

The Phils collected 10 runs on 10 hits off four Boston pitchers.

"This park is made for me," a jubilant Morrie Arnovich declared after going 3-for-4 with four RBIs.

Did You Know?

Tim McCarver once hit a grand-slam single. It happened at Three Rivers Stadium in Pittsburgh on July 4, 1976, as America celebrated its Bicentennial.

In the second inning of the first game of a doubleheader with the Pirates, the Phillies' catcher hit a bases-loaded homer into the right-field seats.

But in his exhuberance to get around the bases, McCarver passed Garry Maddox. He was called out and got credit for a single.

July 5, 1977

Phillies 12, Mets 1

Johnstone, McCarver Tear It Up vs. Mets

With their potent lineup clicking on all cylinders and their No. 1 starter in Cy Young form, the Phillies handed the Mets a humiliating defeat at Veterans Stadium.

Jay Johnstone led a relentless 12-hit attack that included four home runs, one with the bases loaded.

Taking advantage of a rare opportunity to bat cleanup, Johnstone hit his first home run in the first inning with Garry Maddox on third.

In the third, the Phillies chased right-hander Pat Zachry after posting four more runs during a rally started by Steve Carlton's leadoff single.

Mike Schmidt drove in three of those runs with a long homer to the upper deck in left.

Not to be outdone, Johnstone followed Schmidt with an even longer bomb to right after Zachry fired a pitch near his head. Umpire Bob Engel gave the right-hander a warning and order was restored—until Johnstone tore into a 2–0 fastball and joined a handful of left-handed hitters to reach the rarified air of the 500 level.

Another heavy hitter was Tim McCarver. The veteran catcher knocked in the seventh run with a single in the fifth and followed Johnstone's run-scoring single in the sixth with his sixth career grand slam. The blast earned him a standing ovation from the crowd of 23,344.

"That's the first standing ovation I ever got in my life," said McCarver. "What's the matter with the fans? Don't they know I've been released twice?"

Meanwhile, the Mets were unable to do anything against Carlton. After giving up a first-inning double to leadoff hitter Lenny Randle, Lefty no-hit the Mets for seven innings.

At a Glance

WP: Carlton (11–4)

HR: Johnstone 2 (3,4), Schmidt (24), McCarver (2)

Key stat: Johnstone 3-for-5, 4 RBIs; Schmidt 2-for-3, 3 RBIs; McCarver grand slam; Carlton 1-hit allowed

"I feel good, and when you feel good you throw good," he said. "And I've got some extraordinary people playing (behind) me."

Tim McCarver greets Jay Johnstone after one of Johnstone's two home runs on July 5, 1977.

JOHNSTONE
21
11
20
25

Rookie Whiz Kid Miller Moves to 8–0

While Roberts, Simmons, and Konstanty were grabbing the headlines through the early part of the summer of 1950, rookie pitcher Bob Miller was quietly putting together a spectacular first half of the season for the Whiz Kids.

The 24-year-old right-hander improved his record to 8–0 following this win over the New York Giants at Shibe Park.

Miller was supported by a 10-hit attack that included six extra-base hits.

Catcher Andy Seminick led the way with a 4-for-4 day. His second-inning double scored Willie Jones with the Phillies' first run and his leadoff homer in the fifth lit the fuse that blew the game wide open.

The game was tied 1–1 when Seminick belted Sheldon Jones' offering into the left-field bleachers.

Jones drilled the next batter, Mike Goliat, who then scored on Richie Ashburn's 400-foot triple to center. Ashburn walked home when Granny Hamner hit his fifth home run of the season.

The Giants made a pitching change but the Phillies kept on swinging as they scored three more in the bottom of the sixth.

Now staked to an 8–2 lead in the seventh, Miller got careless with his location, and the Giants made him pay. Five hits and three runs later, Miller was gone.

Jim Konstanty struck out Bobby Thompson to end the inning then pitched the final two to pick up his 11th save.

Miller got the win to remain unbeaten. He was by far one of the top rookies in the league, with five complete games and a 2.38 ERA.

Unfortunately for Miller and the Whiz Kids, he had reached the high-water mark of his season.

At a Glance

WP: Miller (8–0)

HR: Jones (16), Seminick (7), Hamner (5)

Key stat: Jones 4-for-4, 2 RBIs, 2 runs; Jones 2-for-4, 2 runs, RBI; Hamner 2-for-4, 3 RBIs

In August he hurt his back and tried to play through the pain, leading to an arm injury that occurred during a game against Cincinnati in September. He was never the same after that.

Following his win over the Giants, Miller won just three more games to finish his rookie season with a record of 11–6, a career best.

Redus, Samuel Stop Fans in Their Tracks with Homers

More than 18,000 fans had barely settled into their seats at Veterans Stadium when they had to jump back up to their feet and cheer as Gary Redus and Juan Samuel became the second Phillies tandem to open a game with consecutive homers.

They also tied the major league mark for most homers leading off a team's first at-bat, a record that fell in 1987 when the San Diego Padres started three games in a row with a home run.

Redus came back in the second inning and whacked a two-run homer to give Shane Rawley all the help he would need.

The Braves scored a pair in the fourth, but the Phils answered back in the bottom of the inning when Greg Gross opened with a single and John Russell blasted the team's fourth home run of the night.

At a Glance

WP: Rawley (11–4)

HR: Redus 2 (3), Samuel (7), Russell (7)

Key Stats: Redus 2-for-4, 3 RBIs, 2 runs

Rawley battled the oppressive July heat and a potent Braves lineup to raise his record to 11–4.

"Both physically and mentally, this was an exhausting game for me," he said. "I didn't have my best stuff. It was so hot out there and Atlanta is such a good hitting club, this one was really tough."

Rawley worked out of a number of jams in his grueling eight-inning stint.

He came out for the ninth but was lifted after surrendering a leadoff walk to Dale Murphy and a single to Bob Horner.

"I gave him the chance to take himself out after the eighth," said manager John Felske. "But Shane wanted to go out and try and finish."

Steve Bedrosian came in and quickly ended the threat by retiring the next three batters.

© Temple University Libraries, Urban Archives

Kewpie Adds to His Lore with 14-Inning Shutout

Meet Dick "Kewpie" Barrett, a long-forgotten journeyman and Pennsylvania native who etched his name in Phillies history when he threw a 14-inning shutout against Cincinnati.

Barrett was a colorful character. Born in Montoursville, Pa., his birth name was Tracy Souter Barrett but he pitched under several pseudonyms, including Dick Kewpie and Dick Oliver. His squat stature and puffy face made him look more like a middle-aged plumber than a professional ballplayer, and his age was in question.

A three-sport athlete at the University of Illinois, the hard-throwing Barrett broke in with Connie Mack's A's in 1933, appearing in 15 games.

He moved to the Boston Braves the next year before washing out and heading to the Pacific Coast League, where he became a legendary star for the

Pennsylvania legend Kewpie Barrett pitched a 14-inning shutout in a 1–0 victory against the Reds on July 8, 1943.

Seattle Rainiers and Indians, winning 20 games seven times. Barrett came back to the major leagues in 1943, hooking up with the Cubs. But after going 0–4, he was released at the end of June.

Desperate for pitching, the last-place Phillies quickly signed him. In his first start, Barrett pitched eight strong innings, giving up just two earned runs in a losing effort against his former team.

His ironman performance came in the second game of a doubleheader against the Reds at Shibe Park.

Barrett gave up nine hits, walked five and had to work his way out of a bases-loaded jam three times. But he continued to hold Cincinnati scoreless, inning after inning.

Reds starter Ray Starr and reliever Joe Beggs were equally impressive. Starr pitched 10 scoreless innings while Beggs sat down the Phillies through the 11th, 12th, and 13th.

The sun was going down as the Phils came to bat in the bottom of the 14th. With two outs and runners on first and second, umpire George Magerkurth was about to call the game.

Barrett was the next scheduled batter but manager Bucky Harris called him back in favor of pinch-hitter Pinky May. It turned out to be a brilliant move when May poked a single into left to bring Coaker Triplett home with the winning run.

At a Glance

WP: Barrett (1–5)

Key stat: Barrett 14 IP; Triplett 2-for-5, run

Barrett went on to have a career-best season with the Phils, going 10–9 with a 2.39 ERA.

The next season, Barrett lost 18 games and in 1945, he retired after going 8–20.

Roberts Magical in Picking Up 150th Win of His Career

On the road to his sixth consecutive 20-win season, Robin Roberts paused in Pittsburgh to mark a milestone. This win over the Pirates was the 150th of Robbie's glittering career. And he was nothing short of brilliant.

Roberts threw just 84 pitches, gave up three hits, all in the same inning, surrendered no walks and struck out four. He also helped himself at the plate with two hits, including his first home run of the season.

The Phillies opened the scoring with two outs in the first inning. Stan Lopata singled, moved to third on a base hit by Del Ennis and scored on a wild pitch thrown by Pirates lefty Dick Littlefield. Puddin' Head Jones knocked in Ennis with a double to right.

The Pirates bunched all three of their hits in the second inning to score their only run of the game. Dale Long opened with a triple to left. Roberts got the next two batters before giving up back-to-back singles to Johnny O'Brien and Dick Groat.

From that point on, Roberts was untouchable as he sat down the next 22 batters in a row.

At the same time, the Phils continued to wear down the Bucs. They scored once in the third when Lopata walked and Ennis tripled, and again in the fourth when Andy Seminick hit a leadoff home run.

At a Glance

WP: Roberts (13–7)

HR: Seminick (7), Roberts (1)

Key stat: Roberts earns 150th career win; Ennis 4-for-5, RBI; Seminick 2-for-4, RBI; Lopata 2-for-3, 3 runs

The Phillies were holding a 5–1 lead when Roberts came to bat in the eighth inning and decided to swing from the left side against Pirates righty Laurin Pepper.

Robbie jacked it into the right-field stands.

Third Pinch-Homer in a Row Lands Unser in Record Books

Del Unser got two thrills for the price of one while providing fans with one of the most memorable moments in Phillies history.

His three-run walk-off homer not only beat the San Diego Padres, it made Unser the first player in major league history to hit three consecutive pinch-home runs.

Unser, who was signed by the Phillies just before the start of the '79 season, started his streak on June 30 in St. Louis with a two-run homer off George Frazier. On July 5 he did it again, delivering a two-run shot against the Mets.

When the 34-year-old outfielder stepped into the batter's box with two outs in the ninth, 30,234 fans stood and hollered out their encouragement.

The Phils began the inning trailing 5–1. But they strung together consecutive hits by Jose Cardenal, Manny Trillo, Bob Boone and pinch-hitter Tim McCarver to cut the Padres' lead down to two.

Now it was Unser's turn and the 12-year veteran jumped on a Rollie Fingers fastball, sending it high and deep over the wall in left-center field. At first he didn't think the ball was going to leave the yard.

"It felt good and I knew the center fielder would have to go back for it. But out? Uh, uh," said Unser. "I looked for the first-base bag first—to make sure I touched it. Then I looked up and it was gone."

At a Glance

WP: Bird (1–0)

HR: Unser (4), Schmidt (30)

Key stat: Unser sets record with 3 straight pinch HRs

A deafening roar went up as he circled the bases. The crowd continued to applaud and cheer as teammates pounded Unser on the back and helmet on their way into the clubhouse.

But the fans weren't ready to leave. They began stomping their feet in rhythm, pleading for a curtain call. Moments later, Unser came back out, tipped his cap and took a bow.

"As far as thrills go, this is A-1—the biggest," a beaming Unser said. "I haven't felt this good about a baseball game in I don't know how long . . . I've finally done something that's gonna make people remember me."

Johnson Goes Homer, Homer, Homer, Homer

In the midst of his most productive season in a career that spanned 16 years, Deron Johnson continued a two-game tear that saw him join the short list of big leaguers who have hit four consecutive home runs.

Phillies fans had little to cheer about during the spring and summer of 1971, but one player they could always count on was the slugging first baseman, one of the franchise's great reclamation projects.

Originally signed by the New York Yankees in 1956, Johnson became an All-Star third baseman for the Cincinnati Reds. In 1965 he led the National League in RBIs with 130.

But his numbers steadily declined after that season. He moved on to Atlanta, where he batted just .208 in 1968 and was sold to the Phillies after the season ended. This time, the change of scenery did wonders for Johnson, who hit 17 homers in 1969 and 27 in 1970.

He was enjoying his finest all-around season in '71 when the Montreal Expos came to town. On July 10th, Johnson cracked his 18th homer, an eighth-inning game winner in the second game of a doubleheader. Turns out he was just getting started.

In the Sunday getaway game, Johnson hit a two-run first-inning blast off Expos starter Carl Morton that ricocheted off the scoreboard in left field.

He victimized Morton again in the third, lofting a 3–2 fastball over the right-field wall. The Phillies were losing 5–4 when the 11-year veteran led off the sixth inning with his third home run of the game and fourth in a row, a bomb that disappeared over the 408 sign in center field.

At a Glance

WP: Champion (1–1)

HR: Johnson 3 (19, 20, 21)

Key stat: Johnson 3-for-5, 5 RBIs, 3 runs; Doyle 2-for-5, RBI

Johnson's record-tying homer put a surge into the entire offense as the Phils posted a season-high seven runs on five hits in the inning. Johnson became just the 11th major leaguer to hit home runs in four consecutive at-bats. He also capped an incredible series against the Expos in which he hit six home runs in five games. He attributed his rampage to extra batting practice and staying disciplined at the plate.

"Ever since I broke in with the Yankees, they've been telling me to go with the pitch," Johnson said. "When I do, I know I'm swinging okay."

Everything Goes Right for Jackson, Phillies

Grant Jackson's only win of the '68 season turned out to be one of the greatest games of his lengthy career, and it came in front of the largest crowd of the major league season to date as 57,011 fans jammed into Shea Stadium for a Bat Day doubleheader.

The 25-year-old southpaw threw a complete game while striking out a career-high 13 batters in a victory that extended the Phillies' winning streak to a season-high six games.

Jackson was helped by a potent offense that banged out 13 hits off three Mets pitchers.

Dick Allen got the Phils on the board in the first with a typically long two-run homer over the right-field wall.

New York cut the lead in half in the bottom of the inning on a double by Phil Linz and a single by Jerry Grote.

John Briggs made it a 3–1 game in the top of the second when he slammed a ball into the bullpen beyond the right-field fence.

At a Glance

WP: Jackson (1–2)

HR: Allen (18), Briggs (3,4)

Key stat: Jackson 13 Ks; Pena 3-for-5, 2 runs; Briggs 2-for-3, 3 RBIs

After the Mets scored their second run in the bottom of the third, Jackson settled into a groove and retired nine batters in a row, five on strikeouts.

The Phillies turned the game into a rout in the seventh inning by scoring four times on five hits, including a double to center by Tony Taylor.

Jackson, making only his second start of the season, looked like he might be fading when Greg Goossen belted a double to lead off the ninth inning.

But he reached back and finished with a flourish. Jackson whiffed whiffing pinch-hitter Bud Harrelson on a called third strike and struck out Tommie Agee swinging. Al Weis then hit a fly-out to left to end the game.

Jackson's gem followed a fine pitching performance in the first game from Rick Wise, who also went the distance in a 5–3 win.

Allen again led the offensive attack, going 2-for-4 with a home run, double and theee RBIs. For the day, he was 3-for-7 with two homers and six RBIs.

With their doubleheader sweep, the Phils moved into third place in the National League with a record of 44–40.

July 15, 1911
Phillies 2, Pirates 1

Dead Balls Weren't So Dead for Ludey

In an era when hitting one home run in a game didn't come often, Fred Luderus did the unthinkable and stroked two in this game against the Pirates. Even more mind boggling is that this was the third time in as many weeks that he hit two homers in one game.

Obtained in a trade with the Cubs late in the 1910 season, the left-handed swinging Luderus got off to a slow start in '11. He didn't hit his first home run until the second week of May. But as he became more accustomed to Baker Bowl's inviting right-field fence less than 300 feet from home plate, Luderus' slugging prowess began to kick in.

On July 4, he became the first Phillie to hit two home runs over the fence in an 11–7 win over the New York Giants. Two days later Luderus popped another pair of homers in a 13–9 loss to the Cardinals.

When the Pirates arrived in Philadelphia for a four-game series, they were well aware of their dangerous opponent.

Bobby Byrne gave the Bucs a first-inning lead after reaching first base when shortstop Mickey Doolan bobbled his routine ground ball. Doolan eventually crossed the plate on a wild pitch from Phillies starter George Chalmers.

Facing Pirates starter Babe Adams in the bottom of the second, Luderus slammed a fastball high over the wall in right to tie the score.

At a Glance

WP: Chalmers (6–2)

HR: Luderus (13, 14)

Key stat: Luderus 2-for-4, 2 RBIs; Chalmers 0 ER in 9 IP

The game was still tied in the bottom of the ninth when Luderus stepped up with two outs and hit a tremendous drive off Adams that cleared the wall and sailed all the way across Broad Street. Eyewitness accounts indicated the ball landed on the roof of North Philadelphia train station.

Luderus was mobbed by teammates and fans who had stormed the field. As he tried to break away and sprint to the Phillies' clubhouse beyond center field, the adoring throng tore the shirt off his back. Luderus grinned as he dodged and weaved, but it was no use. Realizing he was surrounded, Luderus surrendered. His fans hoisted him onto their shoulders and carried him to the clubhouse door.

Their admiration had been building for weeks as "Ludey" went on a rampage. His batting average was up to .330, he was leading the league with 175 total bases, and his 14 homers were four more than the league leader had collected over the entire 1910 season.

Luderus was unable to sustain his torrid home-run pace. He hit only two more the rest of the season. But his total of 16 was still more than enough to lead the team and finish second in the league behind Chicago's Wildfire Schulte, who set a major league record with 21 homers.

Did You Know?

As Charlie Manuel's squad began its rise to the top of the baseball world, the Phillies were reaching a dubious landmark.

On July 15, 2007, they became the first pro sports franchise in North America to lose 10,000 games when they dropped a 10–2 decision to the St. Louis Cardinals.

The Phillies racked up large percentage of those losses during the first half of the 20th century. They had losing records from 1918–31, finished above .500 in '32, then began another losing stretch that ran from 1933–48. In many of those seasons the Phillies lost 100 games or more.

Jordan's Debut One of the Few Bright Spots in Miserable 1988 Season

In the midst of a miserable season, the last-place Phillies got a big boost from rookie Ricky Jordan, who had a big-league debut that was right out of Hollywood.

All the 23-year-old first baseman did was hit a three-run homer in his first official at-bat, reach base three times and score the winning run in a 10–4 rout of Houston.

Jordan was an emergency call-up from the minors to replace the injured Von Hayes.

"I was very nervous before the game because getting to the majors is a dream come true for me, and I couldn't believe it when I was told," said Jordan, who was the Phillies' first-round draft pick in 1983.

After walking his first time up in the second inning, he came around again in the fourth with the Phillies losing 2–0.

Mike Schmidt led off the inning with his eighth home run of the year. Chris James followed with a walk and moved to third on a single by Mike Young.

Jordan stepped to the plate with one out to face Astros lefty Bob Knepper. And he arrived armed with some important information.

At a Glance

WP: Tekulve (3–6)

HR: Schmidt (8), Jordan (1)

Key stat: Jordan 1-for-2, HR in first MLB at-bat, 3 RBIs; Schmidt 3-for-5, 4 RBIs; Bradley 2-for-5, RBI; Samuel 2-for-5, RBI

"Schmitty had told me before the game that Knepper throws a lot of curves and changes, and I went up there thinking 'curve' and that's what I got," said Jordan, who knew the ball was gone the instant he hit it. "But there was no way I was going to watch it. I didn't want to hot dog it."

Jordan became the 31st player in National League history to touch 'em all in his first official big-league at-bat, a feat that made his manager, Lee Elia, very proud.

"He was able to respond with all the anxiety that comes with being in your first major league game, and he gave the whole club a big lift when he hit that ball out of here."

The Astros bounced back against Mike Maddux to tie the game in the fifth on doubles by Craig Biggio, Gerald Young, and Bill Doran.

But the Phillies busted out for five more in the bottom of the sixth, and Jordan again was right back in the thick of things.

Showing exceptional poise and patience for a rookie, he led off by drawing his second walk of the game. Jackie Guttierez bunted him over to second, pinch-hitter Keith Miller singled him to third and Juan Samuel brought Jordan home with a base hit.

After Phil Bradley beat out a grounder for an infield single, Schmidt smacked a line drive to center that Young misplayed into a bases-clearing triple. James capped off the big inning with an RBI single.

Jordan used his astonishing debut as a launching point to a terrific rookie season in which he batted .308 with 11 home runs and 43 RBIs in 273 at-bats.

1964 All-Star Game

This was Johnny Callison's big moment in the national spotlight.

Callison's dramatic three-run walk-off homer against Boston's Dick Radatz in the bottom of the ninth at Shea Stadium gave the National League a 7–4 win, making this All-Star Game one of the most memorable in baseball history.

The NL was trailing 4–3 when Willie Mays led off the ninth with a walk and stole second. Mays scored the tying run on Orlando Cepeda's bloop single to right.

Radatz got Ken Boyer to pop out, intentionally walked Johnny Edwards, then fanned Hank Aaron for the second out.

Callison was next and hammered the first pitch over the right-field wall.

He got a hero's welcome at home plate, and a few minutes later, the MVP trophy.

Half-Dollar Coin Does the Trick for Abbott

It looked like it might never end, but Kyle Abbott finally broke a season-long losing streak with a solid outing backed by a torrent of runs from his offense.

Abbott carried an 0–11 record into this game. One more loss would put him in the team record book alongside three other pitchers who lost 12 in a row; Ken Reynolds in 1972, Hugh Mulcahy in 1940 and Russ Miller, who set the standard in 1928.

At times, Abbott pitched well. In seven of his previous 13 starts he gave up three runs or fewer, and in his outing on July 11, he gave up just two runs in seven innings in a 3–2 loss to the Padres.

Abbott tried a number of gimmicks to change his luck, including growing a beard and, just before this game, sticking a half-dollar coin he received from a fan in his back pocket.

Maybe it worked because the Phils gave their starter an early lead, scoring three runs in the second inning.

Back-to-back walks to John Kruk and Darren Daulton and a single by Wes Chamberlain loaded the bases. Mickey Morandini then drove in two runs with a base hit and Len Dykstra knocked in Chamberlain with a two-out single.

The Phillies piled on four more runs in the third, due in large part to the wildness of Dodgers starter Ramon Martinez, who again walked the first two batters before throwing a wild pitch. Chamberlain contributed a run-scoring double and Morandini tripled to knock in his third run of the game.

Abbott, meanwhile, coasted through his first four innings, giving up no runs and three hits.

In the fifth, he got out of a bases-loaded jam. But in the sixth, Abbott started to sag as he gave up a two-run homer to Eric Karros and a solo shot to Carlos Hernandez.

At a Glance

WP: Abbott (1–11)

HR: Hollins (13)

Key stat: Hollins 3-for-4, 2 RBIs, 3 runs; Morandini 3-for-5, 3 RBIs; Millette 3-for-5, 2 RBIs

With the score now 8–3, manager Jim Fregosi decided to replace his starter with Barry Jones.

The Phils scored twice in the bottom of the sixth and four more times in the seventh to salt the game away for Abbott.

"I feel 20 pounds lighter, like a monkey's off my back," he said.

Fregosi was thrilled to see his pitcher get his first win.

"It's not very often that a guy is going for a record and you're glad to see him not get it. . . . Under the circumstances, I give him a lot of credit for the way he's hung in there."

Abbott's first win was his only win of the '92 season. Eventually, he was banished to the bullpen and finished with a 1–14 record and a 5.13 ERA.

Darren Daulton

One of the toughest players and greatest leaders to ever grace a Phillies clubhouse, Darren Daulton presided over "Macho Row" during that brief period when a gritty bunch of throwbacks made a run to the World Series.

Daulton battled knee injuries for most of the 14 seasons he spent in Philhadelphia, but when he was healthy he was one of the best in the business.

A fine catcher and solid hitter with exceptional power, "Dutch" blossomed into an All-Star in 1992, when he hit 27 home runs and became only the fourth catcher in National League history to lead the league in RBIs, when he knocked in 109.

In 1993, he hit 24 homers with 105 RBIs in leading the Phils to the National League pennant.

There's no telling what kind of numbers Daulton would have posted had he been healthy. He finished his Phillies career with 134 home runs, 567 RBIs and a .245 batting average.

Rolen Keeps on Rollin' in 22-Hit Barrage

Scott Rolen was on a roll. The 24-year-old third baseman hit two home runs for the second game in a row to help the Phillies smack Tampa Bay in one of their most one-sided victories of the '99 season.

In addition to his home runs, Rolen cracked a run-scoring double to lead a 22-hit attack that wore out the Rays' pitching staff.

Designated hitter Bobby Abreu, hitting in front of Rolen, had four hits in six trips to the plate. And Rico Brogna, the No. 5 hitter, was 3-for-4. That's a combined 10-for-15, eight runs, and eight RBIs. The middle of a lineup doesn't get more potent than that, which is why the Phils' cleanup hitter waved off suggestions that he was carrying the team.

"We have too many good players to even consider carrying this team," said Rolen, who got the Phillies started with a two-run blast in the first inning and a 429-foot solo shot to lead off the third. Three more hits after Rolen's homer produced two more runs and chased Rays starter Brian Rekar.

In the top of the fourth, the Phils battered reliever Dave Eiland for five runs on five hits, including Rolen's run-scoring double and Brogna's two-run single. It was more than enough help for Chad Ogea, who held the Rays to two runs over seven innings of work.

Rolen came within a few feet of hitting his third home run of the night in the fifth when he belted a ball to deep right-center field. But Bubba Trammell went to the wall and hauled it in.

"I don't mind playing here at all," he said. "I'm seeing the ball better and my swing is shorter."

At a Glance

WP: Ogea (5–9)

HR: Rolen 2 (23, 24)

Key stat: Phillies 22 hits; Rolen 3-for-5, 4 RBIs, 3 runs; Abreu 4-for-6, 2 RBI, 2 runs; Brogna 3-for-4, 2 RBIs, 3 runs; Arias 3-for-4, 3 RBIs

Indeed, Rolen, in two games at Tropicana Field, was 5-for-9 with four homers and six RBIs. His second home run in the eighth inning the night before proved to be a game-winner.

Broken-Bat Single Puts an End to Hudson's No-No Thoughts

Charlie Hudson went out to the mound in the ninth inning needing just three more outs to write his name in the record book. The 24-year-old rookie from Ennis, Texas, had held the Houston Astros hitless for eight innings and was looking to complete the mission.

"No one mentioned it on the bench because that's bad luck," said Hudson. "But I started thinking about it in the fourth, and by the sixth I was just trying to block it out of my mind and just take every batter one at a time."

But some of Hudson's teammates defied the time-honored tradition of avoiding the pitcher.

"Garry Maddox was talking to me on the bench, trying to keep me relaxed," Hudson said. "Mike Schmidt came up to me in the ninth and said 'Relax and good luck.' And Pete (Rose) kept me pumped up all the time."

The night began with a focus on offense. Outfielder Joe Lefebvre, picked up in a trade from San Diego in May, smacked his first career grand slam in the first inning to give the Phils an early lead.

The Phils made it 5–0 in the second when Hudson scored on a wild pitch by Astros starter Mike Scott.

They added a run in the sixth, then tacked on three more in the seventh to put the game out of reach.

After Lefebvre's fifth RBI knocked in the Phils' final run in the eighth, the focus shifted to Hudson.

With 21,052 fans at Veterans Stadium holding their breath, Hudson struck out Harry Spilman leading off the ninth inning.

Astros	AB	R	H	RBI
Moreno cf	4	0	0	0
Walling rf	4	1	1	2
Thon ss	3	1	1	1
Garner 3b	2	0	0	0
Ruhle p	0	0	0	0
Bass ph	1	0	0	0
Cruz lf	3	0	0	0
Knight 1b	3	0	0	0
Pujols c	0	0	0	0
Doran 2b	3	0	0	0
Bjorkman c	2	0	0	0
Spilman 1b	1	0	0	0
Scott p	1	0	0	0
Puhl ph	1	0	0	0
LaCorte p	0	0	0	0
Reynolds 3b	1	1	1	0
Totals	**29**	**3**	**3**	**3**

Phillies	AB	R	H	RBI
Dernier cf	3	0	0	1
Rose 1b	5	2	4	0
Hayes rf	5	0	0	0
Schmidt 3b	5	2	3	0
Morgan 2b	2	1	0	0
Garcia pr-2b	1	1	0	0
Lefebvre lf	3	2	2	5
Diaz c	5	0	1	2
DeJesus ss	4	1	1	0
Hudson p	2	1	1	1
Totals	**35**	**10**	**12**	**9**

	1	2	3	4	5	6	7	8	9		R	H	E
HOU	0	0	0	0	0	0	0	0	3	-	3	3	1
PHI	4	1	0	0	0	1	3	1	X	-	10	12	0

Astros	IP	H	R	ER	BB	SO
Scott L (5-4)	5	5	5	5	3	2
LaCorte	1.2	4	4	2	1	1
Ruhle	1.1	3	1	1	0	0
Totals	**8**	**12**	**10**	**8**	**4**	**3**

Phillies	IP	H	R	ER	BB	SO
Hudson W (3-3)	9	3	3	3	2	9
Totals	**9**	**3**	**3**	**3**	**2**	**9**

E—Houston Walling. DP—Philadelphia. HR—Houston Walling (1), Thon (13); Philadelphia Lefebvre (5). SH—Philadelphia Hudson. SF—Philadelphia Dernier. HBP—Philadelphia Lefebvre, Hudson. LOB—Houston 1; Philadelphia 9. SB—Houston Thon; Philadelphia DeJesus. Attendance: 21,052.

Garry Maddox

The premier center fielder of his day, "The Secretary of Defense" won eight consecutive Gold Gloves while anchoring an outfield that consistently ranked among the finest in baseball.

Maddox came over to the Phillies from the San Francisco Giants in a 1975 trade for Willie Montanez and quickly became an electrifying presence at Veterans Stadium with his glove and his bat.

His best year was 1976, when he batted .330. But Maddox's biggest career hit was his double that knocked in the winning run in the final game of the 1980 National League Championship Series.

In 12 years with the Phillies, Maddox hit .284 with 85 home runs, 566 RBIs and 189 stolen bases.

The young right-hander quickly got ahead in the count, 1–2 to pinch-hitter Craig Reynolds. The next pitch he threw bore in so hard on Reynolds' hands that it shattered his bat. But Reynolds still managed to flare the ball into shallow center field to break up Hudson's masterpiece.

"He hit it off the weakest part of the bat, and it just fell," Hudson said.

Reynolds knew he hit a great pitch.

"If he makes that pitch 10 more times, I'd probably make 10 outs."

After retiring Omar Moreno on an infield pop-up, Hudson surrendered back-to-back home runs to Denny Walling and Dickie Thon. He later admitted that he lost his cool after Reynolds' broke up the no-no.

"When Reynolds' hit fell in, I said to myself, 'There goes the no-hitter,' and then I just wanted to keep the shutout," said Hudson.

After the first home run Hudson said, "All I wanted was to get it over with and get us a win. It is still my biggest thrill in baseball."

The victory was Hudson's third of the season and the first for manager Paul Owens, who came down from the front office to manage the team after firing Pat Corrales.

Werth Shows His Worth in Extending Phils' Streak to 10 Games

Strong pitching, great defense and some extra-inning dynamite from the bat of Jayson Werth propelled the Phillies to their 10th straight win, their longest streak in nearly two decades.

Werth set off a wild celebration at home plate after thumping a three-run, walk-off home run with two outs in the bottom of the 13th. In the locker room after the game, the right fielder had thoughts of the postseason on his mind.

"We have a good thing going right now," Werth said after hitting his 21st homer. "We've just got to keep it going. Everyone in here knows when we are at our best we're tough to beat . . . but we're still not clicking on all cylinders. We're a second half club and I think you'll see our best baseball in September and October."

The Phillies grabbed a 1–0 lead in the third on Jimmy Rollins' eighth home run.

The lead held up until the fourth, when the Cubs tied it after Ryan Theriot singled and scored on a double to left by Kosuke Fukodome.

Manager Charlie Manuel got a strong outing from Joe Blanton, who gave up one run over seven innings, and a stellar contribution from his bullpen as four relievers teamed up to no-hit Chicago over the next six innings.

But the 'pen needed a big wet kiss from lady luck in the ninth to keep that hitless streak going.

With one out, Brad Lidge hit Aramis Ramirez with a pitch. Fukodome then worked the count to 3–2 before hitting a rocket up the middle. Lidge stuck out his right foot, like a goaltender making a kick save, and deflected the ball to shortstop Jimmy Rollins, who was standing right by the second-base bag.

J-Roll grabbed it, stepped on second and relayed to first for the inning-ending double play.

Lidge gave way to Chan Ho Park, who held down the fort by striking out five Cubs in three dominating innings.

At a Glance

WP: Condrey (6–2)

HR: Werth (21), Rollins (8)

Key stat: Werth game-winning HR in 13th

July 21, 2009
Phillies 4, Cubs 1 (13 innings)

Ryan Howard

The most feared slugger in baseball was a late arrival to the major leagues.

Held back in the minors due to the presence of Jim Thome in Philadelphia, Howard had to wait until the age of 25 before he was called up for good. When he got his chance, Thome became expendable in a hurry.

Howard played half a season in 2005, yet still hit 22 homers and drove in 63 runs, good enough to win the National League Rookie of the Year award.

In 2006, he became the first NL player to win Rookie of the Year and MVP honors in consecutive seasons after hitting .313 with a club-record 58 home runs and 149 RBIs.

Howard followed that up with three more seasons of 40-plus home runs while helping the Phillies become World Champions and usher in a second Golden Age of baseball in Philadelphia.

In the bottom of the 13th, Chicago reliever Jeff Samardzija easily retired the first two Phillies batters—Shane Victorino on a fly ball to left and Chase Utley on a flyout to center.

But Samardzija Ryan Howard and Raul Ibanez to give Werth a chance to hit. And Werth took advantage of the opportunity by smoking a 1–1 pitch into the left-field stands.

"It was just a hanger and I was able to stay through it," said Werth. "That's the good thing about CBP. If you get one up in the air there's a good chance it can go."

It was the defending World Champions' 14th win in their last 15 games and extended their lead over the second-place Atlanta Braves to 6.5 games.

Schmidt's Second Chance Does in Astros

The Houston Astros learned the hard way that you should never give Mike Schmidt a second chance.

With two outs and the Phillies and Astros tied in the ninth inning of a tense, back-and-forth game at the Vet, Schmidt hit a routine pop-up in foul territory. Pitcher Jeff Heathcock, catcher Alan Ashby and third baseman Phil Garner converged on the ball. Garner called his teammates off at the last second, but Heathcock bumped into Garner's arm as he tried to get out of the way and the third baseman dropped the ball.

Schmidt drove Heathcock's next pitch off the façade of the upper deck in left field for a walk-off home run.

"It's a funny game," said Schmidt. "Obviously, I deserved to be out."

At a Glance

WP: Carman (3–3)

HR: Russell (3), Schmidt (13)

Key stat: Russell 2-for-4, 4 RBIs, grand slam; Schmidt 2-for-4, 2 runs, RBI

Schmidt may have been the hero, but second-year man John Russell was an important table-setter. The 24-year-old outfielder was hitting just .205 when he faced veteran knuckleballer Joe Niekro with the bases loaded and two outs in the first inning.

Russell watched a few knuckleballs flutter by then whacked one over the left-field wall for his first career grand slam. Russell said he had been pressing too hard for too long.

"I was going beyond what John Russell could do. I was swinging too hard. I was making every play too tough. So I just finally decided to start relaxing and having fun," said Russell, whose slam allowed starter Charlie Hudson to relax.

After pitching a scoreless first, the right-hander gave up a pair of runs in the second, then found his rhythm and shut down the Astros for the next four innings. Hudson was cruising through the seventh when he suddenly ran into trouble. After getting the first two batters out, he gave up back-to-back doubles to Bill Doran and Craig Reynolds, then walked Kevin Bass.

Manager John Felske yanked Hudson for southpaw reliever Dave Rucker, who promptly gave up a three-run homer to the left-handed hitting Jose Cruz. Now leading 6–5, the Astros seemed to be in control. But Russell sparked a seventh-inning, game-tying rally with a leadoff single. He and Derrel Thomas came around to score on a pair of two-out RBI singles from Juan Samuel and Von Hayes.

Ennis Smacks Three Homers in Career Day at the Plate

Del Ennis had some great days at the plate but this one topped them all. The power-hitting outfielder accounted for all seven runs against the Cardinals by cracking three homers in a Saturday afternoon game at Connie Mack Stadium.

His RBI total was one short of the franchise record but it was tops in the National League for 1955.

The 30-year-old outfielder got rolling with a two-run homer in the first inning after Richie Ashburn led off with a single to center.

At a Glance

WP: Roberts (16–7)

HR: Ennis 3 (17,18,19)

Key Stat: Ennis 3-for-4, 7 RBIs

Del Ennis hit three home runs and accounted for all seven of the Phillies' runs in a 7-2 win over the Cardinals on July 23, 1955.

Those were the only runs scored in the game until the top of the sixth, when the Cardinals got on the board after Bill Virdon's double knocked in Stan Musial, who had singled off Robin Roberts.

Ennis made it a 4–1 game in the bottom of the inning when he deposited another missile into the bleachers, this time with Glen Gorbous on first.

He saved his biggest moment of the day for his last appearance at the plate, as if to put an exclamation point on his performance.

With Ashburn on second and Bobby Morgan on first, Ennis hit a vicious drive off Brooks Lawrence that soared over the left-field roof, expanding the lead to 7–1.

Roberts gave up a meaningless home run in the top of the ninth as he wrapped up a ridiculously easy win.

Of the 108 pitches he threw, 82 were strikes. Roberts scattered nine hits in winning his 16th game.

Del Ennis

A homegrown favorite, Del Ennis was signed by the Phillies out of Olney High School in 1943 and patrolling the outfield at Shibe Park just three years later.

The 21-year-old justified his rapid rise to the big leagues by being named the 1946 Rookie of the Year by The Sporting News after hitting .313 with 17 homers and 73 RBIs.

He settled in to the cleanup spot and became one of the top sluggers and run producers in team history.

Ennis' best season was in 1950, when he hit .311 with 31 homers and a league-leading 126 RBIs to help the Whiz Kids win the National League pennant.

He hit 20 or more home runs nine times in his career and drove in more than 100 runs seven times.

Ennis ranks second on the Phillies' all-time home run list with 259 and third in RBIs with 1,124.

Abreu Shows His Power with 1 Hit, 5 RBIs

The Phils turned a 3–1 deficit into a rout, thanks to a nine-run sixth inning and a record-tying performance from Bobby Abreu.

Kerry Wood dominated the first five innings as the Cubs built their lead. Wood gave up just two hits and struck out nine. The only run he gave up was a homer by Todd Pratt.

But in the top of the sixth the Phillies, and Abreu, exploded.

Marlon Byrd led off the inning with a bunt single and moved to third on a base hit by Placido Polanco, who went 4-for-5 with four RBIs. Wood then walked Jim Thome to load the bases.

Abreu was next and sent a high fly ball to right that carried just far enough to clear the wall at Wrigley Field. It was his third career grand slam.

"I was just trying to put the ball in the air," said Abreu. "Not hit a homer, to

Bobby Abreu used a grand slam and a sacrifice fly to drive in five runs on one hit on July 24, 2003. He nearly hit two grand slams in the game, but settled for one.

drive in a run to keep the rally going. I didn't want to hit a ground ball and hit into a double play. It's good when you start rallying against a pitcher like Kerry Wood because you're not going to see that very often. You do that and you want to keep going . . . put the game away."

At a Glance

WP: Padilla (9–8)

HR: Abreu (16), Pratt (2)

Key stat: Abreu 1-for-3, 5 RBIs, grand slam; Polanco 4-for-5, 4 RBIs, 2 runs

The Phils now held a 5–3 lead but they weren't done. After scoring four more times, they loaded the bases with one out. That brought up Abreu again, this time with a chance to hit a second grand slam.

He hit it hard, but not long enough. As center fielder Kenny Lofton settled under the ball, Marlon Byrd crossed home plate with Abreu's fifth RBI of the inning, tying the franchise record set by Von Hayes on June 11, 1985. Hayes collected all his RBIs in the first inning against the Mets.

"The run faucet was on for them and we couldn't turn it off," said Cubs manager Dusty Baker.

The Cubs tried to mount a comeback, scoring three runs in the seventh to cut the lead to 10–6, but the Phillies added two more in the eighth and another pair in the ninth. They scored 14 runs on 14 hits.

Abreu was incredibly efficient, collecting five RBI on one hit.

July 26, 1987
Phillies 7, Braves 3

Back-to-Back-to-Back Plenty against Braves

Milt Thompson, Von Hayes and Mike Schmidt made this an unforgettable game by hitting back-to-back-to-back home runs.

The trio lit up a Veterans Stadium crowd that had to endure a lengthy rain delay and an implosion by starting pitcher Kevin Gross.

The Phils scored a run in the first inning when Thompson singled, stole second and came home on Schmidt's single to center.

Two more runs crossed the plate in the third on a single and stolen base by Juan Samuel, Thompson's double, and Hayes' single.

Gross had a two-hitter going after five when he self-destructed.

An error by Hayes at first made Dion James a leadoff base runner. Gerald Perry hit a grounder to second that appeared to be an easy double play ball—until it took a weird hop and bounced away from Samuel.

With runners on first and third, Gross faked a pickoff throw to third, then turned and caught Perry off the bag. Perry raced to second and Gross threw wild and high, allowing James to score and Perry to move to third.

The right-hander then walked Ken Griffey and gave up a run-scoring double to Gary Roenicke.

After walking Bruce Benedict, Gross committed a balk, bringing Griffey home with the tying run. In the eighth inning the Phillies pulled away as they filled the air with long fly balls.

At a Glance

WP: Tekulve (4–3)

HR: Thomspon (4), Hayes(14), Schmidt (22)

Key stat: Phils hit 3 consecutive home runs

Thompson's leadoff homer gave them the lead again. Hayes followed with his 14th homer, and a very relaxed Schmidt smoked his 22nd home run to left. The shell-shocked victim of all that abuse was Braves starter Doyle Alexander.

"Milt's homer was the tough one," said Schmidt. "After that we were just kind of swinging free and easy, just trying to make contact. That was the important one. The other ones were for the fans."

The Phils almost became the fourth team in big-league history to hit four home runs in a row when the next batter, Chris James, hit a sizzling liner to left off reliever Joe Boever that sent Griffey to the wall.

"I thought it had a chance," said Elia, but Griffey had room to make a leaping catch on the warning track.

Ennis Chalks Up 7 RBIs for Whiz Kids

Del Ennis unleashed some late-inning thunder to turn a tight game into an easy win for the first-place Whiz Kids.

The slugging outfielder knocked in seven runs with a bases-loaded double in the seventh and a grand slam in the eighth.

Before Ennis' outburst, the crowd at Shibe Park was enjoying a duel between pitchers Curt Simmons and Doyle Lade.

Chicago got the early upper hand by scoring an unearned run in the first inning. But the lead didn't hold up for long.

In the bottom of the second, Willie Jones led off with a single. Granny Hamner squared around to bunt, but pulled back at the last instant and swung away. His looping fly ball was just out of the reach of third baseman Bill Serena, who had charged in on the fake and couldn't get back in time to make the catch.

At a Glance

WP: Simmons (14–5)

HR: Ennis (19)

Key stats: Ennis 2-for-5, grand slam, 7 RBIs; Jones 2-for-4; Ashburn 2-for-3

Both runners advanced on a passed ball, then scored on Stan Lopata's ground ball to first and Mike Goliat's sacrifice fly to center.

The Phils added two more runs in the fourth to make it 4–1, but the Cubs cut the lead to two when Andy Pafko led off the sixth with a home run.

The Phillies began to pull away in the seventh.

With Simmons on first and one out, Eddie Waitkus singled and Richie Ashburn followed with a run-scoring double to right.

Cubs manager Frankie Frisch had Dick Sisler intentionally walked to load the bases and set up a force.

Unfortunately for Frisch, the next batter was the National League's top run producer. Ennis cleared the bases with a double to the gap.

The eighth inning turned into a nightmare for the Cubs and reliever Johnny Vander Meer. The aging lefty, who once threw back-to-back no-hitters, let in one run after walking three batters and committing a throwing error.

With two outs and the bases loaded, Vander Meer had to face Ennis. He grooved a first-pitch fastball that Del sent high and deep, into the upper deck in left-center.

July 28, 1951
Phillies 1, Cubs 0

Meyer Extends Starters' Shutout Streak to 4

It was a tough act to follow, but Russ Meyer came through with a brilliant performance that helped the Phillies' starting rotation establish a team record with its fourth consecutive shutout.

Robin Roberts kicked off the streak on July 25 at Sportsman's Park in St. Louis, blanking the Cardinals on four hits.

The next day, lefty Ken Johnson held the Cards to seven hits in a 7–0 whitewash.

Phillies	AB	R	H	RBI
Waitkus 1b	5	0	0	0
Ashburn cf	3	0	2	1
Jones 3b	3	0	0	0
Nicholson rf	3	0	0	0
Sisler lf	3	0	2	0
Brown pr-lf	0	0	0	0
Hamner ss	4	0	2	0
Pellagrini 2b	4	0	2	0
Seminick c	3	1	2	0
Meyer p	3	0	0	0
Totals	31	1	10	1

Cubs	AB	R	H	RBI
Miksis 2b	4	0	2	0
Jeffcoat pr	0	0	0	0
Ramazzotti 2b	0	0	0	0
Cavarretta 1b	4	0	1	0
Baumholtz cf	4	0	1	0
Sauer lf	4	0	0	0
Burgess c	4	0	1	0
Jackson 3b	4	0	0	0
Hermanski rf	3	0	0	0
Smalley ss	3	0	0	0
McLish p	2	0	1	0
Leonard p	0	0	0	0
Connors ph	1	0	1	0
Kelly p	0	0	0	0
Totals	33	0	7	0

PHI	0	0	0	0	1	0	0	0	0	-	1	10	0
CHI	0	0	0	0	0	0	0	0	0	-	0	7	0

Phillies	IP	H	R	ER	BB	SO
Meyer W (8-8)	9	7	0	0	0	3
Totals	9	7	0	0	0	3

Cubs	IP	H	R	ER	BB	SO
McLish L (2-4)	7.1	9	1	1	4	3
Leonard	0.2	0	0	0	0	0
Kelly	1	1	0	0	0	0
Totals	9	10	1	1	4	3

DP—Philadelphia; Chicago 3. 2B—Philadelphia Seminick. SH—Philadelphia Seminick, Meyer. LOB—Philadelphia 9; Chicago 6. SB—Philadelphia Ashburn 3. Attendance: 10,806.

Bubba Church took the mound on the 27th at Wrigley Field in Chicago and threw a five-hitter as the Phils beat the Cubs 2–0.

Now it was Meyer's turn and the right-hander came up big as he scattered seven hits without ever getting into serious trouble.

The Phils scored their lone run in the fifth inning. Andy Seminick led off with a double off the wall in left field and moved to third on a sacrifice bunt by Meyer.

Richie Ashburn's single through the left side of the infield brought Seminick home. Whitey had a big day at the plate with two singles and a walk, three stolen bases and an RBI.

The Phils had several other chances to pad their lead, but untimely double plays killed those opportunities.

None of that mattered, though, as Meyer mesmerized the Cubs' lineup.

Before the game, the starters worked out an agreement that whoever allowed the streak to be broken would have to buy dinner for everyone.

That turned out to be Roberts, but only after he stubbornly held the Cubs scoreless for five innings the next day. Chicago erupted for three runs against the Phillies' ace in the sixth and went on to win 5–4.

You Want Strikeouts? How 'Bout 26 of 'Em

The Phils and Pirates established a new major league mark for futility in a nine-inning game by striking out a combined 26 times in this game at Forbes Field. But give the pitchers some credit because they were very good.

Right-hander Ray Culp delivered his finest outing of the season, a two-hit shutout with 10 strikeouts and no walks. Pirates lefty Bob Veale blew away 14 Phillies batters in seven innings while relievers Al McBean and Frank Carpin each struck out one.

Culp, who threw a one-hitter against the Cubs in '64, got off to a wobbly start. After leadoff hitter Bob Bailey flied out, Bill Virdon ripped a line drive that one-hopped off the wall in right, but a hustling Johnny Callison quickly picked up the ball and relayed it back to the infield, holding Virdon to a single. Culp beaned the next batter, Roberto Clemente, then struck out Willie Stargell and got Donn Clendenon to ground into a force play to end the inning.

Veale was downright overpowering through the first four, holding the Phillies in check with his flaming fastball. He struck out seven, including three in a row in the third inning.

> **At a Glance**
>
> **WP:** Culp (7–6)
>
> **Key stat:** Culp 9 IP, 2 hits, 10 Ks; Corrales 3-for-4, RBI; Rojas 2-for-4, RBI

However, the Phils found some answers to Veale's heat in the top of the fifth, and the bottom of the lineup instigated the rally.

No. 7 hitter Pat Corrales hit a one-out single and went to third on a base hit by shortstop Bobby Wine. Culp struck out. But Cookie Rojas hit a high chopper through the middle to score Corrales. Wine moved to third then dashed home after Veale threw a wild pitch.

"That's what made us a good team last season," said manager Gene Mauch. "When somebody wasn't doing it, somebody else was."

Culp continued to mow down the Bucs, at one point retiring 15 batters in a row. Bailey picked up the Pirates' second hit on a swinging bunt toward third with one out in the bottom of the sixth, but was left stranded at first when Virdon and Clemente both flied out.

The Phils put the game out of reach by scoring three runs in the top of the eighth. The big blow was a two-run double off the left-field scoreboard by Wes Covington. After Bailey's single back in the sixth, Culp retired the last 11 batters in a row.

Phils Begin Unlikely 13-Game Winning Streak

The Phillies ended a lengthy losing streak and launched a historic winning streak with this victory over the Padres at Veterans Stadium.

Few people would have predicted that this team was capable of such a dramatic turnaround. At the time, the Phils were in last place, 21.5 games out of first with a record of 40–58. They had lost seven in a row, having scored a total of 11 runs in those games.

So no one was surprised to look up at the scoreboard and see the Phillies trailing San Diego 1–0 through five.

Starting pitcher Jose DeJesus had gotten into several jams but managed to avoid disaster.

The Padres scored their lone run in the top of the third on a pair of doubles by Thomas Howard and Bip Roberts.

On the other side, San Diego lefty Dennis Rasmussen looked unbeatable as he surrendered just two hits.

Things seemed to get worse for the Phillies when Lenny Dykstra was thrown out of the game in the fifth for arguing a call on a 3–2 check swing.

Incensed, Dykstra charged umpire Mike Winters and had to be restrained by teammates and manager Jim Fregosi.

The Phillies finally broke through and tied the game with two outs in the sixth when Randy Ready singled and scored after Wes Chamberlain whacked a double to left-center.

At a Glance

WP: DeJesus (7–4)

Key stat: Chamberlain 2-for-4, RBI

In the seventh, they went ahead on John Kruk's RBI double. DeJesus gave way to Mitch Williams, who held off the Padres in the ninth to preserve the win and break the streak. The final out triggered nothing more than a mild celebration from a bunch of relieved ballplayers.

"It's something we needed," said infielder Dave Hollins, unaware winning was about to become the new normal for a couple of weeks.

After beating the Padres again the next night, 9–3, the Phillies went to Montreal and swept their four-game series with the Expos, came back home and took three straight from the Cubs, then won four more against Montreal at the Vet.

The Phillies didn't lose another game until August 13, when the Pirates beat them 4–3.

Lee All of That and More in Debut with Phillies

Cliff Lee was in vintage form as the 2008 Cy Young Award winner lived up to the hype in his Phillies debut.

Acquired with outfielder Ben Francisco in a trade with the Cleveland Indians two days earlier, Lee was superb as he held the Giants to four hits and one run while throwing a complete game.

He had a no-hitter going after five but Juan Uribe broke it up with a one-out double to the right-field corner in the sixth.

"I'm kind of glad I didn't throw a no-hitter," Lee said. "If I do that on the first try, I would have to be living up to some high expectations."

His performance was far more impressive than manager Charlie Manuel had expected.

"First time out, he goes out and gives nine innings," Manuel said. "He's going to fit in real good."

Lee also helped himself at the plate, going 2-for-4 with a single, double and run scored.

At a Glance

WP: Lee (1–0)

HR: Werth (22)

Key stat: Lee's first win as a Phillie; Werth 2-for-5, 3 RBIs

It was a close game through six innings as two Giants pitchers held the Phillies to a single run, which came in the second on Jayson Werth's 22nd homer. But the Phillies blew it open with a three-run seventh and increased their lead to 5–0 in the eighth when Lee doubled and scored on Francisco's sacrifice fly.

Lee gave up his only run in the eighth when Aaron Rowand hit a leadoff double, advanced to third on a bunt and scored on Uribe's sacrifice fly to right.

In the ninth, Lee surrendered a leadoff single to Eugenio Velez, but got Pablo Sandoval to pop out and Bengie Molina to ground into a game-ending double play.

Werth said he had a lot of fun playing defense behind the southpaw.

"He gets the ball and he knows what to do. He throws strikes. He attacks the hitters. He's good."

Lee said the transition from Cleveland to Philadelphia was easy.

"It's a loose clubhouse," he said. "I was more worried about getting to know the guys and getting comfortable with the situation than actually pitching."

Lee was just getting started. He would post a record of 7–4 and become a major factor in the Phillies' drive to their second consecutive National League pennant.

AUGUST

Ryan Howard, a key member of the 2008 World Series championship team, is the only Phillie to hit at least 40 homers for three consecutive seasons. He was named National League Most Valuable Player in 2006.

Phillies 6, Astros 5 (10 innings)

© Temple University Libraries, Urban Archives

Allen's Walk-Off Homer Memorable for Wrong Reasons

Johnny Callison hit two home runs but Dick Allen's walk-off inside-the-park homer is what everyone remembered, not only for its dramatic timing but the horrifying injury that came along with it.

Callison, sporting eyeglasses for the first time in his career, hit his first homer of the game in the fourth inning off Bob Bruce to give the Phils their first lead. He led off the sixth with his second home run to ignite a three-run inning.

The Phils led 5–2 after eight, only to see it disappear in the final frame.

Ray Culp had pitched brilliantly through eight innings. But after giving up singles to the first two batters in the ninth, manager Gene Mauch replaced him

Dick Allen had plenty of memorable moments with the Phillies, including his inside-the-park home run on Aug. 1, 1966. He was NL Rookie of the Year in 1964.

with Larry Jackson. The veteran right-hander promptly gave up a game-tying three-run homer to the first batter he faced, Bob Aspromonte.

The Astros nearly took the lead in the 10th. Jimmy Wynn, who hit a monstrous home run over the roof in left-center earlier in the game, led off with a double.

Sonny Jackson walked, and Chuck Harrison singled to load the bases.

With two outs, Wynn gambled and attempted to steal home but was called out by umpire Ed Vargo. Wynn jumped up and irately argued the call but to no avail.

Allen faced Astros reliever Jim Owens to open the bottom of the 10th and quickly fell behind in the count after taking two mighty swings. On the third pitch, the Phils' slugger connected with a 420-foot blast to center field.

Wynn raced back and to his right. But instead of playing the ball safely off the carom, he gambled again and went for the catch. Wynn reached out on the dead run, got the tip of his glove on the ball, stumbled on the gravel warning track and slammed into the wall with a sickening thud. He crumpled to the ground as the ball bounced away and Allen circled the bases with the winning run.

At a Glance

WP: Fox (3–2)

HR: Allen (25), Callison (7,8)

Key stat: Callison 2-for-5, 2 RBIs; Dalrymple 2-for-4, 3 RBIs; Dick Allen 3B

But there was no big celebration waiting for the Phillies slugger at home plate. The Phillies joined the Astros and even some spectators who rushed to the outfield where Wynn lay unconscious with a fractured elbow and wrist. He was carried out on a stretcher to a local hospital, his season over.

"The way he hit the wall, I was afraid to go out there," said pitcher Jim Bunning. Mauch called Wynn "one of the real fine players in the game today. I hate to see him get hurt."

Andersen's Scoreless Innings Streak Comes to an End at 33

Larry Andersen's record-breaking string of consecutive scoreless innings for a reliever came to an end in this game, but not before he added one more zero to his mark.

LA was acquired by the Phillies in July 1983 after kicking around the minors and majors with Cleveland and Seattle. Now, in his first full season in Philadelphia, he was pitching with a newfound confidence.

"I felt like I was wanted. This was a team that liked me and I was pitching well throughout the year," the veteran set-up man recalled.

Andersen's amazing run began on June 21 with 1 ⅓ innings of scoreless relief in a 10–7 loss to the Mets. The next night in Pittsburgh, the Phils lost 7–6 in 13 innings, but LA did his job well, giving up just one hit while shutting down the Pirates for three innings.

The zeros continued to pile up through the end of June and all through July, though Andersen didn't think much about it.

"I didn't know I was nearing a record until the writers started asking me and that was probably a week or so before I gave up the streak," he said. "So it was probably about late July. It's almost one of those things where you don't want to start thinking about it. It takes away from the team when you do that."

At a Glance

WP: Rawley (4–3)

Key stat: Andersen scoreless innings streak ends at 33 innings

On the night his scoreless streak came to a halt, Andersen was making national headlines as the hottest relief pitcher in baseball.

He was called in to bail out Shane Rawley, who had pitched seven shutout innings against the St. Louis Cardinals.

With the Phils holding a 3–0 lead in the bottom of the eighth, Rawley was lifted after walking leadoff batter Lonnie Smith.

Andersen got the first two batters then threw a wild pitch, allowing Smith to move to second. Mike Jorgensen singled to knock in Smith. The run was charged to Rawley. He got Terry Pendleton to end the inning on a ground-out.

The streak came to an end with one out in the ninth. LA could only blame himself.

“David Green hit a line drive back to me,” he remembered. “I knocked it down, which is about as good as I’m gonna do with a ball back to me. I picked it up and I threw it down the right-field line.”

Green scooted to third on the two-base error. The next batter, Tommy Herr, singled to score Green.

Al Holland was brought in to replace Andersen and retired the next two batters in order to preserve the victory.

With his scoreless streak stopped at 33 innings, Andersen felt a strong sense of relief.

“The last couple of weeks, every time I pitched there were questions about it. I felt it was a distraction from what we were doing as a team. . . . Obviously I would like to have kept it going but I was relieved.”

His streak topped Robin Roberts’ streak of 32 $^{1}/_{3}$ scoreless innings in 1950. And he finished not far behind the all-time leader, Grover Cleveland Alexander, a starter who threw 41 $^{2}/_{3}$ consecutive scoreless innings as a rookie in 1911.

August 3, 2006
Phillies 8, Cardinals 1

Utley, Hamels, Coste All Have a Hand in Win

Two young guns and the oldest rookie in baseball helped the Phillies move to within 2.5 games of the wild-card lead in this blowout of the eventual World Series champs.

Chase Utley extended his hitting streak to 34 games, rookie Cole Hamels threw seven dominating innings and 33-year-old rookie Chris Coste collected four hits for the first time in his brief career as the Phils completed a three-game sweep.

More importantly, the entire team was showing new energy in the wake of a clubhouse shakeup that saw the departure of veteran players such as David Bell and Bobby Abreu. This was their sixth victory in their last seven games.

Hamels sensed a team that was more relaxed "and anytime you're relaxed you'll play better," he said. "With the pressure of the trade deadline over, everyone knows their roles. They can go with the flow and play."

The Phils got on the board first, scoring three times in the third on a pair of walks and three singles off Cardinals righty Jason Marquis.

Hamels was in command from the first pitch, holding the Cardinals to two hits while striking out 12. The only run he gave up gave up came on a sacrifice fly from Scott Rolen in the bottom of the fourth.

"I'm starting to figure out things more," said Hamels. "When you have that confidence, things seem to fall into place."

The Phils were on cruise control with a 5–1 lead when they added three more runs in the ninth on four hits, including Aaron Rowand's 12th home run.

> **At a Glance**
>
> **WP:** Hamels (4–5)
>
> **HR:** Rowand (12)
>
> **Key stat:** Coste 4-for-5, 2 RBIs; Utley 3-for-6, RBI; Rowand 3-for-5, RBI, 2 runs; Hamels 12 Ks

They rapped out a total of 16 hits, with Coste going 4-for-5 and Utley collecting three hits in six trips to the plate.

Coste was living a dream that few ballplayers ever experience. After bouncing around the minor leagues for a decade, he finally got his big break and was brought up to the big club in May. Determined to make the most of his opportunity, Coste was now batting .375 with four home runs.

Utley was coming to the end of one of the longest hitting streaks in team history. At 34 games, he finished two behind the all-time leader, Jimmy Rollins.

Phils Drop Dodgers, Take Over NL East Lead

After chasing Chicago most of the season, the Phillies finally moved into first place in National League East with a dramatic come-from-behind win over the Dodgers in front of more than 47,000 frenzied fans at Veterans Stadium.

Trailing 3-1, the Phillies scored seven times in the eighth inning to seal the win, the first of a three-game sweep of the eventual Western Division champs.

Pitching defined this game through the first seven innings as Jim Lonborg and Rick Rhoden each gave up only one run.

The Dodgers scored twice in the top of the eighth to break the tie, but in the bottom of the inning the Phils struck back and grabbed this game by the throat.

> **At a Glance**
>
> **WP:** Garber (5–5)
>
> **HR:** Luzinski (27)
>
> **Key stat:** Schmidt 4-for-4, 2 RBIs; Sizemore 1-for-3, 2 RBIs

After Mike Schmidt led off with a walk, Greg Luzinski got ahold of a 3–2 Rhoden fastball and seared it deep into the night. The ball thumped off the left-field foul pole in the upper deck.

"He'd been staying away from me all night," said Luzinski. "Everything was on the outside corner. Then he finally came in."

His blast ended an 0-for-14 slump, which was a welcome sight for manager Danny Ozark, who felt that his slugger had been trying to carry the team on his shoulders.

Luzinski agreed.

"I was trying to do too much with the baseball. I was trying to drive, give us a lift."

The Bull had redeemed himself from an earlier defensive blunder when he lost Bill Russell's fly ball in the lights. Russell ended up on second with a double and scored on Reggie Smith's double.

Rhoden was replaced by left-handed reliever Lance Rautzhan, who got into trouble immediately.

Richie Hebner singled to center and Garry Maddox followed with a chopper over the head of third baseman Ron Cey to put runners on first and second. Bob Boone, attempting to bunt the runners over, popped up to Cey instead. But No. 8 hitter Ted Sizemore picked him up with a clutch single to left-center to give the Phils their first lead.

"I'll remember this one, definitely," Sizemore said, "because we went into first place."

The Phils added four more runs on singles by Tim McCarver and Jay Johnstone, and a two-run double by Schmidt.

It was perhaps their biggest win of the season to date and a sign of things to come. They were now in first place by a half-game over Chicago.

"We are," said Ozark, "where we belong."

Ex-MVP Murphy Shows a Last Gasp with Walk-Off Slam

They didn't get very far playing small ball, so the Phillies turned to the long ball to beat the Chicago Cubs in a thriller at Veterans Stadium.

The Phils were losing 2–1 going into the ninth inning, having squandered numerous scoring opportunities throughout the game. In the first three innings alone they left eight runners on base.

But in the ninth, Lenny Dykstra neutralized all that ineptitude with one swing of the bat. Facing Paul Assenmacher, The Dude was looking for a pitch that he could drive.

"We needed an extra base hit because we'd been struggling to score runs all night," said Dykstra, who got what he was looking for, a middle-in fastball.

He turned on it and drilled the ball into the right-field stands. With the score now tied, the game moved into extra innings.

At a Glance

WP: Williams (4–3)

HR: Dykstra (3), Murphy (14)

Key stat: Murphy 2-for-5, 4 RBIs; Thon 2-for-4, RBI

Charlie Hayes led off the 10th inning with a single and moved into scoring position on a sacrifice bunt by Randy Ready. He made it to third after Dickie Thon grounded to first but was left stranded after pinch-hitter Dave Hollins flied to center.

In the bottom of the 11th, Dykstra led off with a walk. Darren Daulton dumped a fastball into left to put runners at first and third. With one out, the Cubs chose to intentionally walk John Kruk and pitch to the aging Dale Murphy.

"It's happened quite a bit, that they walk a guy to get to me," said Murphy, a former MVP who was batting just .243 in his final full season.

All he wanted to do was hit a fly ball deep enough to score the runner from third. Instead, Murphy got all of a Les Lancaster fastball and smoked it over the left-field fence, a walk-off grand slam.

Everything seemed to be breaking right for the Phillies after a terrible first half of the season. They had now won seven in a row and would go on to win their next six, tying the team record for consecutive wins with 13.

August 7, 1943
Phillies 9, Giants 6

Stewart Picks Fine Time for Only 2 Homers of His Career

You don't see many teams bang out 18 hits and lose a game, but the New York Giants managed to do just that against a grateful and beleaguered Phillies pitching staff.

Despite pounding the ball all afternoon, the Giants couldn't get big hits when they needed them. At the end of the day the Giants had tied a major league record by leaving 18 runners on base, two in every inning.

The Phillies got a boost from Glen Stewart, a little known shortstop who hit the only two home runs of his career in this game.

Chester, Pa., native Danny Murtaugh got things started for the Phillies in the first with a leadoff single off Johnny Wittig. Buster Adams bunted for a hit and scored behind Murtaugh on a double by Jimmy Wasdell. Later in the inning, they increased the lead to 4–0 on a bases-loaded single by No. 8 hitter Pinky May.

The Giants cut the lead to 4–1 in the bottom of the first after starter Dick Conger walked three batters and gave up a run-scoring single to Joe Medwick.

Conger was knocked out in the second after the Giants scored three more runs to tie the game.

Stewart hit his first big-league homer in the third, a solo shot, and the Phils added another in the fourth to take a 6–4 lead.

Stewart struck again in the seventh with a three-run belt to the upper deck of the Polo Grounds to make the score 9–5.

At a Glance

WP: Karl (1–2)

HR: Stewart 2 (2)

Key stat: Stewart 3-for-5, 4 RBIs; Murtaugh 3-for-4; Wasdell 2-for-4, 2 RBIs

The Giants couldn't keep up, but not for a lack of effort as they battered relievers Anton Karl and Schoolboy Rowe.

But their rallies continually fell short. The Giants scored a meaningless run in the ninth inning when Mel Ott doubled home Johnny Rucker.

Of their 18 hits, it was the Giants' only extra-base hit of the game. As Whitey Ashburn used to say, "Hard to believe, Harry."

Scoring Gaffe Keeps Wise from No-Hitter

A blown call by the official scorer early in the game cost Rick Wise a date with immortality as the 22-year-old right-hander had to settle for a one-hitter in this nail-biter at Dodger Stadium.

The controversial call was made in the third inning after Bart Shirley hit a high chopper that bounced off the glove of shortstop Roberto Pena.

It appeared to be an error by everyone who saw the play. But the scorer went the other way, deciding that the ball took a bad hop. Pena disagreed. "I messed it up," he said. "That play has to be an error. It went right off my glove."

> **At a Glance**
>
> **WP:** Wise (8–8)
>
> **HR:** Allen (23)
>
> **Key stat:** Wise CG one-hitter

Wise refused to complain.

"The man called it as he saw it," he said. "I'm not disappointed. I was happy enough to win the ball game."

Wise had just finished one of the most intense pitching duels of the season with Bill Singer, who held the Phillies to four hits and no runs up to the start of the ninth inning.

Wise overpowered the Dodgers with a high, hopping fastball. He threw little more than a dozen curves.

"The Dodgers didn't show me they could hit my fastball so why should I give them my off-speed stuff?"

Only one batter hit the ball hard, and Shirley was the only Dodger to reach second base. Still, after eight innings the game remained tied and Wise was mentally preparing himself for extra innings in the ninth . . . until Dick Allen stepped up.

The Wampum Walloper had been in an extended slump and failed to get the ball out of the infield his first three at-bats.

But in his fourth trip to the plate he ripped into a Singer fastball and sent it soaring 450 feet into the left-center field bleachers.

The breathtaking smash was Allen's 23rd homer of the year and a game-changer for his pitcher.

Wise came out in the bottom of the ninth determined to finish the job.

"I felt I was working on a no-hitter and I wanted to get those last three batters out—even though I knew they wouldn't change that earlier scoring decision."

Phillies 4, Pirates 2

Myers Loses His Cool But Not the Game

Jimmy Rollins went 4-for-4 with two triples and Brett Myers got into a memorable argument with manager Charlie Manuel in the Phillies' win over Pittsburgh.

Rollins slammed his first three-bagger to right field to lead off the first inning and scored after No. 2 hitter Shane Victorino ripped a double to right. Ryan Howard's single to center brought in Victorino.

The Pirates made it a 2–1 game in the top of the fourth, scoring their only run off Myers, who gave up just five hits in 7 2/3 innings.

Rollins and Victorino combined for another Phillies run in the seventh when J-Roll led off with a triple and scored on Victorino's base hit to left.

In the top of the eighth, Manuel decided to make a move to the bullpen after Chris Gomez slammed a one-out double and Freddy Sanchez hit a hard liner right at Rollins.

Myers wasn't happy. He turned his back as Manuel walked out, then stalked off the mound to a standing ovation.

When Manuel returned to the dugout he and his pitcher got into a heated argument in front of the TV cameras. They cleared the air after the game.

Myers blamed himself for losing his cool.

"I missed a month here with the team (due to an injury) and I wanted to prove to myself again that I can pitch in the big leagues," said Myers. "And I wanted to stay out there as long as I could."

"He's fine," Manuel said. "He just wanted to stay in the game and I like that. I'll tell you something: his confidence got back. That's why I took him out of the game. . . . He was leaving on a high note."

At a Glance

WP: Myers (5–9)

Key stat: Rollins 4-for-4, 2 triples, 2 runs; Victorino 2-for-3, 2 RBIs; Dobbs 2-for-3, RBI

Manuel was also happy to see the Phillies' offense show some life again after going 23 consecutive innings without scoring a run. During that stretch they collected just 11 hits in 76 at-bats for an average of .145 while suffering back-to-back shutouts for the first time since 1999.

But this victory signaled that the bats were coming back, just in time for an unforgettable stretch run.

"It got the monkey off their back," said Manuel.

'Sandpaper Game' Leaves Gross Roughed Up with Suspension

This was the infamous "Sandpaper Game," a most embarrassing moment for pitcher Kevin Gross, who took desperate measures to break out of a lengthy winless streak by gluing sandpaper to his glove. Gross was caught red-handed and suspended for 10 games.

The 26-year-old right-hander came into the game with a record of 6–10 and had not won a game in his previous seven starts.

Ironically, the sandpaper didn't seem to help very much. Gross was roughed up for two second-inning home runs by Jerry Mumphrey and Jody Davis.

Still, Chicago manager Gene Michael didn't like what he was seeing. He'd been complaining the entire game about Gross scuffing the baseballs. In the fifth, Michael came out to lodge a formal protest with home-plate umpire Charlie Williams.

Williams and crew chief John Kibler walked to the mound for an inspection, and sure enough, found sandpaper glued to the heel of Gross' glove.

Kibler threw him out of the game but held on to the glove so league officials could give it a thorough inspection.

Gross pleaded the fifth after the game.

"I have nothing to say right now. I'm going to wait and see what happens before I say anything. Was there something in my glove? I don't know. I don't have anything else to say."

At a Glance

WP: Frohwirth (1–0)

HR: Hayes (18), Parrish (12)

Key stat: Samuel 2-for-3, RBI; Parrish 2-for-4, 2 RBIs

Manager Lee Elia was stunned.

"I had no idea that something like that was in the thought patterns of any of our pitchers," he said before taking back that statement.

"And I couldn't really find a scuff on the ball they showed me. I have a drawer full of balls that are really scuffed by other pitchers around the league. There wasn't enough on the ball to have him checked, in my opinion."

With the sudden ejection of his pitcher, Elia had few options. It was too early in the game to call on the back end of his bullpen, so the skipper called on rookie Todd Frohwirth, who had just been called up from the minors. It turned out to be a terrific move. With the Phillies holding a 4–2 lead, Frohwirth, a right-handed submariner, struck out the dangerous Andre Dawson on three pitches, then got Jerry Mumphrey to ground out to end the inning. Frohwirth pitched a scoreless sixth before giving way to Kent Tekulve and Steve Bedrosian.

Frohwirth said things happened so fast he didn't have time to think.

"I just had to get in there and get loose in front of the most people I've ever played in front of. It was really a strange feeling."

As for facing Dawson, Frohwirth said he was still relying on instinct.

"I just wanted to throw strikes and I threw him sinkers and sliders. And then I end up with a win in my first game, which right now makes me more excited than I've ever been in my life."

Bunning Hit the Century Mark in NL, Too

It wasn't a classic Jim Bunning performance, but the veteran right-hander was good enough to beat Houston and join Cy Young on the very short list of pitchers to win 100 games in both the National and American leagues.

The 38-year-old Bunning downplayed his accomplishment after it was over, calling it "much ado about nothing," and seemed relieved to reach the milestone after three previous failed attempts.

The Phillies jumped out to a 3–0 lead in the first inning, thanks to an error by second baseman Joe Morgan on Tony Taylor's leadoff grounder.

With two outs, Astros starter Jack Billingham walked a pair of batters to load the bases before giving up back-to-back singles to Don Money and Larry Bowa. All three runs were unearned.

Billingham walked John Briggs to lead off the sixth. Deron Johnson then hit what appeared to be a double-play grounder to second, but the ball took a bad hop off Morgan's leg. Briggs scored, Johnson wound up on second and soon came in to score on a double by Money.

Meanwhile, Bunning had a stranglehold on the Astros through eight innings as he held them to one run on six hits.

"I had great control and a good fastball until the ninth inning. Then I got tired and ran out of gas."

Joe Morgan led off the ninth with a home run to make the score 6–2. After retiring Jimmy Wynn on a pop-up, Bunning gave up three straight singles and saw the lead cut in half.

Cesar Cedeno hit a run-scoring grounder to first for the second out, and Johnny Edwards knocked in the Astros' fifth run with a single to center.

Relievers Joe Hoerner and Dick Selma came in to close it for Bunning.

Phillies	AB	R	H	RBI
Taylor 2b	4	1	1	0
Gamble cf	5	0	0	0
Briggs lf	4	2	1	0
Johnson 1b	3	2	2	2
Stone rf	4	1	0	0
Money 3b	4	0	2	3
Bowa ss	4	0	2	1
Ryan c	3	0	1	0
Bunning p	4	0	0	0
Hoerner p	0	0	0	0
Selma p	0	0	0	0
Totals	35	6	9	6

Astros	AB	R	H	RBI
Alou rf	5	0	1	1
Morgan 2b	4	1	1	1
Wynn lf	4	0	0	0
Mayberry 1b	4	1	1	0
Menke ss	4	1	3	0
Rader 3b	4	1	1	1
Cedeno cf	4	1	1	1
Edwards c	4	0	3	1
Cook pr	0	0	0	0
Billingham p	1	0	0	0
Geronimo ph	1	0	0	0
DiLauro p	0	0	0	0
Miller ph	0	0	0	0
Howard ph	1	0	1	0
Totals	36	5	12	5

PHI	3	0	0	0	0	2	1	0	0	-	6	9	0
HOU	0	0	1	0	0	0	0	0	4	-	5	12	1

Phillies	IP	H	R	ER	BB	SO
Bunning W (9-11)	8.2	11	5	5	0	5
Hoerner	0	1	0	0	0	0
Selma S (16)	0.1	0	0	0	0	1
Totals	9	12	5	5	0	6

Astros	IP	H	R	ER	BB	SO
Billingham L (9-11)	8	8	6	3	4	5
DiLauro	1	1	0	0	1	1
Totals	9	9	6	3	5	6

E—Houston Morgan. DP—Philadelpia 2; Houston. 2B—Philadelphia Money, Johnson; Houston Alou. HR—Houston Morgan (4). SH—Houston Billingham. HBP—Philadelphia Taylor. LOB—Philadelphia 8; Houston 5. Attendance: 18,184.

Broxton Blows Another as Phils Mount Wild Comeback in Late Innings

A sold-out crowd spent most of the night watching Phillies pitchers get lit up and runners being stranded. But the hometown fans got a huge reward for their patience when the Phillies staged an incredible rally against the Dodgers and their fearsome closer, Jonathon Broxton.

Trailing 9–2, the Phils scored four in the eighth and four more in the ninth to beat L.A.

It was an unthinkable finish to a game the Phillies seemed destined to lose. Joe Blanton gave up three runs in the first inning and the Dodgers methodically built on their lead from there, while the Phils failed to cash in on several scoring opportunities.

For Broxton, Citizens Bank Park had become a House of Horrors. He was appearing there for the first time since blowing Game 4 of the 2009 National League Championship Series. And the effects of that game, along with the memory of Matt Stairs' pinch-hit homer in the '08 NLCS, seemed to have a carryover effect as Broxton blew a three-run lead in the final inning, leading to one of the more memorable games in Phillies history.

At a Glance

WP: Baez (3–3)

Key stat: Ruiz 3-for-5, 3 RBIs; Werth 2-for-4, 2 RBIs; Polanco 2-for-4, 2 runs; Sweeney 2-for-4

Staked to a three-run lead in the ninth, the burly Broxton faced five batters and failed to retire one of them.

After plunking leadoff hitter Placido Polanco on his third pitch, Broxton walked the next two batters, Mike Sweeney and Jayson Werth.

He got Ben Francisco to hit what appeared to be a certain double-play ball to Casey Blake at third. But Blake didn't get his glove down in time. The ball went through his legs, allowing Polanco and Sweeney to score.

"Tonight, I looked like an idiot," said Blake. "I've got to make that play, bottom line."

With the fans now on their feet, Carlos Ruiz stepped in and smoked a 1–1 pitch into the gap in left-center field.

Werth paused momentarily at second base to make sure the ball was going to drop and was nearly passed by Francisco, who was running at the crack of the bat.

As Francisco streaked across home plate with the winning run, Ruiz rolled into second, saw his teammates rushing out of the dugout and turned to run the other way. "Chooch" didn't get far, though, as he was surrounded and pounded in a slap-happy celebration between second and first.

Ruiz said he went up to the plate relaxed.

"I was thinking (Charlie Manuel) was showing his confidence to get a big hit right here, because right there you have a bunt situation. So I said, 'You have to do something.' I definitely was looking for a good pitch to hit, and he threw me a slider right down the middle, and I made good contact."

Did You Know?

Ryan Howard is the only Phillie to hit 40 home runs in three straight seasons. He walloped 58 in 2006, 47 in '07 and 48 in '08. Howard made it four years in a row in '09 when he hit 45 homers.

Chuck Klein, Mike Schmidt and Jim Thome each had back-to-back 40 home run seasons.

10-Run First Inning Holds Up against Giants

It was a record-breaking day at Shibe Park as the Phillies threw an early knockout punch against Leo Durocher's Giants by scoring 10 runs in the first inning.

In doing so, the Phils set a new a major league mark by putting their first 10 batters on base before registering an out.

The Giants initially got the upper hand, scoring three times in the top of the first. They got some help from Phillies rookie Curt Simmons, who made a wild throw on what should have been a double play, and a pair of bloopers that fell in for hits.

But the Phils came roaring back in the bottom of the inning as they sent 14 batters to the plate.

Richie Ashburn led off with a single up the middle and scored after Granny Hamner hit one off the scoreboard for a triple.

Infielder Granny Hamner, right, spent 15 seasons with the Phillies and was a key player on the 1950 National League pennant team.

Hamner scored the second run when Johnny Blatnick singled to center. Dick Sisler followed with a base hit to right, and Bert Haas made it five hits in a row when his blooper down the right-field line fell in.

At that point, Durocher decided to make a pitching change, replacing Ray Poat with Alex Konikowski, but the results were the same.

Eddie Miller cleared the bases with a line-drive double down the left-field line to give the Phils a 5–3 lead.

The seventh batter, Del Ennis, hit a routine grounder to short, but Johnny Kerr mishandled it. When Konikowski walked Andy Seminick to load the bases again, Durocher dipped into his bullpen once more, bringing in Andy Hansen.

But there was no stopping the Phillies as Simmons singled to left. Miller and Ennis scored easily, and when outfielder Bobby Thomson bobbled the ball, Seminick raced home and Simmons moved to third.

Still there was no one out and the top of the lineup came around to bat again. Ashburn continued the relentless hit parade, lashing a double to right-center to knock in Simmons with the ninth run.

Hamner ended the amazing on-base streak at 10 when he unsuccessfully tried to bunt for a hit. Blatnick then popped up for the second out. But Sisler singled in Ashburn with the 10th and final run of the incredible inning.

At a Glance

WP: Simmons (6–11)

Key stat: Phillies 17 hits; Ashburn 3-for-4, RBI, 3 runs; Miller 2-for-4, 3 RBIs; Hamner 3-for-4

It may have seemed like overkill at the time, but the Phils needed all those runs after the Giants made things interesting by scoring four runs in the sixth to make the score 10–7.

The Phils bounced back with a run in the bottom of the sixth and another in the eighth while reliever Walt Dubiel shut down the Giants the rest of the way.

Schmidt's 300th Career Homer, Moreland's 5 RBIs Save the Day

Mike Schmidt reached a new milestone in hitting his 300th career home run, but the offensive star of this game was Keith Moreland, who knocked in five of the Phillies' eight runs.

Moreland, a catcher in his second full season with the team, was playing only sporadically behind All-Star Bob Boone.

With the offense in a funk, manager Dallas Green decided to shake things up and inserted Moreland into the lineup.

The 27-year-old Texan responded by stroking a two-out, two-run single into right in the first inning.

Schmidt unloaded a two-run, tape-measure homer in the third to give the Phils a 4–1 lead. At 31, he became the youngest active player to hit 300 career homers.

"Well, I'm a power hitter, so I guess power statistics are the only things I'll ever be able to amass in terms of long-range goals," said Schmidt, who still had more than 200 homers ahead of him. "I'm never going to get 3,600 hits, no question about that."

In the sixth, Schmidt and Gary Matthews each walked with one out, bringing up Moreland again. Mets starter Mike Scott grooved a first-pitch fastball and Moreland pounced on it. His three-run homer increased the Phillies' lead to 7–2.

At a Glance

WP: Christenson (3–6)

HR: Schmidt (17), Moreland (3)

Key stat: Moreland 2-for-5, 5 RBIs; Schmidt 300th HR

Larry Christenson pitched six solid innings, giving up four runs while striking out nine with an overpowering curveball. Reliever Mike Proly pitched three hitless innings to pick up his second save.

Moreland's situation created a dilemma for the front office. He knew he could hit but also knew he wouldn't have much of a chance as long as Boone was still around.

"At the end of the year," he said, "I'll evaluate my situation."

The situation was eventually resolved when the Phillies traded Moreland to the Cubs after the season for starting pitcher Mike Krukow.

Mulholland Gets Emotional with No-Hitter vs. Giants

Terry Mulholland wrote his name in the record books with his first career no-hitter, while also becoming the first Phillie in the 20th century to pull off the rare feat in front of his own fans.

Mulholland, a former Giant who was picked up midway through the 1989 season in a deal for Steve Bedrosian, completely handcuffed his old team with a blazing fastball and sharp slider.

He had a perfect game going until Rick Parker reached on an error by

Terry Mulholland pitched the first no-hitter at Veterans Stadium on Aug. 15, 1990.

third baseman Charlie Hayes leading off the top of the seventh. The Phils gave Mulholland all the run support he would need when John Kruk singled home Darren Daulton with one out in the bottom of the first.

They added three runs in the fifth on an RBI double by Lenny Dysktra and Darren Daulton's two-run homer.

After the Phils scored two more in the sixth to make it a 6–0 game, the focus shifted to Mullholland as tension began to build in the stands and on the field.

"I was nervous as hell," said Kruk. "I'm not gonna lie, I was scared to death."

"I never played in a no-hit game in professional baseball . . . that was just unbelievable."

Outfielder Von Hayes began to visualize the outcome early in the game.

"There was just something about this night," he said. "When the seventh inning ended . . . there was no doubt in my mind he was gonna get it. I really felt destiny was on his side."

The 27-year-old Mulholland didn't start thinking seriously about a no-hitter until the eighth inning.

In the ninth, he retired the first two Giants on ground-outs. The final batter, pinch-hitter Gary Carter, hit a line drive over the third-base bag. Charlie Hayes reached to his right and snared it, setting off a joyous celebration at the mound and a thunderous ovation from more than 32,000 fans.

"You can't imagine what went through my head when he caught that ball," Mulholland said. "There was a rush of emotion, and I am not an emotional person."

Mulholland became just the seventh Phillie in team history to throw a no-hitter and the first to throw one at home since Red Donahue beat Boston 5–0 on July 8, 1898.

Giants	AB	R	H	RBI
Parker cf-rf	3	0	0	0
Anderson 2b	3	0	0	0
Downs p	0	0	0	0
Clark 1b	3	0	0	0
Mitchell lf	3	0	0	0
Williams 3b	3	0	0	0
Litton rf-2b	3	0	0	0
Kennedy c	2	0	0	0
Bathe ph	1	0	0	0
Uribe ss	3	0	0	0
Robinson p	2	0	0	0
Kingery cf	0	0	0	0
Carter ph	1	0	0	0
Totals	**27**	**0**	**0**	**0**

Phillies	AB	R	H	RBI
Dykstra cf	4	1	1	1
Daulton c	3	2	1	2
Hayes lf	2	0	0	0
Murphy rf	4	0	0	0
Kruk 1b	4	1	2	1
Herr 2b	3	1	1	0
Hayes 3b	4	0	1	1
Thon ss	4	1	1	0
Mulholland p	3	0	1	1
Totals	**31**	**6**	**8**	**6**

SF	0	0	0	0	0	0	0	0	0	0	0	0
PHI	1	0	0	0	3	2	0	0	X	6	8	1

Giants	IP	H	R	ER	BB	SO
Robinson L (8-4)	6	7	6	6	4	3
Downs	2	1	0	0	0	0
Totals	**8**	**8**	**6**	**6**	**4**	**3**

Phillies	IP	H	R	ER	BB	SO
Mulholland W (7-6)	9	0	0	0	0	8
Totals	**9**	**0**	**0**	**0**	**0**	**8**

E—Philadelphia Hayes. DP—Philadelphia 1. 2B—Philadelphia Kruk, Dykstra. HR—Philadelphia Daulton (10). LOB—Philadelphia 5. Attendance: 32,156.

Phils' Longest Winning Streak Ever Reaches 13 Games in Montreal

The Phillies extended their longest winning streak in club history to 13 games with this victory at Olympic Stadium in Montreal.

For a while it looked like the streak might be broken as the Phils fell behind 5–2 after seven frustrating innings in which they collected 11 hits off Expos starter Jackie Brown, but left 12 runners on base.

The Expos built their lead at the expense of Jim Kaat. They roughed up the Phillies' lefty for four runs in four innings. Andre Dawson's fifth-inning homer off reliever Warren Brusstar gave the Expos their fifth run.

In the eighth, the Phillies' bench provided the spark that ignited a five-run explosion.

Tommy Hutton, batting for Brusstar, started the rally with a walk then moved to second on a single by Bake McBride. Hutton scored on a base hit by Larry Bowa and McBride dashed home on Mike Schmidt's sacrifice fly.

At a Glance

WP: Brusstar (4–2)

Key stat: Bowa 3-for-6, RBI; Schmidt 2-for-4, RBI; Johnson 1-for-1, 2 RBIs

After Greg Luzinski walked, lefty reliever Will McEnaney was brought in to face left-handed hitting Richie Hebner, prompting manager Danny Ozark to counter with a right-handed pinch-hitter.

It was Davey Johnson, who smoked a first-pitch fastball into left field for a base hit. Del Unser tried to make a play as Bowa rounded third. But as he reached out with his glove, the ball hit a seam on the slick artificial turf, skipped past the startled Unser and rolled to the wall.

Bowa scored, Luzinski scored, and Johnson wound up on third with a triple. Bob Boone then provided an insurance run with a two-out RBI double to left.

In the locker room after the game, there was an atmosphere of invincibility.

"The way we're going, we might never lose again," said Bowa.

The Phillies lost the next night, but went on a six-game winning streak after that to make it 19 out of 20.

August 17, 1972
Phillies 9, Reds 4

15-Game Winning Streak by Carlton Gets 'Em Talking

Steve Carlton continued his other-worldly first season in Philadelphia by picking up his 20th victory and extending his winning streak to a franchise-record 15 games.

Carlton was the talk of the town all summer as he cranked out one dominating performance after another for a last-place team.

And so there was great anticipation at Veterans Stadium when "Lefty" strode to the mound to a standing ovation from the crowd of 53,377. Third baseman Don Money said he got goose bumps, and shortstop Larry Bowa got a knot in his stomach.

"I wanted Carlton to win that game so badly," he said.

Carlton also admitted he was excited.

"It was a combination of things—all the people who support me, the streak, the Reds."

The Big Red Machine was the only team that Lefty hadn't beaten. But that was about to change.

Deron Johnson gave the Phillies an early lead with a two-run homer to right-center in the second. Carlton retired the first six batters he faced before running into trouble in the third as the Reds roughed him up for three runs on four hits.

At a Glance

WP: Carlton (20–6)

HR: Johnson (7), Montanez (12)

Key stat: Luzinski 3-for-4, RBI; Johnson 2-for-4, 2 RBIs; Robinson 3-for-3, RBI

But in the fifth, the Phils put up three more, reclaiming the lead for good.

Terry Harmon opened the inning with a single off starter Ross Grimsley and stole second. Bowa beat out a bunt as Harmon raced to third.

Money hit a line drive to center that was caught, but it was deep enough to bring Harmon home with the tying run.

Willie Montanez was the next batter, and the flashy center fielder belted one over the fence in right-center for a two-run homer. The Phillies added two runs in the sixth and two more in the seventh to put the game away.

When Pete Rose grounded out to end the game, the crowd went berserk as Carlton and his teammates shook hands and retreated to the clubhouse.

But no one in the stands was ready to leave. They began chanting, "We Want Steve!" until Lefty came back out to acknowledge the curtain call.

He stayed out there for quite awhile, chatting and signing autographs.

"Wasn't that something," said Carlton. "It was pretty touching. It never happened to me before. I also want to thank my teammates for their super support. They scored runs, they got big hits, they played great defense."

Steve Carlton

Arguably the greatest pitcher in team history, Steve Carlton developed into Hall of Fame material in his first season in Philadelphia.

Relying on his signature slider, Carlton won 27 of the team's 59 victories in 1972. He also struck out a career-high 310 batters and compiled an earned-run average of 1.97 to win the first of four Cy Young Awards.

A six-time 20-game winner, Lefty won 329 games and struck out 4,136 batters in a career that spanned 24 years.

In 1980 he went 3–0 in the postseason and was the winning pitcher in the deciding game of the World Series.

Carlton was inducted into the Baseball Hall of Fame in 1994.

McMillon's Introduction Includes Grand Slam

The Phillies scored runs in big bunches thanks to a pair of grand slams from Billy McMillon and Mike Lieberthal.

McMillon, a highly touted rookie playing in his first game for the Phils since being acquired from Florida in a trade for Darren Daulton, made an immediate impact.

He singled to right off Giants starter Mark Gardner his first time up. In the third inning, the left-handed hitting outfielder came up with the bases loaded and hammered a 3–2 fastball over the wall in right to give the Phils a 4–0 lead.

"I feel like I have to wake up and turn over. It's a dream," said McMillon. "I'm just trying to contribute. I know everybody says that, but I sincerely mean that."

McMillon received a standing ovation his third time up after hitting a long drive that was caught at the warning track in the fifth inning.

Lieberthal hit his first career grand slam in the sixth. The Phils had already scored two runs and loaded the bases when the young catcher stepped to the plate with one out and crushed a fastball into the left-center field seats off former Phil Terry Mulholland to increase the lead to 10–2.

The slams provided a comfortable cushion for starter Matt Beech. The second-year lefty went seven strong innings, striking out five while limiting the National League West-leading Giants to one run on three hits.

At a Glance

WP: Beech (2–7)

HR: McMillon (1); Lieberthal (18)

Key stat: McMillon 3-for-5, grand slam, 4 RBI; Lieberthal 2-for-5, grand slam, 4 RBIs

Roberts Adds to Legend with Sixth 20-Win Season in a Row

More than 35,000 fans jammed Connie Mack Stadium to watch Robin Roberts beat Brooklyn and become one of a handful of pitchers in big-league history to win 20 games six years in a row.

The Phillies' ace won this game in dramatic fashion, thanks to some late-inning heroics by his teammates.

Roberts' mound opponent, Don Newcombe, had shut down the Phillies through seven innings on two hits. At one point he set down 15 batters in a row.

The Dodgers threatened a number of times but Roberts managed to work his way out of trouble, helped in large part by three double plays in the first four innings. He gave up one run in the fifth and a solo home run to Roy Campanella in the seventh.

The Phils finally got on the board in the eighth on successive singles from Eddie Waitkus, Jim Greengrass and Andy Seminick. However, Roberts killed any hopes of a big inning by hitting a tapper back to Newcombe, who threw to second for the start of a double play.

Robbie retired the Dodgers in order in the ninth to give his team one more chance against the hard-throwing Newcombe, who came into the game with a record of 18–3.

At a Glance

WP: Roberts (20–9)

Key stat: Hamner 2-for-4; Seminick 2-for-3, RBI

Bobby Morgan, a former Dodger, led off the inning with a line-drive double down the left-field line. He moved to third when Granny Hamner singled to right.

Del Ennis hit a bouncer right back to Newcombe, who faked a throw to third in an effort to hold the runner, then fired to second to start a double play. But his throw was wild and sailed into center field.

Morgan scored the tying run and dashed into the dugout, where teammates greeted him with pats on the back for his heads-up play.

"Bobby acted like he was taking off for home," said Smith. "He startled Newcombe. Then, when the pitcher tried for the double play at second, he threw the ball away."

Richie Ashburn

More than a decade after his death, Richie "Whitey" Ashburn remains a beloved figure in Philadelphia.

Ashburn was signed as a catcher out of Tilden, Neb., in 1945. But his blazing speed made him a natural for the outfield.

Soon after his arrival in Philadelphia in 1948, the 21-year-old Ashburn put together a fabulous rookie season in which he batted .333 with 32 stolen bases. He went on to win two batting titles in 1955 and '58 and was one of the top center fielders in the game.

After retiring in 1962 with 2,574 hits and a .308 batting average, Ashburn began a new career as a Phillies broadcaster, eventually teaming up with Harry Kalas to form one of the legendary play-by-play tandems in baseball history.

Ashburn was inducted into the Hall of Fame in 1995.

Willie Jones ended the game after belting a Newcombe fastball into left field to score Hamner.

Roberts became just the fifth pitcher in modern history to win 20 or more games for six successive seasons, joining such luminaries as Lefty Grove, Walter Johnson, Mordecai (Three Finger) Brown and Christy Mathewson.

In his typically understated style, the big right-hander took it all in stride. When asked how he felt, Roberts replied: "I don't know. But it sure was nice to win that one."

Misery Ends as 23-Game Losing Streak Is Finally Halted

Finally! The longest losing streak in modern big league history was mercifully over. After 23 games of misery, the last-place Phillies won a ballgame, something they hadn't done since July 28.

It was a streak that was so inconceivable, so off-the-wall that hundreds of fans showed up along with a five-piece band at Philadelphia International Airport at 1 AM to greet the team as conquering heroes.

The end of the losing streak came on a Sunday afternoon in Milwaukee in the second game of a doubleheader.

The Phils had just lost a 5–2 decision in the opener as Warren Spahn won his 302nd career game.

But they came back to win the nightcap behind John Buzhardt, who happened to win the game that preceded the start of the losing streak.

Buzhardt said he had a hunch before he went out to pitch.

"I figured I was due. We were all due."

After seven innings the Phils were clinging to a 3–2 lead. But in the top of the eighth, they busted out for four runs.

Don Demeter led off the inning with a single. Pinch-hitter Ken Walters made two failed attempts to bunt, then took a full swing and singled.

Lee Walls grounded into a force at second and Clay Dalrymple walked to load the bases.

Bobby Malkmus followed with a run-scoring single to right. Buzhardt then laid down a bunt as Walls broke from third, a perfectly executed suicide squeeze. Tony Taylor knocked in the final two runs of the inning with a base hit to right.

At a Glance

WP: Buzhardt (4–13)

HR: Covington (8)

Key stat: Phils break 23-game losing streak; Dalrymple 3-for-3, RBI; Walls 2-for-5, 3 runs

The Braves came back to scored a run in the eighth and another in the ninth. But Buzhardt hung tough and got the last out to end the historic losing skid.

In the locker room after the game, the Phillies chowed down on ribs and shared a few laughs for the first time in weeks.

"Did anyone check the score to make sure we won?" asked infielder Charley Smith.

Dalrymple quipped: "I had dreams of this thing—but they were a week ago."

Malkmus predicted the plane ride back to Philly "will be a lot smoother for all of us."

But as the plane approached the runway, some of the players grew anxious.

When pitcher Frank Sullivan looked out the window and saw the crowd, he cracked: "They're selling rocks for $1.50 a bushel. We'd better go out in single file so they can't get us all in one burst!"

Instead, the team was astonished to find a throng of screaming supporters. Some brought signs that read: "Who said it couldn't be done—Phils 7 Braves 4." And this: "Just Relax Fellas, You're Home Now."

One of the last to leave the plane was 35-year-old manager Gene Mauch, who was quickly surrounded by the adoring mob, lifted onto their shoulders and carried through the terminal.

With tears in his eyes, Mauch thanked the crowd.

"It's really something," he said. "I've never seen even a winning team try harder than the Phillies during the streak. If we ever win 23 out of 24, they'll have to build a bigger airport."

Bake's Game-Winner Ends It in the 17th

It took 17 grueling innings and a little over five hours for the Phillies to pull this one out over San Diego.

Bake McBride became the man of the hour when he slammed his second triple of the day to bring Mike Schmidt around from first base with the winning run.

There were early indications that this was going to be a wacky game. In the first inning, Phils rookie Bob Walk walked the first two hitters en route to giving up three runs.

The Padres were winning 2–0 and had a man on when Gene Tenace hit a drive to the warning track in left. Lonnie Smith leapt up and had the ball in his glove until he slammed into the fence and slumped to the ground. The ball popped out and Tenace raced to third with an RBI triple.

Walk was taken out of the game after giving up two more runs in the third. His replacement, Randy Lerch, was stellar, limiting the Padres to one run over six innings while giving his team time to mount a comeback against Rick Wise.

That comeback included a two-run homer by Mike Schmidt in the third and Larry Bowa's inside-the-park home run in the sixth.

At a Glance

WP: Saucier (6–3)

HR: Schmidt 2 (33, 34); Bowa (2)

Key stat: McBride 3-for-8, 3 RBIs; Schmidt 3-for-6, 3 RBIs; Smith 3-for-4, 3 runs

The Phillies had an 8–6 lead heading into the ninth inning, but reliever Ron Reed was unable to hold it as he walked leadoff hitter Broderick Perkins and gave up a game-tying home run to Dave Winfield.

The Phils had a great chance to end the affair in the bottom of the 13th.

Pete Rose started off the inning with a double and Schmidt was intentionally walked. McBride bunted the runners into scoring position, but Padres lefty Dennis Kinney escaped by getting Garry Maddox and Bowa to pop-up.

In the bottom of the 17th, Kinney got Rose to ground out then gave up a ground ball single to Schmidt. McBride ripped a long fly ball into the gap in right-center, just out of the reach of center fielder Jerry Mumphrey. The ball rolled to the wall and McBride rolled into third as Schmidt trotted home to end one of the longest games in Phillies history.

Bruntlett's Unassisted Triple Play Ends a Wild One against Mets

Eric Bruntlett's game-ending unassisted triple play was the incredible capstone to a wild and crazy game that included enough up-and-down moments to cause motion sickness.

The Phillies staked Pedro Martinez to a 6–0 lead in the first on a pair of three-run homers from Jayson Werth and Carlos Ruiz.

In the bottom half of the inning, left fielder Raul Ibanez helped turn Angel Pagan's ground-rule double into an inside-the-park homer.

Pagan hit a ball that got stuck under the padding of the fence in left-center. Shane Victorino trotted over and raised his arm to signal "dead ball" to the umpires. But Ibanez raced over, dug the ball out and threw it back to the infield, making it a live ball as Pagan circled the bases. The Mets scored another run on a Jeff Francoeur triple to close the gap to 6–2.

The Phils scored twice in the top of the third but the Mets came right back with two of their own, then scored another run in the bottom of the seventh to make it an 8–5 game.

There were two outs in the ninth when another weird play unfolded. Bruntlett hit a liner to Francoeur in right and wound up on third after the umpire ruled "no catch." Mets manager Jerry Manuel came out to argue the call, the umpire crew conferred and reversed the call.

At a Glance

WP: Martinez (2–0)

HR: Werth (29), Ruiz (8)

Key stat: Werth 2-for-5, 3 RBIs; Bruntlett 3-for-5, unassisted triple play; Ruiz 1-for-4, 3 RBIs

Out came Charlie Manuel, who let the umps have it and was thrown out of the game.

Disaster loomed for the Phils in the bottom of the ninth when Brad Lidge came in for the save. Ryan Howard's error allowed Pagan to scoot all the way to third. He scored when Bruntlett booted Luis Castillo's grounder to second.

Daniel Murphy then hit a ball up the middle that Bruntlett called "one of those strange balls.... You're not real sure whether to go to the bag or go get the ball. It was obviously my ball."

He knocked it down but couldn't make a play.

Francouer stepped to the plate next and hit a liner up the middle as Castillo and Murphy took off in an attempted double steal.

Shane Victorino was watching the play unfold from his vantage point in center field. As he saw Bruntlett reach out to catch the hot shot he shouted, "Touch everybody. Touch everybody."

Bruntlett stepped on second for a force and turned to tag the helpless Murphy for the third out.

He became the 15th player in major league history to pull off an unassisted triple play, the first in National League history to end a game with one and just the second in big-league history to end a game with a triple play.

"It was huge," said Bruntlett, "especially because I was part of the reason we got into such a bad spot there in the ninth. So it feels extra special that it happened there to finish off the game."

August 24, 2008

Phillies 5, Dodgers 2 (11 innings)

Feliz Carries Phils with Tying, Winning Hits

The Phillies were about to lose to the Dodgers and fall 1.5 games behind the Mets until Pedro Feliz came to the rescue and single-handedly led them to a miraculous come-from-behind win in front of a rabid, sold-out crowd at Citizens Bank Park.

With two outs in the ninth, Feliz singled in the tying run, then hit a game-winning three-run homer in the bottom of the 11th. It was the third baseman's second career walk-off home run but by far the most significant.

All signs were pointing to a Phillies loss until the ninth-inning drama unfolded.

The Phils were held to a scratch run by Dodgers starter Hiroki Kuroda through six innings.

Joe Blanton, acquired in a trade with Oakland in July, flirted with disaster in the first inning after loading the bases with one out. But after giving up a run-scoring single to James Loney, the right-hander retired the next two batters.

Los Angeles took a 2–1 lead in the seventh when Jeff Kent singled home Andre Ethier.

The Phillies mounted their game-tying rally against Jonathon Broxton, an otherwise dominant closer who, in this game, picked up the first of many scars inflicted by his tormenters from the City of Brotherly Love.

Shane Victorino opened the ninth with a single to center and moved to second on Eric Bruntlett's sacrifice bunt.

At a Glance

WP: Durbin (5–2)

HR: Feliz (13)

Key stat: Feliz 2-for-3, 4 RBIs; Victorino 2-for-4

Broxton struck out Jayson Werth, then walked pinch-hitter Andy Tracy. That brought up Feliz, who poked a singled into right. Victorino scored and the crowd erupted.

The Dodgers blew a golden opportunity in the 10th when they loaded the bases with nobody out. But reliever Chad Durbin wiggled his way out of the seemingly impossible jam by getting Casey Blake to hit a grounder to third. Feliz stepped on the bag and threw out Manny Ramirez at home for a double play. Durbin then retired Russell Martin on a fly ball to right to end the inning.

Victorino again was the catalyst in the 11th. "The Flyin' Hawaiian" opened the inning with a soft liner to left and never broke stride when he noticed left fielder Manny Ramirez make a half-hearted attempt to retrieve the ball and throw it back to the infield.

Dodger reliever Jason Johnson walked Chris Coste, and Werth moved the runners into scoring position after grounding out to second.

Feliz stepped into the box with two outs and went after the first pitch, driving it high and deep to the seats in left-center. There was a huge contingent of smiling, back-slapping teammates waiting for him by the time he arrived at home plate.

Did You Know?

The Phillies' record for most extra-inning home runs is held by Mike Schmidt. The Hall-of-Fame third baseman hit nine, three better than runner-up Dick Allen.

Jefferies, Juden Help Phils Get a Jump

Everyone got in on the act in this mauling of the Dodgers and rookie sensation Hideo Nomo. But Gregg Jefferies and Jeff Juden stood above all others for their individual contributions.

Jefferies became the first Phillie to hit for the cycle in 32 years, while Juden threw a complete game and hit a grand slam.

Hitting a single, double, triple and home run in the same game is about as rare a feat as pitching a no-hitter. Johnny Callison was the last Phillie to do it, on June 27, 1963.

But Jefferies needed only four at-bats to join Callison, Chuck Klein (twice), Cy Williams, Sam Thompson and Lave Cross on that illustrious list.

His first hit was a two-run homer off Nomo that landed in the right-field seats at Veterans Stadium.

In the third inning, Jefferies came to the plate with Mickey Morandini on third and Jim Eisenreich on first. He hit a high fly ball that sliced away from left fielder Roberto Kelly and bounced into the corner for a triple. The Phillies were winning 7–2 in the fourth when Jefferies laced a single to right with Eisenreich on first. He eventually scored as the Phils extended their lead to 14–2.

Juden highlighted the inning when he swung at a 3–2 fastball and hit a bullet into the Phillies' bullpen with the bases loaded.

One inning later, the switch-hitting Jefferies turned around to the right side to face lefty reliever John Cummings. This time he ripped a ball down the left-field line for a stand-up double.

With the cycle complete, the home crowd stood and cheered along with Jefferies' teammates and manager Jim Fregosi, who could relate to what Jefferies had done. Fregosi hit for the cycle twice when he played for the Angels.

At a Glance

WP: Juden (2–1)

HR: Jefferies (9), Juden (1)

Key stat: Jefferies 4-for-5, 4 RBIs, hits for cycle; Juden 1-for-5, 4 RBIs, grand slam

Juden, a 6-foot-7 right-hander, gave up four runs in the middle innings before settling down and coasting to his second win of the year.

After the game, Jefferies had no time to talk about his historic performance. In fact, he really didn't have to think about it. That's because his pregnant wife was experiencing labor pains, and he had to drive her to the hospital.

It's All Wilber, All the Time against Reds

Del Wilber, a journeyman backup catcher, had the game of his life as he became the only player in major league history to hit three home runs in as many at bats and to drive in and score all of his team's runs.

Wilber hit all three home runs off Reds lefty Ken Raffensberger.

"The first one I hit was a high fastball inside, the next was some kind of breaking ball inside and low and the third was a low, inside curve," said Wilber. "I guess Raffy thought I was a setup for inside stuff. He oughtn't to pitch me that close."

Ironically, Raffensberger gave up the first two of Phils catcher Andy Seminick's three home runs in one game two years earlier.

Wilber hit his first homer in the third inning, a towering drive that soared over the left-field roof at Shibe Park.

His second shot hit the roof in the fifth and his third homer flew into the upper deck in the seventh.

Wilber's unexpected power surge made a winner out of his battery mate, Ken Johnson.

At a Glance

WP: Johnson (5-4)

HR: Wilber 3 (5,6,7)

Key stat: Wilber 3-for-3, 3 RBIs; Ashburn 2-for-4

The left-handed curveball specialist pitched one of his best games of the year, shifting strategies along the way.

"We used a pattern early in the game," said Wilber. "He got the first strike with a fastball, then broke that crazy curve over. We got by that way for three innings."

When the Reds loaded the bases in the fifth, Wilber says they changed the pattern "and went to two fastballs in succession, then the curve ball."

Johnson gave up only one hit after the fifth inning. He struck out eight and walked two.

His brilliant performance followed another shutdown effort from Jocko Thompson, who limited the Reds to three hits.

Thompson and Johnson are one of only eight starting duos in team history to throw doubleheader shutouts.

© Temple University Libraries, Urban Archives

Wise Chalks Up 11 Ks, Shows Bat Prowess with Pair of Homers

In his complete game victory over the Giants, Rick Wise struck out 11 batters and once again demonstrated that he was much more than a pitcher.

Wise slammed two home runs—the second with the bases loaded—to power the Phillies to a 7–3 win.

It was the second time in the '71 season that Wise hit two homers in a game. The first was during his no-hit masterpiece against Cincinnati on June 23.

Wise was that rare breed of pitcher who took pride in his hitting. "I worked at it," he recalled. "I know I stayed in a lot of games I would have been pinch-hit for if it wasn't for my ability to swing the bat."

Rick Wise trots around toward home plate after another August homer. Wise set a franchise record for pitchers by hitting six home runs in 1971.

The Giants jumped out to a 2–0 lead, but the Phillies cut it in half in the bottom of the second when Deron Johnson doubled and scored on a single by Bobby Pfeil.

Byron Browne tied the game in the fourth with a home run to the upper deck in left field.

There were two outs and nobody on in the fifth when Wise unloaded for the first time with a shot that left the park in a hurry to give the Phils a 3–2 lead. The ball thumped against the backdrop above the bullpen in left.

San Francisco came back to tie the game in the top of the sixth after Bobby Bonds reached first on an error by shortstop Larry Bowa, stole second and scored on a double by Al Gallagher.

In the seventh, the Phillies loaded the bases on walks to Browne, Roger Freed and Tim McCarver. That brought up Wise, who was looking to hit a fly ball long enough to score the go-ahead run. He got his fly ball . . . and then some.

"I knew when I hit it, I'd get the run in from third," said Wise. "I really didn't think it was going out but it had just enough to clear the left-field fence."

It was his sixth home run of the season and the 11th and final homer of his Phillies career.

Wise shut down the Giants through the seventh, eighth, and ninth innings. He ended the game with a flourish by striking out the great Willie Mays.

Giants	AB	R	H	RBI
Henderson lf	4	0	1	0
Fuentes 2b	4	0	1	0
Bonds rf	4	2	1	0
McCovey 1b	4	1	1	1
Gallagher 3b	4	0	3	2
Healy c	2	0	0	0
Dietz ph	1	0	0	0
Speier ss	3	0	0	0
Rosario cf	3	0	1	0
Kingman ph	1	0	0	0
Cumberland p	3	0	0	0
McMahon p	0	0	0	0
Mays ph	1	0	0	0
Totals	**34**	**3**	**8**	**3**

Phillies	AB	R	H	RBI
Bowa ss	3	0	1	0
Harmon 2b	4	0	0	0
Montanez cf	4	0	0	0
Johnson 1b	4	1	1	0
Browne lf	2	1	1	1
Gamble pr-lf	1	1	0	0
Freed rf	2	1	0	0
Pfeil 3b	4	0	1	1
Ryan c	2	0	0	0
McCarver ph-c	0	1	0	0
Wise p	3	2	2	5
Totals	**29**	**7**	**6**	**7**

SF	2	0	0	0	0	1	0	0	0	-	3	8	0
PHI	0	1	0	1	1	0	4	0	X	-	7	6	1

Giants	IP	H	R	ER	BB	SO
Cumberland L (7-3)	6	5	5	5	2	1
McMahon	2	1	2	2	3	5
Totals	**8**	**6**	**7**	**7**	**5**	**6**

Phillies	IP	H	R	ER	BB	SO
Wise W (14-10)	9	8	3	2	2	11
Totals	**9**	**8**	**3**	**2**	**2**	**11**

E—Philadelphia Bowa. DP—San Francisco; Philadelphia 2. 2B—San Francisco Gallagher 2, Bonds, McCovey; Philadelphia Johnson. HR—Philadelphia Wise 2 (5,6), Browne. LOB—San Francisco 6; Philadelphia 3. SB—San Francisco Bonds. Attendance: 33,012.

Hayes Hits 3 Homers, Drives in All 6 Runs

Having rediscovered his batting stroke, Von Hayes put on one of the greatest performances of his career as he bashed three homers and drove in all six of the Phillies' runs.

The Giants would have been better off pitching around Hayes, who hit a solo shot his first time up in the top of the second. San Francisco got its only run in the bottom of the inning on a home run from Matt Williams. Hayes did it again his next time at the plate. This time there were two on in the fourth when the veteran outfielder connected off Giants right-hander Don Robinson.

While Hayes handled the offensive load, Bruce Ruffin took care of keeping the Giants' bats in check.

The 25-year-old southpaw gave up four hits and struck out four in seven innings. Not bad, considering that he wasn't even sure if he could pitch that night because of stiffness in his left shoulder.

"Maybe I should go into every start feeling like that," said Ruffin, who made the decision to pitch after warming up.

"I was really tentative at the beginning, but once I got out of the first inning, I settled down and went after them," he recalled.

Ruffin wasn't sure he'd make it out of the first. Brett Butler led off the game with a walk and Robby Thompson followed with a sharp single to right. Hayes' throw to third got by Charlie Hayes but luckily for Ruffin, the ball hit umpire John McSherry, allowing Hayes to recover it and hold Butler at third.

At a Glance

WP: Ruffin (4–8)

HR: Hayes 3 (19, 20, 21)

Key stat: Hayes 3 HRs, 6 RBIs

Will Clark hit a line smash to first baseman Ricky Jordan, who stepped on the bag to double up Thompson. Ruffin then got Kevin Mitchell to end the inning on a pop-up.

Roger McDowell relieved Ruffin in the eighth and picked up a two-inning save.

Hayes hit his third and final home run in the ninth off Craig Lefferts.

"I have never had a night like this, that's for sure," said Hayes.

Hayes' third homer gave him 21, tying his career high. He would finish the '89 season with 26.

Phils Make It a 4-Game Sweep of Mets

In a preview of the upcoming stretch drive, the Phillies came from behind and literally stole this game to complete a four-game sweep of their hated rivals.

Jayson Werth and Tad Iguchi were the thieves who put themselves in position to score the tying and winning runs off former Phillies closer Billy Wagner in the ninth inning.

The Phils appeared to be on their way to a blowout early in the game. Ryan Howard opened the scoring with his 36th home run after Jimmy Rollins led off with a double.

In the fourth, Pat Burrell and Aaron Rowand each went deep to build the lead to 5–0.

But the Mets responded with three runs in the fourth, driving starter Kyle Lohse out of the game, and scored two more times in the fifth to tie it.

The Phillies regained the lead in the bottom of the inning. Successive singles from Carlos Ruiz, Shane Victorino and Rollins plated three more runs.

The game remained 8–5 until the top of the eighth, when the Phillies' bullpen imploded. The Mets scored five runs, helped by three walks and an error, to take a 10–8 lead.

"We had kind of a meltdown in the eighth inning," said manager Charlie Manuel.

At a Glance

WP: Gordon (2–2)

HR: Howard (36), Burrell 2 (23,24), Rowand (22)

Key stat: Werth 2-for-4, 2 SBs, 2 runs; Burrell 2-for-5, 3 RBIs; Utley 2-for-5, game-winning RBI

The Phils got one back in the bottom of the eighth on Burrell's second homer of the game, this one off Wagner, who was brought in early by his desperate manager, Willie Randolph.

Wagner broke Werth's bat with a sizzling inside fastball, but the right fielder still managed to dump it into right for a leadoff single in the ninth. That's when the fun began.

With 42,552 screaming fans on their feet at Citizens Bank Park, Werth talked strategy with first-base coach Davey Lopes and made up his mind to steal.

"It was a situation where I need to be on second," said Werth. "I got a couple of reads on him. I took off and got the steal."

It turned out that Werth made the bag easily because Wagner was focusing exclusively on the batter. Realizing this, Werth took off for third on the very next pitch. And he made it.

Iguchi rewarded his hustle by belting a 1–2 pitch into right field for a game-tying single.

With Rollins now batting, Iguchi swiped second, prompting the Mets to intentionally walk the All-Star shortstop and set up a double play.

The strategy backfired when Chase Utley pounded a 3–2 fastball into right to score Iguchi with the winning run.

After the game, the Phillies were jubilant and had a lot to say about their fan support.

"This was as loud as I've ever heard it with Chase up," said Burrell.

Manuel said: "When fans are that loud, they don't let you get down, they don't let you quit or let you let up. Believe me they do play a role in the game."

It's Out with Ozark, In with Green

It was an emotional day in Atlanta as the Phillies won a ballgame but lost a manager.

Just hours before they beat the Braves to snap a five-game losing streak, the front office announced that Danny Ozark had been fired after nearly seven years on the job.

He had guided the team through its most sustained period of success in franchise history to date, having won three straight Eastern Division championships in 1976, '77 and '78. But injuries and indifference caused the team to backslide in '79. So Ozark's firing came as no surprise.

The Phillies' infield in 1979 consisted of, from left, shortstop Larry Bowa, third baseman Mike Schmidt, first baseman Pete Rose, and second baseman Manny Trillo. The foursome, however, couldn't stop an August firing of manager Danny Ozark.

He was informed of the front office's decision the day before and could have quietly left town. Instead, Ozark decided to stick around and face the cameras at a news conference.

"I understand the reasons for this, I guess," said Ozark. "The people in the front office know this team's a hell of a lot better than it's shown the last couple of days and they don't want it to fall flat on its face."

His replacement was Dallas Green, the team's farm director and polar opposite of Ozark in terms of temperament and personality.

"I held a team meeting with the club and I told them the truth," Green said. "I'm not after anybody's butt, but I want to see why we haven't been winning. There's got to be a reason with all this talent. My job is to figure it out."

Green was a winner in his managerial debut as the Phils plastered three Braves pitchers for 13 hits and six runs.

The Phils scored one in the first when Bake McBride singled, stole second, went to third on an errant throw and scored on Manny Trillo's sacrifice fly.

Mike Schmidt hit a two-run homer in the third to give starter Doug Bird a 3–0 lead.

In the fifth, the Phils scored three more runs on five consecutive singles, with Schmidt, Greg Luzinski and Bob Boone picking up RBIs.

Bird got Dale Murphy to pop up for the first out in the bottom of the sixth. At that point the rains came and the game was called, a fitting ending to a dreary, dismal day in Phillies history.

Larry Bowa may have summed it best when he said: "If this were a fair world, 18 players would get fired."

At a Glance

WP: Bird (2–0)

HR: Schmidt (41)

Key stat: Schmidt 2-for-4, 3 RBIs; Rose 2-for-4, 2 runs; Trillo 2-for-3, RBI

SEPTEMBER/ OCTOBER

Schilling Strikes Out 16 Yankees in Gem

The New York Yankees came to town for an interleague series with the Phillies, but Curt Schilling stole the spotlight as the right-hander dominated the defending World Champions with a 16-strikeout performance.

As a jacked-up crowd of nearly 51,000 fans looked on, along with a nationally televised audience, Schilling overpowered the Bombers with a fastball that was consistently clocked in the upper 90 mph range.

He set the tone in the first inning by blowing away leadoff hitter Derek Jeter with three straight heaters, then tore through the heart of the Yankees lineup, striking out five of the first six batters he faced.

The Phils bunched a pair of runs together in the first and three more in the fourth, providing a big boost for Schilling, who allowed just seven hits and walked none through his eight brilliant innings.

He saved his best stuff for the Yankees' Big Three; Jeter, Paul O'Neill, and Tino Martinez. In 12 trips to the plate, they struck out 10 times.

Jeter whiffed four times and could only shake his head when asked his assessment of Schilling.

At a Glance

WP: Schilling (14–10)

HR: Barron (3)

Key stat: Schilling 16 Ks; Morandini 3-for-4; Rolen 2-for-4, RBI

"You're asking the wrong person. I didn't even it see it, man."

"He chewed us up and spit us out," marveled Yankees manager Joe Torre.

Schilling's 16 strikeouts were the most for a Phillies pitcher since Steve Carlton punched out 16 Chicago Cubs on June 9, 1982. He may have tied Art Mahaffey's club record of 17 strikeouts, or even the National League mark of 19 had he not been taken out after the eighth inning. But Schilling did not disagree with manager Terry Francona's move to bring in Ricky Bottalico.

"Terry and I talked, "Schilling said. "We decided if I had an easy eighth, I'd go out for the ninth. But the eighth wasn't that easy."

Schilling struck out the first two batters before giving up back-to-back singles to Wade Boggs and Bernie Williams. He fanned Martinez for the third time to end the inning.

In addition to picking up his 14th win of the season, Schilling ended the day as the league leader in strikeouts with 280. Later in the month he broke Steve Carlton's club record of 310 strikeouts and finished the season with 319.

Phils End Marathon on Rocky Mountain High

The Phillies were unable to put anything together at hitter-friendly Coors Field for six innings, then exploded for nine runs in the seventh and held on to beat the Rockies.

Charlie Manuel and his troops were on their way home from a wildly successful West Coast trip when they parachuted into Denver for a quick make-up game with the Rockies. Instead, they became embroiled in a four-hour marathon that featured a combined 35 hits, six homers, 23 runs and 14 pitchers used.

Colorado rocked Joe Blanton for six runs on 10 hits, including a pair of second-inning home runs from Chris Iannetta and Dexter Fowler. Blanton was removed with one out in the fifth.

At a Glance

WP: Bastardo (1–0)

HR: Howard (25), Utley (12), Werth (19)

Key stat: Utley 2-for-4, 6 RBIs; Werth 3-for-5, RBI, 3 runs; Ibanez 2-for-5, RBI

Meanwhile, Rockies rookie Jhoulys Chacin held the Phillies scoreless and hitless until the fourth, when Raul Ibanez smacked an RBI single to center.

The Phillies trailed 7–3 when Placido Polanco led off the seventh with a double to left. Chase Utley knocked him in with a single and advanced to second on a wild pitch by reliever Joe Beimel.

Ryan Howard then delivered a two-run homer and Jayson Werth followed with a game-tying solo blast to left.

"With what we've accomplished over the past few years and what we've done here, you can't count us out. We're resilient," said Werth.

The hits kept coming. Ben Francisco's RBI single gave the Phils their first lead, and Utley capped the amazing inning with a grand slam. He finished the day with a career-high six RBIs.

The Phils were now holding a 12–7 lead. They would need every one of those runs. Chad Durbin was rocked for three runs on four hits in the seventh. He was replaced in the eighth by Jose Contreras, who got out of a bases-loaded jam.

That set the stage for Brad Lidge's nail-biting ninth. Fowler reached on an error by Howard, moved to third on a single to right by Carlos Gonzalez and scored on Troy Tulowitzki's grounder to second to make it a one-run game.

But Lidge struck out Clint Barmes and got Ryan Spilborghs to ground into a force at third to end the game and pick up his 19th save.

September 3, 1917
Philadelphia 9, Robins 3 (Game 2)

© National Baseball Hall of Fame

Alexander the Great Starts, Completes, Wins Doubleheader

There was little fanfare when Grover Cleveland Alexander walked off the mound after beating the Brooklyn Robins. After all, baseball fans were used to seeing the great right-hander do amazing things year after year since he broke into the majors in 1911. He was about to complete his third consecutive season with at least 30 wins.

But no one today could conceive of even attempting to do what Alexander the Great accomplished on a Monday afternoon at Ebbets Field.

It was Labor Day, and the 30-year-old right-hander was the hardest working man in baseball as he started, completed and won both ends of a doubleheader.

Grover Cleveland Alexander's 1915 season is the stuff of legends: a 31-10 record with a 1.22 ERA. He ranks tied for third all-time in major league wins with 373.

In Game 1, Alexander threw a four-hit shutout to lead the Phils to a 5–0 win.

He got all of 15 minutes to relax, then went right back out for the start of Game 2.

Dode Paskert gave Alexander a comfortable three-run cushion when he hit a bases-loaded triple off Robins starter Jack Coombs in the top of the second.

The Phillies got another run in the third when Fred Luderus was hit by a pitch and scored on George "Possum" Whitted's triple to the left-field corner. Whitted attempted to extend his hit to an inside-the-park home run but was tagged out at the plate.

The Robins finally broke through, scoring their first run of the day off Alexander in the bottom of the fourth. Myers led off the inning with a double. Alexander got the next two batters to fly out before giving up an RBI single to Zach Wheat.

But the Phillies quickly squashed any thoughts of a comeback when they scored again in the fifth on a double by Milt Stock and a run-scoring single by Fred Luderus.

Brooklyn scored its second run in the bottom of the sixth. After putting runners at the corners, Frank O'Rourke hit a two-out tapper to third. Stock was unable to come up with the ball as Jim Hickman raced home.

Ed Delahanty

He was a five-tool player in a four-tool era. "Big Ed" Delahanty could do it all, and then some.

He started his career with the Phillies in 1888, but Delahanty didn't really distinguish himself until 1892, when he batted .306.

After that, Big Ed dominated the decade, hitting for both average and power. He batted .400 or better three times, with a career-best .410 average in 1899, led the league in slugging percentage four times and was tops in RBIs three times. His .346 lifetime batting average is fourth-highest in major league history.

Delahanty also led the National League twice in home runs, three times in RBIs, and four times in doubles. In 1896, he became just the second player to hit four homers in one game.

In addition to his prowess at the plate, Big Ed was one of the finest outfielders of his generation, with exceptional range and a powerful arm.

Once again, though, the Phillies demoralized Brooklyn by scoring a run their next time up.

They added three more runs in the ninth to wrap up the unforgettable double-dip victory for their pitcher.

Alexander's numbers for the day were staggering: 18 innings pitched, three runs, 13 hits, one walk.

At a Glance

WP: Alexander

Key stat: Whitted 3-for-4, RBI; Paskert 2-for-5, 3 RBIs

Estalella Sets Rookie Mark with 3 Homers

Bobby Estalella put on an astonishing display of raw power as the 23-year-old became the first rookie in team history to hit three home runs in a game.

Manager Terry Francona had a hard time believing what he had seen after the Phillies beat the Expos at Olympic Stadium.

"I'm not sure it's supposed to be that easy," he said. "The most home runs I ever hit in one season was three. He did it in an hour and a half. And look who he did it against."

Estalella brutalized Pedro Martinez, the eventual 1997 Cy Young Award winner. And he was blissfully ignorant about his mound opponent.

"I didn't know that much about him," Estalella confessed. "They tell me he's pretty good."

The muscular catcher hit his first homer in the top of the second, a first-pitch solo blast that tied the game 1–1.

In the sixth, Estalella surprised Martinez by swinging at a 3–0 fastball. His two-run rocket into the left-field stands gave the Phillies a 5–4 lead. Francona gave him the green light.

"Why not?" asked the Phils' skipper. "He showed us he's not afraid, didn't he?"

Estalella chiseled his name into the team record book in the ninth inning with another solo shot, giving him three home runs and four RBIs for the game. Not bad for a guy who had just been called up to the big club from Triple A.

At a Glance

WP: Beech (4–8)

HR: Estalella 3 (1,2,3); Brogna (17)

Key stat: Estalella 3-for-4, 4 RBIs; Brogna 2-for-4, RBI

"This really hasn't sunk in yet," Estalella said. "I was just trying to do my job and things ended up working out better than I expected."

Estalella was also solid behind the plate, guiding lefty Matt Beech to his fourth win of the season.

LC Uses Arm, Allen's Bat to Halt Woes

Demonstrating the maturity of an old pro, 22-year-old Larry Christenson ended the first-place Phillies' eight-game losing streak with his arm and Dick Allen's formidable bat.

Christenson hit two homers and held the Mets to one run over 8 $^{2}/_{3}$ innings; impressive numbers, considering that he almost didn't survive the first inning.

"We were already going downhill and I loaded the bases and ended up giving up a run but got out of the jam," Christenson recalled.

LC tied the game with his first home run in the third, using Allen's war club.

"I broke both of my 36-inch, 36-ounce bats in batting practice. Bobby Wine sawed me off and he's laughing at me. But I don't have a bat," Christenson said.

So he approached Allen.

"He always walked around with a bat in his hand. And he handed me this bat of his and he said, 'Son, if you can swing it, you can use it.'"

At a Glance

WP: Christenson (11–8)

HR: Christenson 2 (1,2)

Key stat: Christenson 2-for-3, 2 RBIs; 2 runs

The Phils took a 2–1 in the sixth after Garry Maddox led off with a single, advanced to third and scored on a sacrifice fly by Greg Luzinski.

Christenson produced the Phillies' final run with another tape-measure job in the eighth, using Allen's bat again. The bat was 36 inches long and weighed 42 ounces, but Christenson had no problems using it.

"Joe Torre, the Mets third baseman, told me both home runs added up to 900 feet," he said.

Allen was also impressed.

"They were major league homers," he said.

Both were hit off Mickey Lolich. After the second one, Christenson remembered a bizarre development.

"Lolich ends up walking off the mound. Not being taken out of the game but walks off the mound. When I crossed home plate on the second home run he kept walking. And I'm going, 'That's really weird!'"

The veteran southpaw came back to pitch to one more batter. But after Dave Cash singled, Mets manager Joe Frazier came out and removed his humiliated starter.

The victory was huge for the Phils, who were beginning to hear whispers about the blown pennant of 1964 after watching their 15.5-game lead over the second-place Pirates melt away.

Coupled with the Pirates' loss to Montreal, they were now 7.5 games in front, three weeks away from winning their first division championship.

Did You Know?

The team record for position players who have hit home runs in consecutive games is five.

Dick Allen set the standard in 1969. Mike Schmidt matched it in 1979. Twenty-six years later, Bobby Abreu turned the trick, and Chase Utley did it twice in 2008.

September 8, 1998
Phillies 16, Mets 4

7 Homers Puts '98 Phils in Record Book

They weren't considered a power-hitting team, but the 1998 Phillies put on a one-game slugging exhibition unequaled in franchise history.

In their 16–4 battering of the Mets, the Phils set a team record by hitting seven home runs.

Marlon Anderson was the unlikely hitter to break the record. The rookie second baseman was up for the first time as a big leaguer when he slammed a pinch-hit two-run homer into the Phillies' bullpen.

"This is unbelievable," he said. "I could never have dreamed anything like this could happen in my first big league at-bat."

Rico Brogna got the long-ball parade started in the first inning with a solo homer.

In the third, Kevin Sefcik and Bobby Estalella each went yard as part of a five-run inning that ended a miserable night for Mets starter Hideo Nomo, who gave up seven runs.

Brogna hit his second homer of the night and 20th of the season in the bottom of the fifth, a two-run blast off Brad Clontz. It also gave him 100 RBIs for the first time in his career.

"This was a magic night," said Brogna. "Home runs are in the air. Everyone has caught the fever."

Including Sefcik, who came into the game with one homer all season. In the bottom of the sixth, he hit his second of the night.

"It's kind of amazing," he said.

At a Glance

WP: Byrd (3–2)

HR: Brogna 2 (19,20), Estelella 2 (6,7), Sefcik 2 (2,3), Anderson (1)

Key stat: Phillies set team record with 7 HRs

Estalella was no stranger to multiple-home run games, having hit three in game as a rookie in 1997.

He blasted his second of the game in the bottom of the seventh.

Scott Rolen, the Phillies' home run leader, failed to connect, but still managed to get involved in this magical game, joining Brogna by driving in his 100th run of the season. The 23-year-old third baseman also became the youngest Phillie in modern history to reach the 100 RBI mark.

Phillies 5, Pirates 4 (14 innings)

Squeeze Bunt Gives Phils Surge to World Series

It took 14 excruciatingly tense innings for the Phillies to finally dispatch their division rivals in one of the most thrilling games in team history.

It was a game that ended not with a bang, but with a gentle squeeze—as in bunt. Bob Boone laid it down as Garry Maddox slid head first into home with the winning run.

The Phils put themselves into position to win after scuffling back from a 4–2 deficit.

Pittsburgh broke up a 2–2 tie in the seventh by roughing up Steve Carlton for a pair of runs.

Garry Maddox barrels into home plate following Bob Boone's bunt on Sept. 9, 1980.

Phillies 5, Pirates 4 (14 innings)

But the Phillies' big boppers sparked a two-out rally in the eighth. Mike Schmidt brought the Vet Stadium crowd to life by slamming a two-out run-scoring triple to left off reliever Kent Tekulve. Greg Luzinski then singled to bring Schmidt home with the tying run.

The Pirates had a chance to go ahead in the 12th. With Mike Easler on first and Matt Alexander on second, Bill Madlock hit a one-out grounder to third. Schmidt threw to Manny Trillo as Easler slid hard into the bag to break up the double play. Trillo dropped the ball but the ump ruled he held on long enough for the force-out.

Meanwhile, Alexander kept running and made a dash for home. Trillo retrieved the ball and threw a laser to Boone in plenty of time to tag the runner and end the inning.

Maddox opened the 14th inning with a double to the gap in left-center. Larry Bowa made two failed attempts to bunt him over to third, then got the job done by hitting a chopper to first.

Manager Dallas Green was thinking "squeeze" from the moment Bob Boone stepped out of the on-deck circle.

As Maddox took off, the veteran catcher squared around and bunted reliever Mark Lee's first pitch back toward the mound. Lee, in a panic, threw the ball over catcher Ed Ott's head as Maddox slid across the plate with the winning run.

At a Glance

WP: Brusstar (2–0)

Key stat: Luzinski 2-for-4, RBI; Maddox 2-for-6

"That, gentleman, was a very, very satisfying win, I'll tell you that," said manager Dallas Green. "That's called grinding it out. I couldn't be prouder right now."

The win effectively eliminated the Pirates from the pennant race and gave the Phillies a surge of momentum that would carry them into the playoffs and World Series.

In the locker room, Lee Elia went out on a limb and made this prediction:

"I think we're going to win it. The coaches have been talking about it lately. They guys are showing enthusiasm out there—and it's rubbing off on everybody."

Bystrom Overcomes Pennant Fever with Shutout vs. Mets

Making his first big-league start in the thick of a pennant race, 22-year-old Marty Bystrom gave a spectacular performance, holding the Mets to just five hits as he tossed a complete game shutout.

Bystrom made his major league debut a few days earlier, throwing one scoreless inning against the Dodgers.

He wasn't supposed to start against the Mets. But with Larry Christenson down with an injury, manager Dallas Green needed a body, so he turned to the rookie who had turned heads in the spring.

"I was pretty much penciled in as a starter in big-league camp but I pulled a hamstring and missed half the season," recalled Bystrom. "I didn't really pitch until July. In August I ripped off six straight wins in Oklahoma City and got called up in September."

The Phillies gave their young starter plenty of room to maneuver by scoring three runs in the first. Pete Rose opened the game with a double and scored on Bake McBride's single. After Mike Schmidt grounded out, Greg Luzinski knocked in McBride with a double to left then scored on a single to center by Garry Maddox.

At a Glance

WP: Bystrom (1–0)

Key stat: Bystrom's first big-league win

Bystrom took the mound in the bottom of the inning and struck out the first hitter he faced, Mookie Wilson. Frank Taveras singled and stole second but advanced no further as Bystrom retired the next two hitters.

The 6-foot-5 right-hander was cool and calm all night as he banged the strike zone with four pitches and got ahead of the hitters.

Only two of the five hits Bystrom surrendered left the infield, and not one Mets base runner reached third.

"Pitching's all about confidence and I had a lot of it at that time, which makes all the difference in the world."

Manager Dallas Green didn't seem surprised at Bystrom's performance.

"I've known he could do this for some time," he said. "The thing that I really like about him is his demeanor out there, the way he conducts himself."

Bystrom said he didn't know much about the Mets but didn't really care. "I had pretty good stuff and I didn't get real nervous about it. . . . But this has to be the tops of all time for me—at least for now."

Bystrom was just getting cranked up. He would go on to win his next four starts, helping the Phillies win a division title, and make two appearances in the postseason.

His amazing six-week ride in the big leagues would end on a float—in a parade down Broad Street.

Did You Know?

Only eight players have spent their entire career with the Phillies.

Mike Schmidt tops the list with 18 years of service. Larry Christenson is a distant second with 11.

Terry Harmon and Bob Miller each played 10 years. Putsy Caballero had eight while John Boozer, George Chalmers and Jack Meyer played all seven of their big-league seasons in Philadelphia.

Festival of Homers Puts '04 Phils at the Top

Home runs dominated this wacky extra-inning game at Shea Stadium.

Todd Pratt's second-inning blast was the Phillies' 187th of the season, breaking the team record set in 1975. September call-up Ryan Howard hit his first major league homer. And David Bell's second home run of the day, a two-run shot in the 13th, won the game.

The Phillies celebrated by shaving the head of manager Larry Bowa, who told the players they could grab the clippers and razor and have at it if they won five games in a row, something they hadn't accomplished all season.

"Everybody got a piece of me," Bowa said after watching his troops play catch-up for much of the afternoon.

They had to dig out of an early hole after starter Eric Milton gave up six runs in five innings. David Bell made it a 6–3 game with his first home run in the top of the sixth, and Howard, batting for pitcher Geoff Geary, uncorked his first big-league blast in the seventh.

"It was great," said the 24-year-old rookie, "because both teams were battling and it helped us."

His two-run homer brought the Phils to within one. In the eighth, Pat Burrell put the Phillies in front for the first time with a two-run blast. But the lead didn't last long as the bullpen saw its 28-inning scoreless streak come to an end.

At a Glance

WP: Hernandez (3–5)

HR: Pratt (1), Bell 2 (14,15), Howard (1), Burrell (21)

Key stat: Bell 4-for-7, 4 RBIs; Pratt 2-for-6, 2 RBIs; Howard 1-for-1, first big-league HR, 2 RBIs

Rheal Cormier gave up a single and a walk and was replaced by right-hander Tim Worrell, who surrendered a two-out game-tying single to Jeff Keppinger.

In the ninth, the Phils bunched together four singles to take a 9–7 lead. And then, things turned weird. Billy Wagner came in, blew the save and was thrown out of the game after throwing a 1–0 fastball up and in to Cliff Floyd. Umpire Dana DeMuth believed he was throwing at the batter.

Wagner got into a heated argument with DeMuth and had to be restrained. He was escorted to the dugout, where the enraged lefty grabbed a water cooler and threw it onto the field, followed by some paper cups.

The game moved into extra innings and was finally decided by Bell's home run.

September 12, 1961
Phillies 19, Dodgers 10

Demeter Thrives as Last-Place Phils Explode against Koufax

Sitting on the worst record in baseball, the last-place Phillies unleashed a season's worth of frustration as they bombarded the Dodgers for 19 runs on 17 hits at L.A. Memorial Coliseum. They also got to play the role of spoiler by dropping the Dodgers 4.5 games behind the first-place Cincinnati Reds.

> **At a Glance**
>
> **WP:** Short (6-10)
>
> **HR:** Demeter (19, 20, 21), Amaro (1), C. Smith (11)
>
> **Key stat:** Demeter 4-for-5, 7 RBIs, 5 runs; Amaro 3-for-4, 2 RBIs, 3 runs; Dalrymple 3-for-5, 3 RBIs

Don Demeter and Ruben Amaro spearheaded the hitting barrage. Demeter had his finest hitting performance as a pro, going 4-for-5 with three homers

Don Demeter, shown waiting for a late throw as Willie Mays slides in safely to third base in 1962, put on a game to remember on Sept. 12, 1961. Demeter smacked three home runs and drove in seven runs in a 19–10 win over Sandy Koufax and the Dodgers.

and seven RBIs, while Amaro had three hits, including his first career home run. Demeter got started right away, belting a two-run homer in the first. The Dodgers came back with four in the bottom of the inning as they knocked Phils starter John Buzhardt out of the game. The big blow was a three-run homer by Wally Moon.

But there was no stopping the Phils, who gave Sandy Koufax one of the worst beatings of his career.

Amaro set the tone with a leadoff triple. Six hits, one error and nine runs later, the Phillies had an 11–4 lead. Koufax retired only one batter in the second before he was lifted. His line: 1 $\frac{1}{3}$ innings, 5 hits, 6 runs.

The onslaught continued in the third with the Phils plating three more runs. Their bats cooled down through the middle innings before heating up again in the seventh.

After a double by Bobby Malkmus and a single by Charley Smith, Demeter unloaded his second home run of the game to increase the lead to 17–5.

The Dodgers scored two in their half of the inning, only to see the Phils score another run in the eighth on Amaro's first big-league homer.

Demeter fittingly capped the scoring in the top of the ninth with his third home run of the game. He was now the hottest hitter in the majors with five homers and 14 RBIs in his last four games.

Moreover, the soft-spoken outfielder had just completed the greatest game of his career against the team that traded him to the Phillies.

"I enjoyed every minute of it," he said.

Chris Short

One of the top power-pitching lefties of the 1960s, Chris Short put together some magnificent seasons during his 14 years in Philadelphia.

Short's breakout year was 1964, when he went 17–9 with a career-best earned-run average of 2.20 and represented the Phillies at the All-Star Game.

He was a 20-game winner for the only time in 1966, but Short's best all-around season was in '65, when he went 18–11 with 237 strikeouts and a 2.82 ERA.

Short is fourth on the Phillies' all-time wins list with 132.

Short Trumps Koufax, Dodgers Behind 14 Ks

In a battle between two flame-throwers, Chris Short out-dueled Sandy Koufax setting a franchise record for strikeouts by a left-hander in the process.

Koufax, winner of 23 games, gave up five hits and struck out eight in seven innings. Short mowed down 14 Dodgers while allowing only four hits over nine.

Amazingly, both pitchers came into this game on only two days' rest, yet were still able to overpower the hitters.

The Phils manufactured a run off Koufax in the seventh, thanks to some heads-up base running from Don Hoak. The veteran third baseman singled to right with one out. When Koufax threw a breaking ball that bounced away from catcher John Roseboro, Hoak took off for second and kept going to third when he noticed Roseboro was slow to retrieve ball near the seats behind home plate.

Bob Oldis then surprised the Dodgers' infield by dropping a bunt down the third-base line, allowing Hoak to cross home plate standing up.

At a Glance

WP: Short (7–11)

Key stat: Hoak 2-for-3, run; Gonzalez 2-for-4, run; Short 14 Ks

Short carried a two-hit shutout into the ninth, only to see his masterpiece disintegrate in a matter of minutes. Tommy Davis led off the inning with a single up the middle. Frank Howard, the 6-foot-8 power hitter who had struck out in his three previous at-bats, tomahawked a high fastball into the upper deck in left, silencing the crowd at Connie Mack Stadium.

"When he hit that home run I almost died," Short said. "That was the only pitch that I made to him all night that was over the plate, and he hit it into the seats."

Manager Gene Mauch marveled at Howard's strength.

"Nobody else in the world could hit a baseball that high and get it out of the park in that wind."

The ninth began with Tony Gonzalez ripping a single to center off Larry Sherry, who had replaced Koufax in the eighth inning. Roy Sievers squared around to bunt and was hit by a pitch.

Sherry was lifted for left-hander Ron Perranoski, causing Mauch to respond by sending in right-handed pinch-hitter Ruben Amaro, who bunted both runners into scoring position.

Hoak was intentionally walked to load the bases and set up a double play. It was a strategy that appeared to work when Bob Oldis hit a grounder right at second baseman Junior Gilliam, who flipped to Maury Wills for the force.

But Hoak got a great jump at first and barreled into the shortstop in a desperate attempt to break up the double play.

An off-balance Wills threw wildly past first base, allowing Gonzalez and pinch runner Dick Allen to dash home with the tying and winning runs.

The Dodgers stood slack-jawed as the crowd roared and the Phillies celebrated at home plate.

September 14, 1962

Phillies 2, Cardinals 1

Callison's Back-to-Back Walk-Off Homers a First

The Phillies' long history is filled with batters who've hit game-winning home runs. No one had ever hit a walk-off in successive games until Johnny Callison came along.

On September 13, the young, talented right fielder took Hall of Famer Warren Spahn deep with one out in the bottom of the ninth to give the Phils a thrilling 2–1 win over the Milwaukee Braves at Connie Mack Stadium.

The next night, he did it again. Callison's victims this time were the St. Louis Cardinals.

Rookie Dennis Bennett was sensational as he struck out 13 while holding the Cardinals to five hits. But veteran right-hander Larry Jackson was equally impressive, limiting the Phillies to just three hits over eight innings. Neither pitcher issued a walk.

The Phillies struck first when Tony Taylor led off the game with a single, stole second and scored on Callison's single.

After that, Jackson put the Phillies' lineup into a coma, retiring the next 20 batters. Bennett had a one-hitter through six and carried a shutout into the ninth.

Red Schoendienst, batting for Jackson, led off the final inning with a single to center and pinch runner Bob Gibson was forced out at second on Julian Javier's bunt. Javier then moved to third on a base hit by Stan Musial.

Javier scored the tying run when Curt Flood grounded into a force at second.

At a Glance

WP: Bennett (7–9)

HR: Callison (21)

Key stat: Callison 2-for-4, 2 RBIs; Bennett 13 Ks

In the bottom of the ninth, Jackson was relieved by Lindy McDaniel, who quickly retired Taylor on a grounder to third and struck out Bobby Klaus.

But Callison was another matter. The 23-year-old laid into a fastball, sending it far over the right-field fence by the scoreboard, and went into his victory trot around the bases for the second night in a row.

It was the 21st home run for Callison, who was enjoying a breakout season in which he batted .300 with 23 homers and 83 RBIs.

Ennis Provides the Drama in 19-Inning Affair against Reds

The longest game in Shibe Park's history was also one of the most exciting and nerve-wracking.

The Whiz Kids scored two runs in the bottom of the ninth to force extra innings, then tied it again with two runs in the bottom of the 18th before winning the game in the 19th inning on a bases-loaded single by Del Ennis in the second game of a doubleheader. The Phillies also won the opener 2–1.

The Reds looked like they were going to have an easy win after building a 5–0 lead against Robin Roberts through six innings.

But in the bottom of the seventh, the Phillies began to show a pulse as they scored two runs off Reds starter Howie Fox.

They were trailing 5–3 in the bottom of the ninth when Ennis smacked a one-out single to left. Stan Hollmig, batting for left fielder Jackie Mayo, came up with a big double to put runners on second and third, and Granny Hamner followed with a two-bagger to tie the game.

The focus was now on the bullpens. Herm Wehmeier and Jim Konstanty each entered the game for their respective teams in the ninth and settled in for what turned out to be an epic battle of relief pitchers.

Wehmeier went 9 $^{2}/_{3}$ inninngs, Konstanty 10. Neither got the decision, though Konstanty nearly got tagged with the loss. In the 18th, he walked the bases loaded, then gave up a two-run single to Ted Kluszewski. The right-hander avoided further damage by getting Joe Adcock to ground into an inning-ending double play.

Konstanty faced 41 batters, allowed two runs on six hits, struck out three and walked six.

In the bottom of the inning, the Phils struck back. Ennis doubled and went to third on Dick Sisler's single. After Hamner flied to center to score Ennis, Stan Lopata cracked a triple to score Sisler with the tying run.

Blix Donnelly, in relief of Konstanty, held the Reds scoreless in the 19th, setting the stage for the dramatic finish.

Wehmeier's replacement, Eddie Erautt, gave up a leadoff single to Eddie Waitkus. Richie Ashburn laid down a sacrifice bunt that turned into a single when the ball rolled down the line, hit a pebble and stopped in fair territory. An

September 15, 1950
Phillies 8, Reds 7 (19 innings) (Game 2)

irritated Erautt then walked Willie Jones to load the bases for Ennis. The Reds drew their infield and outfield in, but could only watch helplessly as Ennis hit a scorching liner over their heads to the wall in left. His fifth hit of the game was the game-winner.

The next day's *Philadelphia Evening Bulletin* described the moment this way:

"Never will a louder cheer go up at any game than the one which saluted Ennis when he cracked the single in the 19th inning with the bases loaded, scoring Eddie Waitkus from third with the winning run."

The victory completed a doubleheader sweep of Cincinnati and gave the first-place Phillies a 7.5-game lead over the Brooklyn Dodgers.

Reds	AB	R	H	RBI
Merriman cf	8	2	3	1
Hatton 3b	7	1	3	0
Wyrostek rf	8	1	0	0
Kluszewski 1b	6	1	2	2
Adcock lf	9	0	3	2
Usher lf	0	0	0	0
Ryan 2b	9	0	1	0
Stallcup ss	9	0	1	1
Howell c	9	1	2	0
Fox p	4	1	0	0
Raffensberger p	0	0	0	0
Wehmeier p	4	0	0	0
Tappe ph	1	0	0	0
Erautt p	0	0	0	0
Totals	**74**	**7**	**15**	**6**

Phillies	AB	R	H	RBI
Waitkus 1b	9	2	5	0
Ashburn cf	9	0	2	0
Jones 3b	9	0	1	1
Ennis rf	10	2	5	2
Mayo lf	4	0	0	0
Hollmig ph	1	0	1	0
Caballero pr	0	1	0	0
Sisler lf	4	1	1	0
Hamner ss	8	1	2	3
Seminick c	2	0	1	0
Lopata c	4	0	1	1
Goliat 2b	9	1	2	0
Roberts p	2	0	0	0
Whitman ph	1	0	0	0
Brittin p	0	0	0	0
Bloodworth ph	1	0	1	1
Johnson pr	0	0	0	0
Konstanty p	4	0	1	0
Silvestri ph	1	0	0	0
Donnelly p	0	0	0	0
Totals	**78**	**8**	**23**	**8**

CIN 0 0 3 1 1 0 0 0 0 0 0 0 0 0 0 0 0 2 0 - 7 15 1
PHI 0 0 0 0 0 0 2 1 2 0 0 0 0 0 0 0 0 2 1 - 8 23 4

Reds	IP	H	R	ER	BB	SO
Fox	7.1	9	3	1	4	2
Raffensberger	1	0	0	0	0	2
Wehmeier	9.2	11	4	4	2	1
Erautt L (3-2)	0	3	1	1	1	0
Totals	**18**	**23**	**8**	**6**	**7**	**5**

Phillies	IP	H	R	ER	BB	SO
Roberts	7	8	5	2	1	3
Brittin	1	0	0	0	0	1
Konstanty	10	6	2	2	6	3
Donnelly W (1-4)	1	1	0	0	0	0
Totals	**19**	**15**	**7**	**4**	**7**	**7**

E—Cincinnati Ryan; Philadelphia Hamner 3, Waitkus. DP—Philadelphia 2. 2B—Cincinnati Howell, Ryan; Philadelphia Hamner 2, Ennis, Hollmig, Waitkus 2, Goliat. 3B—Philadelphia Lopata. LOB—Cincinnati 17; Philadelphia 23. SB—Cincinnati Merriman, Hatton; Philadelphia Ashburn. Attendance: 20,673.

Native Philadelphian Del Ennis chalked up 126 RBIs to lead the Phillies to the 1950 National League pennant, their first in 35 years. He was a three-time All-Star.

Phillies

Schmidt's First Homer Comes with Parents in Attendance

The greatest third baseman in baseball history began his journey to the Hall of Fame with his first career home run in this game against the Montreal Expos.

At the time, minor leaguer Michael Jack Schmidt was just another September call-up hoping to make an impression on the front office.

The Phillies were trailing 1–0 in the seventh inning when Terry Harmon kick-started the winning rally with a single and went to third on a perfectly executed hit-and-run with Greg Luzinski.

Joe Lis hit a hard liner to the left side but shortstop Tim Foli made a diving catch and easily doubled up Luziniski, who was running with the pitch.

Roger Freed was the next batter, but Expos manager Gene Mauch went against conventional wisdom and ordered an intentional walk to get a crack at the unknown third baseman.

With his parents in attendance at Veterans Stadium, watching him play in a big-league uniform for the first time, the 22-year-old Schmidt launched a towering fly ball off Balor Moore that sailed over the 371 foot sign in left-center for a three-run homer.

At a Glance

WP: Twitchell (4–8)

HR: Schmidt (1)

Key Stat: Schmidt first career HR

His timely hit made a winner out of first-year starter Wayne Twitchell.

"It was a big thrill, for me and my parents," said Schmidt, who was promoted to the big club after hitting 26 home runs in the Pacific Coast League.

"I consider myself a power hitter in the sense that a power hitter is someone who doesn't have to get all of the ball to hit it out," said Schmidt. "I didn't get all of that one tonight. I got it down on the end of the bat. I really didn't have any idea it was going out."

Schmidt also didn't know that he was going to hit 548 career home runs.

But as the saying goes: "The journey of a thousand miles begins with a single step."

Rollins Shows Signs of an MVP in Debut

In his big-league debut, Jimmy Rollins gave Phillies fans a glimpse into the future.

Flashing the electrifying talent that would someday make him an MVP, the speedy shortstop went 2-for-4, stole the first base of his career and scored his first two runs to spark the Phils to a 6–5 win over Florida.

Manager Terry Francona liked what he saw: "You certainly don't judge a guy by one game, but it looks like with his speed and what he does at shortstop, it may give us another dimension."

The 21-year-old switch-hitter drew a walk in his first at-bat and scored his first run when Bobby Abreu whacked his 24th home run of the season.

"Getting that first at-bat out of the way and getting on base took a little edge off for me," Rollins said.

In the bottom of the third he unleashed his blinding speed after ripping a Chuck Smith fastball into the right-field corner. As he approached second, Rollins kicked it into high gear, rounded the bag and raced into third with a triple. However, he was left stranded after Abreu, Pat Burrell, and Travis Lee each struck out.

At a Glance

WP: Wolf (11–7)

HR: Abreu (24)

Key stat: Rollins 2-for-4, 2 runs, SB; Abreu 2-for-4, 2 RBIs, 2 runs

The Phillies were clinging to a 3–2 lead when Rollins jump-started a seventh-inning rally with a leadoff single and stolen base. After Abreu walked, J-Roll scored on a single by Burrell.

Pinch-hitter Brian Hunter and Kevin Jordan each followed with RBI singles to give the Phils a 6–2 lead.

The Marlins nearly tied the game in the ninth inning as they rocked closer Jeff Brantley for three runs. But rookie left-hander Tom Jacquez came in and struck out Mark Kotsay to end the game and an eye-opening debut for the heir apparent at shortstop.

"It all depends on who you talk to," said Francona. "A couple of months ago, it didn't seem like he was going to be ready, but as the season progressed, it seemed like the reports got better."

Rollins admitted he was so excited about the prospect of playing in his first big-league game that he had trouble sleeping the night before.

September 18, 1971
Phillies 4, Cubs 3

Wise Back Up to His Antics with 32 Outs in a Row vs. Cubs

Rick Wise did it again. Three months after the Phillies' right-hander became the only pitcher in big-league history to throw a no-hitter and hit two home runs in the same game, he put on another Herculean performance.

Wise retired 32 batters in a row and collected three hits, including the game-winning single in the 12th inning to beat the Cubs at Veterans Stadium.

He left teammates shaking their heads in disbelief.

"That is known as doing it all," said Jim Bunning.

Wise said the no-hitter against the Reds was still his biggest thrill, "but this has to rank right up there because I had to battle back."

He got off to a shaky start, giving up three runs on four hits over the first two innings.

In the top of the first, Pat Bourque hit a hanging curveball for a solo homer. The Cubs added another run on an error by first baseman Greg Luzinski and two singles.

After Frank Fernandez homered to give the Cubs a 3–1 lead in the second, Wise made an adjustment. He ditched his curveball, relying instead on a fastball and slider the rest of the way, and settled into a groove that few pitchers find.

Over the next 10 2/3 innings, Wise dispatched hitter after hitter with nearly robotic proficiency. No hits, walks, errors or runs. He was within range of the all-time record of 36 consecutive outs set by Harvey Haddix when Ron Santo broke up the streak with a single in the top of the 12th.

At a Glance

WP: Wise (16–13)

HR: Gamble (5)

Key stat: Wise 3 hits, retires 32 consecutive batters

The Phillies trailed most of the afternoon, but stayed close with runs in the first and third. They finally tied the game in the bottom of the eighth on back-back singles from Tim McCarver and Deron Johnson, and a run-scoring sacrifice fly by Willie Montanez.

In the bottom of the 12th, Montanez led off with a hot shot to third. Santo dove out and gloved the ball, but threw wildly into the Phillies' dugout, allowing

Montanez to cruise into second. He advanced to third after Luzinski laid down a beautiful bunt.

Cubs manager Leo Durocher walked the next two batters to load the bases and set up a force.

But Wise had other plans. He crowded the plate, fouled off the first two pitches, then punched a low-and-away slider into right over the head of the drawn-in right fielder. Montanez jubilantly crossed the plate as the team streamed out of the dugout to congratulate Wise at first.

Did You Know?

Rick Wise and Larry Christenson share the franchise lead for most career home runs hit by a pitcher. Both hit 11.

Wise, who spent seven seasons in Philadelphia, hit six of his home runs in 1971 and hit two home runs in a game twice that year.

LC racked up his total over 11 years. His season high was three in 1977.

In second place is Al Orth, who hit seven. Bill Duggleby slammed six, and Robin Roberts is in fourth place with five career homers.

Birthday Homer Suits Morgan Fine in Run to Division Title

Joe Morgan celebrated his 40th birthday by giving the Phillies a huge present in their red-hot run to the Eastern Division title.

The future Hall of Fame second baseman led a gutsy comeback with four hits—including two home runs—and four RBIs to lead the Phils to their fourth straight victory and 11th in their last 14 games.

"This is my 19th year, and I can remember hitting a home run on my birthday only once," said Morgan, who had slogged through one of the most difficult seasons of his career until September rolled around. "I felt loose and relaxed at the plate tonight."

The Cubs attacked Marty Bystrom early, scoring three runs in the first off the right-hander. Morgan brought the Phillies back with a two-run homer in the fourth.

But the Cubs scored two more in the sixth to make the score 5–2.

Ivan DeJesus keyed a sixth-inning rally with a two-out triple into the right-field corner. Von Hayes knocked him in with a pinch-hit single and knocked out Cubs starter Dickie Noles.

At a Glance

WP: Reed (8–1)

HR: Morgan 2 (15,16)

Key stat: Morgan 4-for-5, 4 RBIs; DeJesus 2-for-4, 2 RBIs

Lefty Craig Lefferts was Noles' replacement, and Morgan greeted him with a shot to the base of the fence in right-center field. Hayes motored home to make it a 5–4 game.

Chicago tacked on another run in the seventh when Bill Buckner homered off Willie Hernandez. But the Phils kept plugging away.

In the bottom of the inning, they loaded the bases with one out on consecutive singles from Joe Lefebvre, Gary Matthews, and Greg Gross.

Pete Rose struck out looking for the second out. But DeJesus came up big again with a bases-clearing double to tie the game.

Morgan untied it in the bottom of the eighth. Facing closer Lee Smith, he sent a high fly ball to right that cleared the wall to give the Phillies their first lead of the night.

"He threw me either a cut fastball or slider," said Morgan. "Most of my home runs are line drives but the ball was low and away and I got under it."

The crowd at Veterans Stadium erupted, giving Morgan a lengthy standing ovation. The aging second baseman had given them little to cheer throughout the season as he battled a series of leg injuries and struggled just to get his batting average over the .200 mark.

Now, he wanted to put all that behind him.

"All I want, at this point, is to play as well as I can in these last two weeks and help us take this division. And I definitely think we'll win it."

His words were prophetic. The Phillies would push their winning streak to 11 games and complete a sizzling stretch drive that would culminate with another division championship and National League pennant.

Pete Rose

His best years were behind him when he signed a free-agent contract with the Phillies after the 1978 season, but Pete Rose still had a couple of .300 seasons left in him. More important was the enormous championship pedigree he brought to Philadelphia from Cincinnati.

Charlie Hustle helped turn a team of talented also-rans into World Champions in 1980.

In 1981 he broke Stan Musial's National League hit record, and in '83 he led the Phillies to their second pennant in four seasons.

Rose batted .291 and struck out just 151 times in his five seasons with the Phillies.

He remains baseball's all-time hit king but his spot in Cooperstown is still vacant because of a gambling scandal uncovered when he was managing the Reds.

Halladay Ends Drought of 20-Game Winners

Roy Halladay became the first Phillie in 28 years to win 20 games and came one step closer to realizing his dream of pitching in the postseason as he led the Phils to another thrilling win over second-place Atlanta.

A sold-out crowd of fired-up fans at Citizens Bank did their best to create a playoff atmosphere for the big right-hander, by continually waving rally towels and cheering heartily throughout the game.

Halladay gave a gritty performance, allowing seven hits and three runs in seven innings to help the Phils increase their lead over the Braves to five games with 10 left to play and reduce the team's magic number to six.

"It's definitely special," said the Phillies' ace. "But the best part about it is it's been completely secondary for me. Being able to think about getting ourselves into the playoffs and finishing these last couple of weeks strong has been the priority. To be able to go out and pitch in meaningful games at this point in the season makes all the difference."

The Phillies broke a scoreless tie in the third with a dose of their patented long-ball lightning.

Placido Polanco and Chase Utley led off with back-to-back singles off rookie left-hander Mike Minor. After Ryan Howard lined out to right, Jayson Werth got ahold of a fastball and drilled it into the seats in left-center to give the Phils a 3–0 lead.

At a Glance

WP: Halladay (20–10)

HR: Werth (25)

Key stat: Werth 2-for-4, 3 RBIs; Ibanez 2-for-4, 2 RBIs; Halladay 20th win

The Braves battled back, nicking Halladay for a run in the fifth when shortstop Wilson Valdez's relay throw to first on a double-play ball hit Rick Ankiel as he slid hard into second. Alex Gonzalez scored on the errant throw.

Atlanta made it 5–2 in the sixth when Martin Prado scored from third on Derrek Lee's sacrifice fly.

But Raul Ibanez provided some insurance in the bottom of the sixth with a double down the right-field line to score Howard and Werth.

Halladay appeared to tire in the seventh as he gave up a tape-measure home run to rookie Freddie Freeman before finishing the inning.

Ryan Madson pitched a scoreless eighth and Brad Lidge sat the Braves down in the ninth to record his 25th save.

It was the ninth consecutive win for the surging Phillies, who improved their record to 91–61, tops in the National League.

"We're right where we want to be," said Werth. "We're going for the best record in baseball. Make no mistake about it. Everyone in here feels like we're the best team in baseball, and we're going to go out and prove it."

"It only gets funner from here on out," said Halladay, who became the first Phillie to win 20 games since Steve Carlton in 1982, and the first right-hander to do it since Robin Roberts in 1955.

Chase Utley

The Phillies have had some great second basemen throughout their history, but none compares to Chase Utley.

After taking over the position in 2005, Utley quickly became one of the top second basemen in the game.

A five-time All-Star, he is that rare breed of middle infielder capable of hitting for average and power.

Utley has hit .290 or better four times, posting a career-high batting average of .332. He's also slugged more than 170 homers and collected 650 RBIs.

Howard Smacks Record-Tying 58th Homer

Wrapping up the greatest single season of slugging in franchise history, Ryan Howard walloped his 58th home run and knocked in three runs to help the Phils beat the Marlins.

Howard's blast tied the all-time record for most homers in a season by a Philadelphia player. Jimmie Foxx hit 58 with the Athletics in 1932. It was also Howard's 29th homer at home, tying the mark set by Chuck Klein, also in '32.

The 6-foot-4, 230-pound first baseman hit No. 58 in the third inning off starter Ricky Nolasco, a line smash to the seats in left-center. Jimmy Rollins and Chase Utley scored ahead of him.

As he circled the bases, the sold-out crowd at Citizens Bank Park broke out their white rally towels and chanted "MVP!" When Howard stepped out of the dugout for a curtain call, the stadium erupted.

"This is the first time I've seen the fans this excited," he said. "It's a great feeling."

Howard's historic homer gave the Phillies a 4–0 lead. They scored one in the first when Rollins smoked a leadoff double and came around on a single to center by Utley.

The early outburst allowed Cole Hamels to settle in and find his rhythm. The rookie southpaw flirted with danger early on. He had at least one runner on in each of the first three innings and got into a bases-loaded jam in the third, but managed to work out of trouble each time.

At a Glance

WP: Hamels (9–8)

HR: Howard (58)

Key stat: Utley 3-for-4, RBI; Conine 2-for-3, RBI; Howard 1-for-2, 3 RBIs

Overall, he was dazzling. In 6 2/3 innings Hamels gave up one run, walked three and struck out 10.

"I'm very pleased, because I definitely know you have to learn from failure to succeed," Hamels said. "It's how you finish. Nobody remembers the beginning. They always remember the end. I just want to finish as strong as I can."

Hamels' strong finish made him a late-season candidate for Rookie of the Year.

And with his gaudy numbers, Howard was an easy choice for National League Most Valuable Player. In addition to his 58 home runs, he led the league with 149 RBIs and batted .313.

11-Run Inning Gives Phils a Comeback Win

A third-inning explosion unlike any in team history vaulted the Phillies to an easy win in a game that saw two teams going in opposite directions.

The defending World Champion Phillies had sealed their playoff position in June by winning their division in the first half of the strike-shortened season. The Cardinals were in the midst of losing seven out of eight and falling out of playoff contention when they ran into a buzz saw at Busch Stadium.

The Cardinals carried a 1–0 lead into the top of the third. By the end of the inning, they trailed by 10 runs.

Manny Trillo began the assault with a leadoff double to right. The next seven batters hit safely as runners circled the bases like a merry-go-round.

Larry Bowa broke the hitting streak by walking, but Trillo followed with a single, his second hit of the inning.

The relentless attack continued for 31 minutes. When it finally ended, the Phillies had pounded out 11 hits. The 11 runs were the most scored in an inning in the major leagues all season. They came up two shy of the club record for most runs in an inning overall, but set a new scoring mark for the third inning.

Mike Schmidt contributed two singles and two RBIs to the third and said an inning like that just happens.

"Everybody's going up there trying not to be the one to end it. Nobody wants to make the last out."

The massacre was a nice present for rookie Mark Davis, who won his first game in the majors.

Phillies	AB	R	H	RBI
Smith cf	3	1	1	1
Maddox cf	3	0	0	0
Rose 1b	5	2	2	0
McGraw p	0	0	0	0
Matthews lf	3	1	3	4
Unser lf-1b	2	0	0	0
Schmidt 3b	3	1	2	2
Aviles 3b	2	1	2	0
McBride rf	4	2	2	2
Aguayo 2b	1	0	0	0
Boone c	5	2	3	3
Bowa ss	2	1	1	0
Sandberg ss	2	0	0	0
Trillo 2b	3	1	3	1
Gross rf	2	0	0	0
Davis p	4	2	1	1
Brusstar p	0	0	0	0
Vukovich ph-lf	1	0	0	0
Totals	**45**	**14**	**20**	**14**

Cardinals	AB	R	H	RBI
Herr 2b	2	0	0	0
Gonzalez 2b	3	0	1	0
Templeton ss	2	0	1	0
Ramsey ss	3	0	0	0
Hernandez lf	2	0	1	0
Roof lf	3	1	2	0
Hendrick cf	2	0	0	0
Green cf	2	1	0	0
Tenace 1b	5	2	2	4
Oberkfell 3b	2	0	1	0
Braun 3b	1	1	1	0
Landrum rf	4	1	2	1
Porter c	0	0	0	0
Brummer c	2	0	0	0
Sanchez c	1	0	0	0
Sorensen p	1	0	0	0
Shirley p	0	0	0	0
Littell p	0	0	0	0
Otten p	1	0	0	0
LaPoint p	1	0	0	0
Iorg ph	1	0	0	1
Bair p	0	0	0	0
Totals	**38**	**6**	**11**	**6**

PHI	0	0	11	0	3	0	0	0	0	-	14	20	0
STL	0	1	0	0	0	0	0	5	0	-	6	11	0

Phillies	IP	H	R	ER	BB	SO
Davis W (1-3)	7	8	4	4	3	7
Brusstar	1	2	2	2	0	1
McGraw	1	1	0	0	0	0
Totals	**9**	**11**	**6**	**6**	**3**	**8**

Cardinals	IP	H	R	ER	BB	SO
Sorensen L (7-7)	2	9	6	6	0	1
Shirley	0	1	1	1	0	0
Littell	0.2	3	4	4	2	1
Otten	3.1	6	3	3	0	0
LaPoint	2	1	0	0	0	1
Bair	1	0	0	0	0	1
Totals	**9**	**20**	**14**	**14**	**2**	**4**

DP—St. Louis. 2B—Philadelphia Trillo, McBride, Aviles; St. Louis Roof. 3B—St. Louis Landrum. HR—Philadelphia Boone (4); St. Louis Tenace 2 (4,5). LOB—Philadelphia 6; St. Louis 8. SB—St. Louis Oberkfell. Attendance: 11,758.

Kruk a One-Man Gang with 2 Homers, 5 RBIs

Maybe the scoreboard should have read, "Kruk 5, Cubs 4." After all, John Kruk put on a one-man show at Wrigley Field as he slammed two homers, including a grand slam, and knocked in all five runs.

The stout first baseman got started in the third inning by hitting a solo home run off righty Shawn Boskie to break a scoreless tie.

In the top of the fourth, the Phillies loaded the bases after Boskie surrendered an infield single to pitcher Tommy Greene and a pair of walks to Mickey Morandini and Wes Chamberlain.

Kruk came up with two outs and blasted a Boskie fastball, sending it over the bleachers in right and out onto the street, a no-doubt-about-it grand slam.

It was his 20th home run of the season and gave Greene lots of breathing room, something he needed as the Cubs began to chip away.

Andre Dawson led off the fourth with a home run and Rick Wilkins took Greene deep in the fifth to make it a 5–2 game.

When Hector Villanueva hit a solo shot to the back of the bleachers in the bottom of the sixth, manager Jim Fregosi had seen enough and decided to change pitchers after the inning.

Southpaw Bruce Ruffin came in to pitch the seventh but got into trouble right away, plunking leadoff batter Doug Dascenzo and giving up a single to Jerome Walton. Dascenzo eventually scored on Ryne Sandberg's sacrifice fly.

Danny Cox pitched a scoreless eighth, giving way to closer Mitch Williams, who picked up his 30th save. Greene got the win to improve his record to a career-best 13–7.

In addition to his homers, Kruk extended his hitting streak to 13 games and won the praise of his manager.

At a Glance

WP: Greene (13–7)

HR: Kruk 2 (19, 20)

Key Stat: Kruk 2-for-5, 5 RBIs, grand slam

"The biggest thing is for a manager to have a player like him," said Fregosi. "He's a throwback to the old school."

Eastern Division Champs at Long Last

The long drought was finally over. After 26 years of frustration, heartbreak, and disappointment, Philadelphians finally had a baseball team they could call a champion.

Greg Luzinski was the hitting star and Jim Lonborg took care of the pitching as the Phillies defeated the Expos at Jarry Park to clinch the National League Eastern Division crown.

The Bull's three-run homer in the sixth proved to be the game-winner while Lonborg held the Expos to four hits.

The veteran right-hander had been in this position before, having led the

The Phillies' 1976 division title was the first of six in an eight-year period. Above, the Phillies celebrate their 1980 crown.

Boston Red Sox to the 1967 American League pennant. Nevertheless, manager Danny Ozark thought about passing him over for this game because he had been having some arm trouble.

"But one thing you know about Lonborg," Ozark said. "If you send him out there with a broken arm and a broken leg, he's still going to give you a professional job as long as he can go."

The game was scoreless in the sixth when Dave Cash drew a leadoff walk from lefty Dan Warthen. Jerry Martin hit a liner to right to put runners on first and second. No. 3 hitter Mike Schmidt hammered a long drive to left but Del Unser caught up to it on the warning track.

That left it up to Luzinski, who had struck out looking with runners on second and third in the fourth inning.

"He'd struck me out with a fastball," said the Bull, "and I knew he was going to come back with one sooner or later. I'm up there waiting for it."

And he got it. Luzinski slammed Warthen's 1–1 pitch into the left-field bleachers for his 21st home run of the season.

Lonborg drove in the final run with a single in the seventh, then returned to the mound and coasted through the final three innings. He wrapped up his gem by striking out Earl Williams.

The 34-year-old right-hander leaped into the air as catcher Bob Boone sprinted out to embrace him. The two were quickly swarmed by a mob of jubilant teammates.

"I never won before, but I like the feeling," said infielder Terry Harmon.

Larry Bowa was on the verge of tears as he reflected on all the struggles that led up to this moment.

"The years of frustration," he said. "Being told I was too small or that I would never be a big-leaguer. Then, all those terrible years of last-place finishes. All that was flashing before me when we needed that final out."

For the first time since 1950, the Phillies were popping champagne corks.

Phillies	AB	R	H	RBI
Cash 2b	3	1	2	0
Martin rf-lf	4	1	1	0
Schmidt 3b	4	0	2	0
Luzinski lf	3	1	1	3
Tolan pr-1b	0	0	0	0
Allen 1b	4	0	0	0
Brown rf	0	0	0	0
Maddox cf	4	1	2	0
Boone c	4	0	0	0
Bowa ss	4	0	1	0
Lonborg p	4	0	1	1
Totals	34	4	10	4

Expos	AB	R	H	RBI
Unser lf	4	0	1	0
Garrett 2b	3	1	0	0
Dawson 2b	4	0	1	1
Valentine rf	4	0	0	0
Williams 1b	4	0	0	0
Parrish 3b	3	0	0	0
Foli ss	3	0	2	0
Foote c	3	0	0	0
Warthen p	1	0	0	0
Cromartie ph	1	0	0	0
Kerrigan p	0	0	0	0
Jorgensen ph	1	0	0	0
Murray p	0	0	0	0
Totals	31	1	4	1

PHI	0	0	0	0	0	3	1	0	0	-	4	10	0
MON	0	0	0	0	0	1	0	0	0	-	1	4	1

Phillies	IP	H	R	ER	BB	SO
Lonborg W (17-10)	9	4	1	1	1	5
Totals	9	4	1	1	1	5

Expos	IP	H	R	ER	BB	SO
Warthen L (2-9)	6	4	3	3	1	6
Kerrigan	2	5	1	1	0	0
Murray	1	1	0	0	0	0
Totals	9	10	4	4	1	6

E—Montreal Dawson. 2B—Montreal Dawson. 3B—Philadelphia Bowa. HR—Philadelphia Luzinski (21). HBP—Philadelphia Luzinski. LOB—Philadelphia 5; Montreal 4. SB—Philadelphia Cash, Maddox.

Make That 4 Eastern Division Titles in a Row

Led by staff ace Roy Halladay and backed by thousands of loyal fans who had trekked to Washington DC, the Phillies rolled over the Nationals to clinch their fourth consecutive Eastern Division title.

There was never really any doubt that they would win; not with Halladay on the mound. The best pitcher in baseball had waved his no-trade clause with Toronto and joined the Phillies in the off-season because he wanted the chance to win a championship.

So here he was, ignoring a steady rain and mowing down the Nationals while his teammates took care of the offense.

Halladay surrendered just two hits in winning his 21st game.

"That guy is a horse," said Shane Victorino. "He's been like that since the season started. Amazing."

Jayson Werth produced the winning run with a long homer to left in the second inning.

When the Phils added three more in the sixth, their traveling fans, who had been sitting in clusters throughout the stadium, became more boisterous as they migrated to the lower level.

By the ninth inning, Nationals Stadium looked more like Citizens Bank Park with fans now gathered in one large block, waving their rally towels and chanting, "Let's Go Phillies!"

At a Glance

WP: Halladay (21–10)

HR: Werth (26)

Key stat: Phillies 4th straight division title; Werth 3-for-5, 4 RBIs; Polanco 3-for-4, RBI; Ruiz 3-for-4, RB

When Halladay struck out Danny Espinosa with a change-up to end the game, they let out a roar as the players streamed out of the dugout to mob their ace.

"We're just starting," Halladay said. "I'm looking forward to moving forward. It should be fun."

The Phillies were in uncharted territory as the first team in franchise history to advance to the postseason four straight years. The Phillies of the mid-1970s won three consecutive division titles.

As the rain continued to fall outside, the locker room inside was soon flooded with champagne and beer. Players slipped on their NL East champion

T-shirts and hats, strapped on their goggles and let loose the bubbly in a celebration that had become old hat for most, and a fresh, new dream-come-true for others.

"I've seen it too much on TV," said Halladay. "It's everything it's cracked up to be."

It was an amazing end to a season that began with sky-high expectations, then ran into a ditch as injuries mounted and took their toll. The low point of the campaign saw the Phillies fall seven games out of first, and hitting coach Milt Thompson, lose his job.

But Charlie Manuel's resilient troops fought on, got healthy, and rebounded in August shortly after Roy Oswalt arrived in a trade with Houston.

In September the Phillies caught fire, compiling a record of 21–6 for the month.

"It's been a long year," said Manuel. "And this is just the first step."

From 'Wheeze Kids' to NL East Champs

A season filled with controversy and upheaval ended with celebratory champagne showers at Wrigley Field as the rampaging Phillies wrapped up the National League Eastern Division title after thumping the Cubs.

No one would have predicted an ending like this a month earlier. The Wheeze Kids, led by aging stars Pete Rose, Joe Morgan, and Tony Perez, had underachieved for most of the season. General manager Paul Owens tried to fire up the troops by firing manager Pat Corrales and moving down to the dugout as his replacement in mid-July. But the results were the same—until September rolled around.

A switch seemed to go off as this group of veterans found their groove and began piling up one victory after another. Going into this game, their record for the month was 20–7, including an 11-game winning streak.

When they took the field to play the Cubs, the Phils appeared to be relaxed and determined to nail down the title.

Mike Schmidt set them on that path by breaking a 3–3 tie in the third with his 40th home run. Bo Diaz, who had a career-high five hits, followed Schmidt with his second homer of the game, a two-run blast that gave the Phillies a 6–3 lead.

At a Glance

WP: Hernandez (9–4)

HR: Schmidt (40), Diaz 2 (14, 15)

Key stat: Diaz 5-for-5, 3 RBIs, 4 runs; Morgan 4-for-4, 3 RBIs; DeJesus 3-for-4, RBI

"Man, it was just one of those days when I saw the ball really good, and I hit some balls that carried," Diaz said. "I've had a tough year, but so have some other guys and we all kept trying to play hard and play together."

The Cubs scored a pair in the bottom of the fourth but they simply could not keep up with a team that was on a mission.

The Phils added two in the fifth and two more in the sixth to make it a 10–5 game.

After scoring three more runs on four hits in the ninth, the Phillies turned to Al Holland to close things out.

The burly, bearded left-hander with the intimidating glare came over to the Phillies along with Joe Morgan in a trade with the Giants and was enjoying the best season of his career.

Holland, who relieved Larry Andersen with one out in the eighth, gave up a leadoff double to Carmelo Martinez and a walk to Ryne Sandberg, then retired the next three batters to nail down the title.

"We've had a lot of problems, a lot of controversy," said Holland. "But we thought in spring training that we would win this thing. And this is just the beginning. We're going after the World Series, now."

Owens was at a loss to explain his team's turnaround.

"But to finally see everything come together is easily the highlight of my baseball life," said Owens.

The Phillies wrapped up the best September in modern franchise history with a record of 22–7 and carried that momentum to their second World Series appearance in four years.

Mike Schmidt

The greatest third baseman to ever play the game, Mike Schmidt was the most dominant power hitter of his generation.

After enduring a 1973 rookie season laced with strikeouts and a dismal .196 batting average, Schmidt blossomed in '74 as he raised his average nearly a hundred points to .282, belted a league-leading 36 homers and collected 116 RBIs.

Schmidt led the Phillies to three straight Division championships in the mid-1970s, and in 1980, slammed a career-high 48 home runs as the Phils won the World Series for the first time in team history. Schmidt was voted MVP of the Series and the National League.

A 12-time All-Star, Schmidt won eight home run titles, second only to Babe Ruth, and 10 Gold Gloves. He was voted NL MVP three times.

Injuries and age forced Schmidt to announce his retirement on May 29, 1989. In 18 seasons with the Phillies, he slammed 548 home runs and drove in 1,595 runs, both tops on the team's all-time list.

Schmidt was selected to the Hall of Fame in 1995.

Allen's Best Day Ever Includes 3 Homers, 7 RBIs against Mets

The Phillies ended their first losing season in seven years with a win behind a jaw-dropping performance from Dick Allen, who enjoyed the biggest day of his career.

Allen slugged three homers and knocked in seven runs to help the Phillies stage a big comeback against Tom Seaver.

The fireballing young righty held the Phillies to one hit through five while striking out eight as the Mets jumped out to a 2–0 lead.

But Allen took over in the sixth inning. After John Briggs led off with a single, he walloped a first-pitch fastball from Seaver over the right-center field fence to tie the game.

In the seventh, the Phils took the lead after Seaver hit leadoff batter Roberto Pena with a pitch and gave up a two-run homer to Clay Dalrymple.

Jerry Grote's RBI single in the bottom of the seventh kept the Mets close, but not for long.

In the top of the eighth, Allen swung at reliever Cal Koonce's first pitch, sending it to the same distant area beyond the center field wall to make it a 5–3 game.

In the ninth, the Phillies blew the game open. Singles by Rick Joseph and Dalrymple, a walk to John Briggs and a base hit by Gary Sutherland brought one run in and Allen to the plate with the bases loaded.

This time, he took the first pitch from Ron Taylor, then scalded the second one over the fence in left for a grand slam, his 33rd homer of the year.

At a Glance

WP: Short (19–13)

HR: Allen 3 (31, 32, 33), Dalrymple (3)

Key stat: Allen 3-for-4, 7 RBIs; Dalrymple 3-for-3, 2 RBIs; Briggs 2-for-4

It was the 16th time in his career that Allen had hit two home runs in a game, but the first and only time he'd hit three. His seven RBIs were also a career high.

Allen's awesome outburst made a winner out of Chris Short, who ended his season with a record of 19–13.

Slow Start Ends with '07 NL East Crown

After three consecutive second-place finishes, the Phillies finally made it to the top of their division, returning to the post-season for the first time in 14 years.

Charlie Manuel's resilient troops had to overcome a slew of obstacles, including a league-worst 4–11 start and a rash of injuries.

By the time September arrived, the Phillies had gathered themselves for a historic stretch run in which they went 13–4 while the first place Mets did an impersonation of the '64 Phillies by *losing* 12 of 17, blowing a seven-game lead.

The teams were tied for first going into the final day of the season. But as the Phillies took the field against the Washington Nationals, a roar went up from the sold-out crowd at Citizens Bank Park after the out-of-town scoreboard showed that the Florida Marlins had scored seven runs in the first inning against the Mets.

Jamie Moyer took the mound without peeking at the scoreboard. He didn't have to.

"(The fans) let me know what was happening," he said. "I really forced myself to focus on what I needed to do and making good pitches."

Spurred on by a rowdy towel-waving crowd, the crafty lefty held the Nationals scoreless in the first, then turned it over to the offense.

At a Glance

WP: Moyer (14–12)

HR: Howard (47)

Key stat: Howard 3-for-4, 3 RBIs; Rollins 2-for-3, RBI, 2 runs

Right on cue, Jimmy Rollins led off with a single, stole second and third, and scored the first run of the game on a sacrifice fly by Chase Utley.

The Phils scored two more runs on two hits in the third and increased their lead to 5–1 in the bottom of the sixth on Rollins' two-out triple. It was the 20th three-bagger of the year for the eventual 1997 National League Most Valuable Player.

Ryan Howard accounted for the Phils' final run by smashing his 47th homer in the bottom of the seventh.

Moyer did a tremendous job on the hill. In 5 1/3 innings he allowed just one

Jimmy Rollins speaks to the fans after the Phillies won the National League Eastern Division championship by defeating the Washington Nationals on Sept. 30, 2007.

League

unearned run on five hits and struck out six. Tom Gordon, J. C. Romero, and Brett Myers took it from there, posting zeroes the rest of the way.

Myers struck out Willy Mo Pena to end the game, threw his glove in the air and was tackled by Pat Burrell as the rest of the team rushed in and piled on.

Screaming fans looked on, high-fived and hugged one another. Similar celebrations broke out like wildfires in homes and bars across the entire region as years of pent-up frustration was released.

The Phillies moved into the clubhouse and popped the corks for the traditional champagne showers.

"I'm at a loss for words," said Myers. Howard noted that a lot of people counted the Phillies out but the players never stopped believing. "That's why they call us the Fightin' Phillies," he said. "We're going to celebrate. The whole town is going to celebrate."

Suddenly the locker room was too small for the big first baseman, who ordered his teammates back onto the field. "Come on, let's go," he commanded. "Let's go yell at the fans."

So out they went, with champagne bottles and beer cans in hand to shake hands and mingle. It was a spontaneous moment of joy rarely seen in the City of Brotherly Love.

The victory made a prophet out of Rollins, who boldly predicted back in January that the Phillies were the team to beat.

"It feels like a blessing," said Rollins. "I guess that was pretty accurate."

October 1, 1950
Phillies 4, Dodgers 1 (10 innings)

High Drama as Sisler's Homer Brings Home the Pennant in 1950

An entire city erupted in delirious celebration after Dick Sisler hit the most dramatic home run in franchise history. Sisler's blow gave the Phillies their first National League pennant in 35 years.

It was the climax to a tension-filled game and two white-knuckle weeks in which the Phillies saw their 7.5-game lead dwindle to one going into the final day of the season.

Sisler was the man of the hour, but there many heroes in this game. Robin Roberts was spectacular, even more so for a pitcher who was making his fourth start in eight days. The right-handed bulldog went all 10 innings to become the first Phillie to win 20 games since Grover Cleveland Alexander in 1917.

Dodgers starter Don Newcombe had matched Roberts pitch for pitch until the fateful 10th inning.

The Phillies scored their first run with two outs in the sixth on three straight singles by Sisler, Del Ennis and Puddin' Head Jones.

But the Dodgers came back and tied the game in the bottom of the inning when Pee Wee Reese hit a fly ball to right-center that got wedged in the base of a wire screen and was declared a ground-rule home run.

It was one of only three hits that Roberts had surrendered over eight innings. In the ninth, things got scary. Cal Abrams opened the inning with a walk and moved to second after Reese lined a single to left. Duke Snider followed with a line single to center. Abrams raced to third and made the turn for home at the urging of third base coach Milt Stock.

Ashburn got a tremendous jump on the ball and rifled a strike to catcher Stan Lopata in plenty of time to nail Abrams, who didn't even bother to

Phillies	AB	R	H	RBI
Waitkus 1b	5	1	1	0
Ashburn cf	5	1	0	0
Sisler lf	5	2	4	3
Mayo lf	0	0	0	0
Ennis rf	5	0	2	0
Jones 3b	5	0	1	1
Hamner ss	4	0	0	0
Seminick c	3	0	1	0
Caballero pr	0	0	0	0
Lopata c	0	0	0	0
Goliat 2b	4	0	1	0
Roberts p	2	0	1	0
Totals	**38**	**4**	**11**	**4**

Dodgers	AB	R	H	RBI
Abrams lf	2	0	0	0
Reese ss	4	1	3	1
Snider cf	4	0	1	0
Robinson 2b	3	0	0	0
Furillo rf	4	0	0	0
Hodges 1b	4	0	0	0
Campanella c	4	0	1	0
Cox 3b	3	0	0	0
Russell ph	1	0	0	0
Newcombe p	3	0	0	0
Brown ph	1	0	0	0
Totals	**33**	**1**	**5**	**1**

PHI 0 0 0 0 0 1 0 0 0 3 - 4 11 0
BRO 0 0 0 0 0 1 0 0 0 0 - 1 5 0

Phillies	IP	H	R	ER	BB	SO
Roberts W (20-11)	10	5	1	1	3	2
Totals	**10**	**5**	**1**	**1**	**3**	**2**

Dodgers	IP	H	R	ER	BB	SO
Newcombe L (19-11)	10	11	4	4	2	3
Totals	**10**	**11**	**4**	**4**	**2**	**3**

DP—Philadelphia; Brooklyn. 2B—Brooklyn Reese. HR—Philadelphia Sisler (13); Brooklyn Reese (11). SH—Philadelphia Roberts. LOB—Philadelphia 7; Brooklyn 5. Attendance: 35,073.

slide. Disaster was averted, for the moment. But Roberts still had to get past some dangerous hitters with runners on second and third.

He intentionally walked Jackie Robinson, then got Carl Furillo to hit a pop-up to first and Gil Hodges to fly out to right to end the threat.

Having weathered the storm, it seemed appropriate that Robbie would lead off the 10th inning with a base hit. Eddie Waitkus' bloop single put runners on first and second. Ashburn attempted to bunt the runners into scoring position but Newcombe threw to third in time to get the force.

That brought Sisler to the plate. After falling behind in the count 1–2, the left-handed swinging first baseman got ahold of an outside fastball, sending it slicing toward left. Abrams went back to the wall and ran out of room as the ball soared into the stands.

Sisler's 13th homer of the season was the biggest of his career. As he followed Waitkus and Ashburn across home plate, the entire team was out there to greet him with bear hugs and back slaps.

In a box seat next to the Dodgers' dugout, George Sisler, the great Hall of Famer, threw his hat in the air and cheered wildly for his son.

The stunned Dodgers were too demoralized to mount a comeback. Roberts retired the side in order, setting off a mob scene at the mound and a riotous celebration back in Philly.

The next day's *Philadelphia Inquirer* captured the scene when the Whiz Kids arrived back home: "Many of the players wives met the train at North Philadelphia and joined their husbands on the ride downtown. There they were met by a joyous mob, which prevented them from reaching the Warwick Hotel, and another celebration, for more than an hour."

Rollins Maintains Streak, But Playoff Hopes Die

The Phillies and Jimmy Rollins ran out of time. In their final game of the season, they blew out the Washington Nationals, but lost out in their bid for a wild-card playoff spot when Houston rallied to beat the Cubs.

Rollins extended his historic hitting streak to 36 games. However, with the season over he was no longer eligible to challenge Joe DiMaggio's single-season 56-game hitting streak.

Rollins got his first hit in the fourth, a leadoff single to right, after Hector Carassco retired the first nine batters. Rollins made it to third after a ground ball and a wild pitch, then scored on Bobby Abreu's sacrifice fly.

Rollins' second hit was a run-scoring double, part of a three-run fifth.

As the Phillies built a 5–3 lead through the middle innings, they began to carefully watch the out of town scoreboard. But the news from Houston wasn't good.

The Astros scored three times in the bottom of the sixth to erase a 4–3 Cubs lead and went on to win 6–4 to punch their ticket to the playoffs. The Phillies won 9–3 but it turned out to be a hollow victory as they finished one game short of forcing a one-game playoff for the wild-card spot.

"I'm very proud of our guys," said manager Charlie Manuel. "I told them that I came here to win and I'll never be

Jimmy Rollins

The heart and soul of some great Phillies teams, Jimmy Rollins has anchored the infield since breaking in with the club in September 2000.

In 2001, J-Roll hit .274 and stole a league-leading 46 bases to earn a spot on the All-Star roster and finish third in Rookie of the Year balloting behind Roy Oswalt and Albert Pujols.

After slumping to .245 in '02, Rollins began stringing together some remarkable seasons. In 2005, he set a team record by hitting safely in 36 consecutive games, and in '07, he was voted Most Valuable Player after posting some unbelievable numbers. Rollins reached career highs with 30 home runs, 20 triples, 212 hits, 139 runs, 94 RBIs, and a .296 batting average.

Rollins is a three-time All-Star and a three-time Gold Glove winner.

satisfied until we win a World Series. We couldn't get it done but we're definitely contenders."

"We fell one game short but there are a lot of positive things to take away from it," said Rollins, who raised his batting average to .404 and his on-base percentage to over .450 for the month of September.

At a Glance

WP: Lieber (17–13)

Key stat: Rollins 2-for-4, 2 RBIs, extends hitting streak to 36 games

J-Roll would pick up where he left off the next season, getting hits in the first two games before his streak was stopped at 38, the longest hitting streak in Phillies history and the eighth-longest in major league history.

Did You Know?

The Phillies ended the 1965 season at Shea Stadium with one of the most remarkable and grueling two-day stretches of pitching in club history.

On Oct. 2, Jim Bunning threw a two-hit shutout to beat the Mets 6–0 in the first game of a doubleheader. In the nightcap, Chris Short threw 15 shutout innings, striking out a franchise-record 18 in a game that was suspended after going scoreless through 18 frames.

The two teams played another twinbill the next day, with the Phils winning both games 3–1. Game 2 went 13 innings.

Your final totals: 49 innings pitched, one earned run.

Phils Couldn't Give Away East Title, So Schmidt Blast Wins It

The Phillies' march to their first World Series championship began with this error-filled, gritty and emotionally draining victory that ended with corks popping at Olympic Stadium.

They arrived in Montreal on Oct. 3 tied for first with the Expos. After pulling out a 2–1 squeaker on Friday night, the Phillies needed one more win to wrap up the Eastern Division title. A loss would throw both teams back into a tie for first, setting up a showdown on the final day of the season.

For much of this game, the Phils did all they could to hand Montreal a victory. They made five errors, committed numerous base-running blunders and left 12 runners stranded. Yet somehow, they found the wherewithal to overcome those obstacles.

With two outs in the third, Bake McBride beat out a grounder for an infield hit and Mike Schmidt hit a laser off the wall in left-center. The fleet-footed McBride was waved home by third-base coach Lee Elia. But the Expos pulled off a perfect relay to nail him at the plate.

At a Glance

WP: McGraw (5–4)

HR: Schmidt (48)

Key stat: Schmidt 3-for-5, 2 RBIs; Luzinski 2-for-4, 2 RBIs; McBride 3-for-5, 2 runs; Rose 3-for-5, 2 runs

The Expos took the lead in the bottom of the third on Jerry White's two-run homer off Larry Christenson.

The Phils scored their first run and had an opportunity to break the game open in the top of the fifth. With nobody out and runners on first and second, Pete Rose ripped a run-scoring single to left. McBride then hit a topper that hugged the third-base line to load the bases. But Schmidt struck out and Greg Luzinski lined into a double play to end the inning.

The Bull redeemed himself with one out in the top of the seventh by bouncing a two-run, bases-loaded single up the middle to give the Phillies a 3–2 lead. They might have gotten more had Schmidt and Luzinski not gotten caught in rundowns on the throw back to the infield.

In the bottom of the seventh, Trillo opened the door for another Expos rally when he dropped Chris Speier's routine pop up with one out. Montreal wound up scoring twice to reclaim the lead.

Phillies 6, Expos 4 (11 innings)

The Phillies were still trailing 4–3 and down to their last out in the ninth when Bob Boone stepped to the plate with a runner on second. The veteran catcher was mired in a 2-for-27 slump. But he embraced the moment and lined a 1–0 pitch off Woodie Fryman into center field for a game-tying single.

"I think if we hadn't made it to the playoffs it was going to be an awfully long winter for me," he said.

Schmidt shuddered at the thought of losing.

"After so much emotion, after all the emotional craziness of the game, after so many highs and lows, leaving so many runners on base. . . . It would have been really hard to regroup tomorrow," said Schmidt.

In the top of the 11th, Rose, facing Stan Bahnsen, led off with a single. McBride popped up and Schmidt stepped into the spotlight.

"I just wanted to hit a gapper," he said. "I just wanted to drive the ball somewhere."

Schmidty drove it, all right. As Phils broadcaster Andy Musser breathlessly described it on the radio, "He buried it!"

Schmidt's 48th home run of the year landed more than a dozen rows back in the lower left-field stands, giving the Phillies a 6–4 lead.

Tug McGraw came out and retired the side in order, ending the game and the pennant race by striking out Larry Parrish.

In the locker room afterward, Rose looked around at the celebration and smiled approvingly.

"This is what I came over here for," said the former Cincinnati Red. "This is what I expected with the Phillies. It took a year but here we are."

Schmidt thoughtfully stepped back from the celebration for some perspective.

"We're excited to win this," he said. "but we want to take the next step against whoever we play. We still have to prove we can win a league playoff and a World Series. That's what everyone in the room is looking for."

POSTSEASON

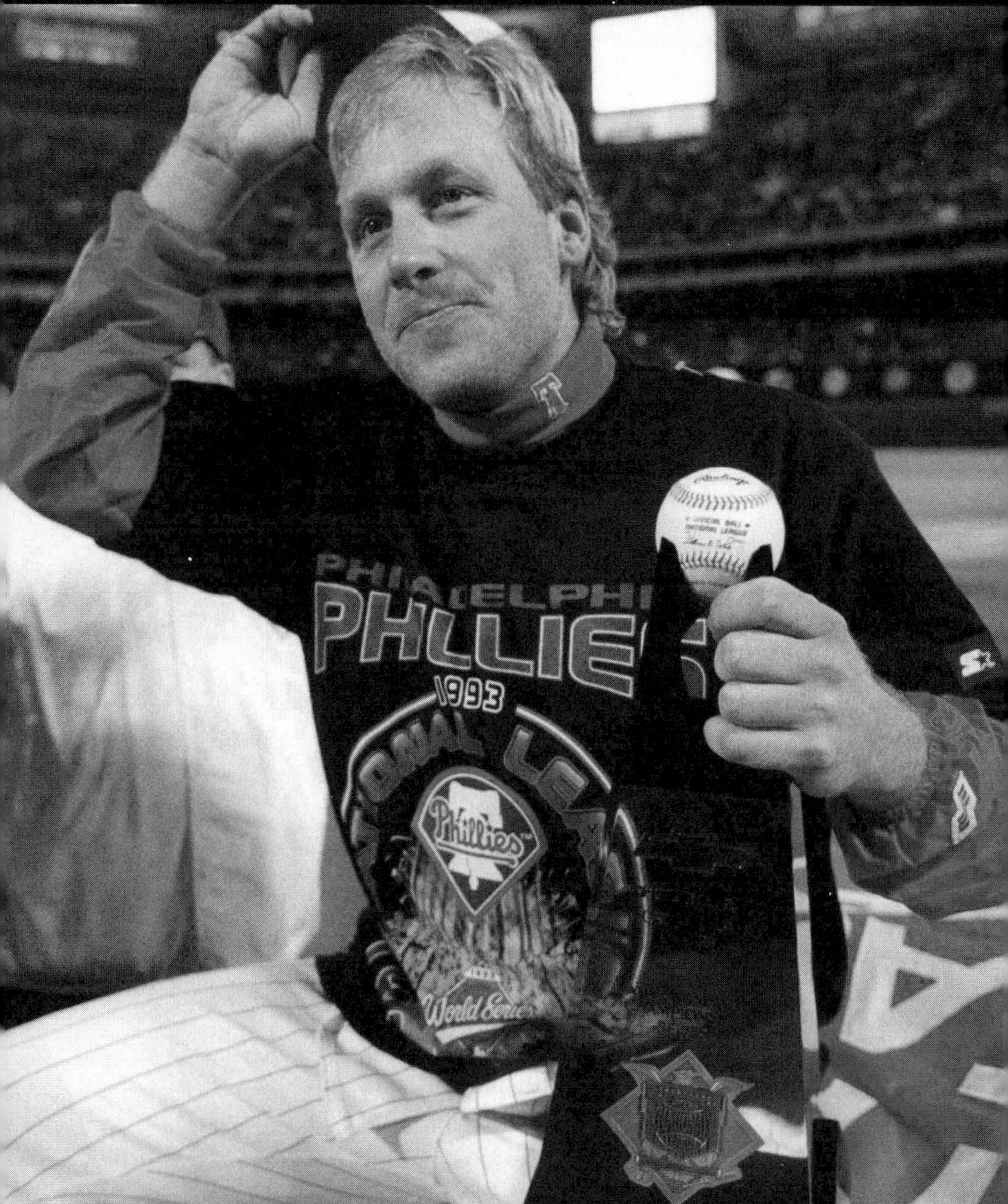

Curt Schilling poses with the National League Championship Series MVP trophy after the Phillies defeated the Atlanta Braves in Game 6 of the National League playoffs.

October 12, 1980
NLCS Game 5
Phillies 8, Astros 7 (10 innings)

Big Comeback Caps Playoff Thriller

This remains the most thrilling and inspiring playoff game in team history as the Phillies crawled back late in the game to beat the Astros and advance to the World Series.

Trailing 5–2 in the eighth inning at the noisy Astrodome, Larry Bowa had the daunting task of leading off against the great Nolan Ryan, who was virtually unbeatable when he had a lead after the seventh inning. But Bowa received words of encouragement from Pete Rose before heading into the batter's box.

"I remember Pete came up and says, 'You get on and we're gonna win this game,'" said Bowa, "and I said, 'I'm getting on.'"

Bowa lined a single to left-center. Bob Boone then hit a hard grounder off Ryan's glove for a hit and Greg Gross surprised everyone, including third-base coach Lee Elia, by bunting for a hit to load the bases.

Larry Bowa (left) and Mike Schmidt ride in the team's victory parade in Philadelphia following the Phillies' 1980 World Series victory.

"I honest to God thought that the world had stopped or was about to ready to stop 'cause everything got very slow," Elia recalled. "You could see the ball bounce, see it spin, no play. It was like 'Holy Geez, how did he think to do that.' It was unbelievable!"

The Phillies erupted. Rose drew a bases-loaded walk to make it a 5–3 game, bringing a sudden end to Ryan's night.

After reliever Joe Sambito got pinch-hitter Keith Moreland to ground into a run-scoring force at second, righty Ken Forsch came in and struck out Mike Schmidt.

But pinch-hitter Del Unser picked everyone up with a game-tying single, and Manny Trillo followed with a triple down the line in left, scoring two to give the Phillies a 7–5 lead.

The Astros, however, were not about to roll over. They scored two runs in the bottom of the seventh to tie it at 7.

The score stayed that way until the 10th, when Garry Maddox smacked a two-out double to score Unser with what proved to be the game-winning run.

Phillies	AB	R	H	RBI
Rose 1b	3	0	1	1
McBride rf	3	0	0	0
Moreland ph	1	0	0	1
Aviles pr	0	1	0	0
McGraw p	0	0	0	0
Vukovich ph	1	0	0	0
Ruthven p	0	0	0	0
Schmidt 3b	5	0	0	0
Luzinski lf	3	0	1	0
Smith pr	0	0	0	0
Christenson p	0	0	0	0
Reed p	0	0	0	0
Unser ph-rf	2	2	2	1
Trillo 2b	5	1	3	2
Maddox cf	4	1	1	1
Bowa ss	5	1	2	0
Boone c	3	1	2	2
Bystrom p	2	0	0	0
Brusstar p	0	0	0	0
Gross lf	2	1	1	0
Totals	**39**	**8**	**13**	**8**

Astros	AB	R	H	RBI
Puhl cf	6	3	4	0
Cabell 3b	5	0	1	0
Morgan 2b	4	0	0	0
Landestoy 2b	1	0	1	1
Cruz lf	3	1	2	2
Walling rf	5	2	1	1
LaCorte p	0	0	0	0
Howe 1b	4	0	2	1
Bergman pr-1b	1	0	0	0
Pujols c	1	0	0	0
Ashby ph-c	3	0	1	1
Reynolds ss	5	1	2	0
Ryan p	3	0	0	0
Sambito p	0	0	0	0
Forsch p	0	0	0	0
Woods ph-rf	1	0	0	0
Heep ph	1	0	0	0
Totals	**43**	**7**	**14**	**6**

PHI 0 2 0 0 0 0 0 5 0 1 - 8 13 2
HOU 1 0 0 0 0 1 3 2 0 0 - 7 14 0

Phillies	IP	H	R	ER	BB	SO
Bystrom	5.1	7	2	1	2	1
Brusstar	0.2	0	0	0	0	0
Christenson	0.2	2	3	3	1	0
Reed	0.1	1	0	0	0	0
McGraw	1	4	2	2	0	2
Ruthven W (1-0)	2	2	0	0	0	0
Totals	**10**	**14**	**7**	**6**	**3**	**3**

Astros	IP	H	R	ER	BB	SO
Ryan	7	8	6	6	2	8
Sambito	0.1	0	0	0	0	0
Forsch	0.2	2	1	1	0	1
LaCorte L (1-1)	2	3	1	1	1	1
Totals	**10**	**13**	**8**	**8**	**3**	**10**

E—Philadelphia Liuzinski, Trillo. DP—Houston 2. 2B—Philadelphia Maddox, Unser; Houston Reynolds, Cruz. 3B—Philadelphia Trillo; Houston Howe. SH—Philadelphia Boone; Houston Cabell. LOB—Philadelphia 5; Houston 10. SB—Houston Puhl. Attendance: 44,802.

October 21, 1980
World Series Game 6
Phillies 4, Royals 1

Highway Escort Gets Phils on Their Way

After 97 years of futility, the Phillies finally reached the mountaintop with this victory over the Royals in Game 6 of the World Series.

They had returned to Philadelphia supremely confident after winning Game 5 to take a three-games-to-two lead.

"When we came back, I told everybody this thing's over," said shortstop Larry Bowa. "It was a feeling I never had before."

The Phillies got their first break of the day hours before the game started when a carload of players and coaches heading to the ballpark was pulled over for speeding on I-95.

"There's six of us in the car," said coach Lee Elia. "And the cop is looking in going 'Holy Geez, there's Lonnie Smith and Dickie Noles. He says follow me, you've got an escort in.'"

A foul pop from Royals batter Frank White is deflected by Phillies catcher Bob Boone as first baseman Pete Rose moves in to make the catch in the ninth inning of their World Series game. Rose was able to hang on to ball for the second out of the inning.

The Phillies built a 4–0 lead behind Steve Carlton, who pitched seven stellar innings before tiring in the eighth, giving way to Tug McGraw. In the ninth, the Royals loaded the bases with one out against the Phillies' closer, who also appeared to be running out of gas. McGraw summoned his catcher to the mound for some sage advice.

"I had no idea what I was gonna say because I couldn't tell what he was doin' wrong," said Bob Boone. "Tug's lookin' at me like 'Bob, I know you know what I'm doing wrong, come out and tell me.' So I walked out and I got to the mound and I said, 'Tuggles, everything's high.' And as I said that I just pivoted and walked back to home plate. He's laughin' and I'm laughin and all of a sudden, whatever that did, he was throwin' strikes again."

McGraw got Frank White to lift a foul pop near the Phillies' dugout. Boone raced over and reached up for the ball as he converged with first baseman Pete Rose in front of the dugout. The ball hit his mitt, then popped out. The crowd gasped.

But Rose, heads-up as always, snagged it. Except Boone said it should have never come to that.

"Charlie Hustle my rear end, I'm the one that hustled on that play," Boone said. "That's Pete's ball all the way. I'm getting over there and I'm waiting for him to call me off and I'm not hearing anything and I'm going 'Come on, Pete.'"

"I reached up to grab the ball. I didn't catch it the normal way I would catch a ball.

When it popped out of my glove I wanted to kill him. And then, all of a sudden his glove whips in front of my eyes and he catches it, and I wanted to kiss him."

McGraw now faced Willie Wilson, a dangerous hitter who was having a horrendous series. After setting him up with a couple of screwballs, McGraw struck out Wilson out on a high fastball to end the series and kick off a city-wide celebration that lingered through the long winter.

Royals	AB	R	H	RBI
Wilson lf	4	0	0	0
Washington ss	3	0	1	1
Brett 3b	4	0	2	0
McRae dh	4	0	0	0
Otis cf	3	0	0	0
Aikens 1b	2	0	0	0
Concepcion pr	0	0	0	0
Wathan c	3	1	2	0
Cardenal rf	4	0	2	0
White 2b	4	0	0	0
Gale p				
Martin p				
Splittorff p				
Pattin p				
Quisenberry p				
Totals	**31**	**1**	**7**	**1**

Phillies	AB	R	H	RBI
Smith lf	4	2	1	0
Gross lf	0	0	0	0
Rose 1b	4	0	3	0
Schmidt 3b	3	0	1	2
McBride rf	4	0	0	1
Luzinski dh	4	0	0	0
Maddox cf	4	0	2	0
Trillo 2b	4	0	0	0
Bowa ss	4	1	1	0
Boone c	2	1	1	1
Carlton p				
McGraw p				
Totals	**33**	**4**	**9**	**4**

KC	0	0	0	0	0	0	0	1	0	-	1	7	2
PHI	0	0	2	0	1	1	0	0	X	-	4	9	0

Royals	IP	H	R	ER	BB	SO
Gale L (0-1)	2	4	2	1	1	1
Martin	2.1	1	1	1	1	0
Splittorff	1.2	4	1	1	0	0
Pattin	1	1	0	0	0	2
Quisenberry	1	0	0	0	0	0
Totals	**8**	**9**	**4**	**3**	**2**	**3**

Phillies	IP	H	R	ER	BB	SO
Carlton W (3-0)	7	4	1	1	3	7
McGraw S (4)	2	3	0	0	2	2
Totals	**9**	**7**	**1**	**1**	**5**	**9**

E—Kansas City Aikens, White. DP—Kansas City; Philadelphia 2. 2B—Philadelphia Smith, Maddox, Bowa. SF—Kansas City Washington. LOB—Kansas City 9; Philadelphia 7. Attendance: 65,838.

October 27-29, 2008
World Series Game 5
Phillies 4, Rays 3

Suspension Only Delays Another Series Crown

Twenty-eight years after winning their last World Series title, the Phillies were champions again, winning a game that took three days to complete.

The Phils had a three-games-to-one lead when they met the Rays for Game 5 in a steady, chilly rain that soon grew into a monsoon. Shane Victorino's two-run single in the first gave the Phils the early lead.

Chase Utley's solid defensive play helped the Phillies win the 2008 World Series. Here, Utley leaps over Tampa Bay's Carl Crawford to turn a double play during the eighth inning in Game 5.

Tampa Bay scored a run in the fourth then tied it in the top of top of the sixth on a run-scoring single by Carlos Pena. At that point, the wind and rain had become too much. With parts of the infield under water, Commissioner Bud Selig suspended a World Series game for the first time in major league history. The storm hung around for another day, holding up the resumption of play until Wednesday.

It was still windy and cold when Geoff Jenkins led off the bottom of the sixth with a booming double off the wall in right-center. Jenkins moved to third on Jimmy Rollins' sacrifice bunt and scored when Akinori Iwamura couldn't handle Jayson Werth's flare behind second.

In the seventh, the Rays tied the game again when Rocco Baldelli homered off Ryan Madson. They would have taken the lead had it not been for a tremendous play by Chase Utley.

With Jason Bartlett on second, Iwamuri smacked a grounder up the middle that Utley backhanded. Knowing he had no shot to get the speedy Iwamuri, Utley pump-faked a throw to first as Bartlett rounded third. His throw to the plate arrived in plenty of time to nail Bartlett. From there, the Phillies seized control of the game.

In the bottom of the seventh, Pat Burrell hit a rocket that just missed clearing the wall in the deepest part of left-center. Pinch runner Eric Bruntlett raced to third on Victorino's ground ball to second, and scored on a single by Pedro Feliz.

J.C. Romero pitched a scoreless eighth before handing the ball to Brad Lidge, who created an unforgettable snapshot moment by striking out Eric Hinske to end the series and dropping to his knees, arms raised to the sky.

Devil Rays	AB	R	H	RBI
Iwamura 2b	4	0	2	0
Crawford lf	4	0	1	0
Upton cf	4	1	1	0
Pena 1b	4	1	2	1
Price p	0	0	0	0
Longoria 3b	4	0	1	1
Navarro c	3	0	1	0
Perez pr	0	0	0	0
Baldelli rf	3	1	1	1
Zobrist ph	1	0	0	0
Bartlett ss	3	0	1	0
Hinske ph	1	0	0	0
Kazmir p	2	0	0	0
Balfour p	0	0	0	0
Howell p	0	0	0	0
Bradford p	0	0	0	0
Aybar 1b	0	0	0	0
Totals	33	3	10	3

Phillies	AB	R	H	RBI
Rollins ss	3	0	0	0
Werth rf	3	1	2	1
Utley 2b	3	1	0	0
Howard 1b	4	0	0	0
Burrell lf	2	0	1	0
Bruntlett pr-lf	0	1	0	0
Victorino cf	4	0	1	2
Feliz 3b	4	0	2	1
Ruiz c	4	0	1	0
Hamels p	2	0	0	0
Jenkins ph	1	1	1	0
Madson p	0	0	0	0
Romero p	1	0	0	0
Lidge p	0	0	0	0
Totals	31	4	8	4

TBR	0	0	0	1	0	1	1	0	0	-	3	10	0
PHI	2	0	0	0	0	1	1	0	X	-	4	8	1

Devil Rays	IP	H	R	ER	BB	SO
Kazmir	4	4	2	2	6	5
Balfour	1.1	2	1	1	0	0
Howell L (0-1)	0.2	1	1	1	0	1
Bradford	1	1	0	0	0	0
Price	1	0	0	0	1	2
Totals	8	8	4	4	7	8

Phillies	IP	H	R	ER	BB	SO
Hamels	6	5	2	2	1	3
Madson	0.2	2	1	1	0	1
Romero W (2-0)	1.1	2	0	0	0	0
Lidge S (7)	1	1	0	0	0	1
Totals	9	10	3	3	1	5

E—Philadelphia Rollins. DP—Philadelphia 3. 2B—Tampa Bay Pena; Philadelphia Burrell, Jenkins. HR—Tampa Bay Baldelli (2). SH—Tampa Bay Howell; Philadelphia Rollins. HBP—Philadelphia Utley. LOB—Tampa Bay 5; Philadelphia 12. SB—Tampa Bay Perez, Upton; Philadelphia Werth, Utley. Attendance: 45,940.

October 6, 2010
NLDS Game 1
Phillies 4, Reds 0

Halladay's Playoff Debut Nearly Perfect with No-Hitter

Roy Halladay made his playoff debut a game for the ages.

Facing the Cincinnati Reds in the opening game of the National League Division Series, the 33-year-old right-hander became only the second pitcher in major league postseason history to throw a no-hitter. Don Larsen of the New York Yankees was the first to do it in 1956 when he pitched a perfect game against the Brooklyn Dodgers in the World Series.

Halladay, who threw a perfect game against the Marlins in Florida on May 29, was nearly perfect again. The only base runner he allowed was Jay Bruce, who walked with two outs in the fifth inning.

But to a man, Phillies players and coaches agreed that he was better in this game.

"He had four pitches throughout nine innings that he pretty much could throw at any time and on both sides of the plate," said pitching coach Rich Dubee.

Halladay threw 25 first-pitch strikes as he completely overmatched the Reds. It was almost unfair.

"When you're trying to thread a needle at the plate, it's miserable," said Reds first baseman Joey Votto. "It's not fun being up there trying to hit nothing."

The Phillies had no trouble hitting Reds starter Edinson Volquez, who was chased from the game with two outs in the second inning.

His problems began in the first when he gave up a double to Shane Victorino. The Flyin' Hawaiian stole third and scored the first run of the series on Chase Utley's sacrifice fly to right.

In the second, Volquez walked Carlos Ruiz and gave up an infield hit to Wilson Valdez. Halladay then helped himself with a line-drive single to left to score Ruiz.

Volquez was lifted after he walked Jimmy Rollins and surrendered a two-

Roy Halladay celebrates with catcher Carlos Ruiz (51) after throwing a no-hitter to defeat the Cincinnati Reds 4-0 in Game 1 of the National League Division Series.

51
R Z
34

run single to Victorino to make it 4–0. As the game moved into the late innings, the sold-out crowd at Citizens Bank Park got louder and more animated. By the ninth, the fans were standing, waving rally towels and cheering every pitch.

Halladay got Ramon Hernandez to hit a pop-up for the first out and Miguel Cairo to lift a pop-up to third baseman Alvarez in foul territory for the second out.

Brandon Phillips was next. He fell behind 0–2 before hitting the top half of a slider on the outside corner.

Catcher Carlos Ruiz leapt out of his crouch and pounced on the ball as Phillips sped down the line.

At a Glance

WP: Halladay (1-0)

Key stat: Halladay no-hitter, 8 Ks

From his knees, Ruiz threw to Ryan Howard at first for the final out, then jumped up and rushed over to embrace Halladay. They were quickly joined by teammates, who streamed out of the dugout and bullpen as more than 45,000 frenzied fans let out a deafening roar.

"It's something I wasn't worried about achieving," said Halladay. "I think if you're not putting too much emphasis on trying to throw a no-hitter, you're going to go out and stay aggressive. It makes it a lot easier."

His main focus was on winning. Halladay came to Philadelphia to achieve his dream of earning a World Series ring.

"The longer you play, the more you think about having that chance and being able to be involved in it," he said.

ACKNOWLEDGMENTS

This book would not have happened without the encouragement and nagging of some very special people.

Many are colleagues of mine at KYW Newsradio. Matt Leon, Mike Denardo, Mark Rayfield, Steve Butler, Greg Orlandini, and Mark Abrams were especially helpful in their prodding.

John Miller at PhillySportsDaily.com stepped up at a time when I was wobbling on the project and ordered me to make the call to Triumph Books and commit. Thanks, John.

I'm also very grateful to Larry Andersen, Curt Simmons, Rick Wise, Larry Christenson, Bob Boone, Lee Elia, and Larry Bowa, who were most cooperative and gracious in sharing their stories of past glory.

Thanks also to my wife, Kimberly, for enduring all those nights after my day job when I'd come home to work some more. My sons, Pete, Chris, Lucas, and Eli all spent time in the bowels of Temple University's Paley Library helping me with my research. And finally, a big thanks to the helpful folks at Temple's Urban Archives, an invaluable resource for those interested in finding out more about Philadelphia's rich and colorful history.

REFERENCES

BOOKS

Bilovsky, Frank, and Rich Westcott. *The Phillies Encyclopedia*. New York: Leisure Press, 1984.

Honig, Donald. *The Philadelphia Phillies: An Illustrated History.* New York: Simon & Schuster, 1992.

Westcott, Rich. *Phillies Essential.* Chicago: Triumph Books, 2006.

WEB SITES

Baseball Almanac (www.baseballalmanac.com)

Baseball Library (www.baseballlibrary.com)

Baseball Reference (www.baseball-reference.com)

Major League Baseball (www.mlb.com)

Philadelphia Phillies (phillies.mlb.com)

Retrosheet (www.retrosheet.com)

Society for American Baseball Research (www.sabr.org)

NEWSPAPERS/WIRE SERVICES

Associated Press

Philadelphia Daily News

Philadelphia Evening Bulletin

Philadelphia Inquirer